The Works

of

Jonathan Swift

Gulliver's Travels

Introduction by
BEN RAY REDMAN

BLACK'S READERS SERVICE

ROSLYN, NEW YORK

PRINTED IN THE UNITED STATES OF AMERICA

CONTENTS

CONTENTS

INTRODUCTION

If you had been in London in the autumn of the year seventeen hundred and twenty-six, and had moved in any but illiterate circles, you could not have missed hearing of a certain extraordinary, brilliant, and vastly diverting book. Coming upon the town anonymously, it had taken all by storm. At Court and in Grub Street, in boudoirs and coffee-houses, it was the topic of the day. Everyone, everywhere, "from the cabinet-council to the nursery," was reading it, laughing at it, and discussing it. The Princess of Wales had read it "with great pleasure," and was later to inform the author orally of her approval. The Dowager Duchess of Marlborough was "in raptures at it," and declared that she could "dream of nothing else since she read it." The Earl of Peterborough and Mrs. Howard were only two of many who were experimenting with the new, strange dialect that the book had made fashionable. Arbuthnot was willing to exchange "all his profits" for title to the volume, and predicted that it would have "as long a run as John Bunyan." It had "passed Lords and Commons, *nemine contradicente*," and had encountered few hostile critics. The Maids of Honour thought the author had dealt with them a little harshly, and Lady Mary Wortley Montagu was characteristically vigorous in her denunciation of the whole production; but the swelling tide of popularity was not to be stemmed by scattered protests. There was no doubt as to the triumphant success of the remarkable book that had been dropped in the dark from a hackney coach at Benjamin Motte's door, according to his own story, and which he had published at the Middle Temple-Gate in Fleet-Street, on October 28, 1726, under the title of "Travels into Several Remote Nations of the World," and as the work of one "Lemuel Gulliver, First a Surgeon, and then a Captain of several Ships."

The authorship of this greatest of English satires, which the world has since called simply "Gulliver's Travels," was unknown at first to the many, but it was guessed at rightly by the sagacious few, and to Swift's most intimate friends it was, of course, no secret at all. As members of the Scriblerus Club, ten years or so before, Pope and Gay and Arbuthnot had collaborated with Swift in drawing up the rough plan of such a satirical book of travels. Martin Scriblerus was to have been the imaginary hero, and he was to have journeyed, as Gulliver later did, first to a land of pygmies, then to a country of giants, then to a realm of mathematicians and philosophers, and finally to a people who would disgust him and his readers with their own species. Taking up the abandoned project around 1720, Swift wrote Pope in the fall of 1725 that he had finished preparing the work for the press; and it was doubtless Pope who arranged, with the mystifications of which he was so fond, the details of publication.

Some masterpieces are conceived in love; a few have been conceived in hate. "Gulliver's Travels" belongs to the second order. "Hatred," says Carl Van Doren, "was native to Swift, as love was to St. Francis." And, despite the fact that a recent editor of Swift has sought to persuade us that the savage dean's biographers have painted him in too dark colors, I see no reason to question the judgment. Nor have we cause to doubt the man himself when he writes: "The chief end I propose to myself in all my labours is to vex the world rather than divert it, and if I could compass that design without hurting my own person or fortune, I would be the most indefatigable writer you have ever seen. . . . I have ever hated all nations, professions, and communities, and all my love is towards individuals. . . . But principally I hate and detest that animal called man, although I heartily iove John, Peter, Thomas, and so forth. This is the system upon which I have governed myself many years." But the world, perversely, refused to be vexed by "Gulliver" and insisted instead on being diverted; nor has it ever ceased to be diverted since. It is the way of the world, for as Swift himself remarked, when satire is aimed at all it offends none, "since every individual person makes bold to understand it of others, and very wisely removes his particular part of the burden upon the shoulders of the world, which are broad enough, and able to bear it."

The life of Jonathan Swift—born in Dublin in 1667; educated at Trinity College in the same city; served as secretary to Sir William Temple, off and on, from 1689 to 1699; author of "The Battle of the Books" and "The Tale of a Tub," published in 1704; rector of Laracor, and later Dean of St. Patrick's, Dublin; pamphleteer extraordinary for the Tory Government of 1710-1711; author of minor satires that swim like porpoises around his great leviathans; cursed with a maximum of human ambition, and condemned to suffer defeat in proportion,—this life may be read in many versions: in the sturdy prose of Johnson, and the sentimental prose of Thackeray; in the bulky volumes of Sir Henry Craik; in the analytical chapter of Sir Leslie Stephen; and in the lively pages of more recent biographers. To touch lightly upon this life is impossible; to approach it is to become involved in its problems and mysteries, particularly in the central problem of Swift's relationship with Esther Johnson, whom he called Stella, and with Esther Vanhomrigh, whom he called Vanessa. And those who have dwelt longest with that problem have come away from it either with unprovable theories or with the frank confession that they left it unsolved. But no mystery, I think, obscures the basic pattern of Swift's history. Thackeray, for all his sentimental meanderings, laid it bare when he wrote: "His youth was bitter, as that of a great genius bound down by ignoble ties, and powerless in a mean dependence; his age was bitter, like that of a great genius, that had fought the battle and nearly won it, and lost it, and thought of it afterwards, writhing in a lonely exile."

BEN RAY REDMAN.

A VOYAGE TO LILLIPUT

A Voyage to Lilliput

CHAPTER I

*The Author Gives Some Account of Himself and Family—
His First Inducements to Travel—He Is Shipwrecked, and
Swims for His Life—Gets Safe on Shore in the Country
of Lilliput—Is Made a Prisoner, and Carried Up the
Country.*

My father had a small estate in Nottinghamshire; I was
the third of five sons. He sent me to Emanuel College in
Cambridge, at fourteen years old, where I resided three
years, and applied myself close to my studies; but the
charge of maintaining me, although I had a very scanty
allowance, being too great for a narrow fortune, I was
bound apprentice to Mr. James Bates, an eminent surgeon
in London, with whom I continued four years; and my
father now and then sending me small sums of money, I
laid them out in learning navigation, and other parts of
the mathematics, useful to those who intend to travel, as
I always believed it would be, some time or other, my fortune to do. When I left Mr. Bates, I went down to my
father; where, by the assistance of him and my uncle John,
and some other relations, I got forty pounds, and a promise

*The "Voyage to Lilliput," the first part of the travels, is
founded upon the ancient fiction of the "Pigmies," known to all
classical scholars, and familiar to children in their modern
representatives—the "fairies." The tale is highly amusing, the
incidents happily conceived, and the adventures wonderfully
captivating.

of thirty pounds a year to maintain me at Leyden; there I studied physic two years and seven months, knowing it would be useful in long voyages.

Soon after my return from Leyden, I was recommended by my good master, Mr. Bates, to be surgeon to the Swallow, Captain Abraham Pannell, commander, with whom I continued three years and a half, making a voyage or two into the Levant, and some other parts.* When I came back I resolved to settle in London; to which Mr. Bates, my master, encouraged me, and by him I was recommended to several patients. I took part of a small house in the Old Jewry; and being advised to alter my condition, I married Mrs. Mary Burton, second daughter to Mr. Edmund Burton, hosier, in Newgate Street, with whom I received four hundred pounds for a portion.

But my good master Bates dying in two years after, and I having few friends, my business began to fail; for my conscience would not suffer me to imitate the bad practice of too many among my brethren. Having therefore consulted with my wife, and some of my acquaintance, I determined to go again to sea. I was surgeon successively in two ships, and made several voyages, for six years, to the East and West Indies, by which I got some addition to my fortune. My hours of leisure I spent in reading the best authors, ancient and modern, being always provided with a good number of books; and when I was ashore, in observing the manners and dispositions of the people, as well as learning their language, wherein I had a great facility, by the strength of my memory.

The last of these voyages not proving very fortunate, I grew weary of the sea, and intended to stay at home with

*The wonderful skill of Swift is shown in this opening. Gulliver gives a brief notice of himself in a manner so simple and so natural that the reader is, at the very outset, impressed with a feeling of the reality of the narrative, and thus prepared to believe the narrator. How admirable is the mention, as it were casually, of such minute circumstances as that he was two years and seven months studying physic; that he took *part* of a house in the Old Jewry, and got £400 fortune with his wife.

my wife and family. I removed from the Old Jewry to Fetter Lane, and from thence to Wapping, hoping to get business among the sailors, but it would not turn to account. After three years' expectation that things would mend, I accepted an advantageous offer from Captain William Prichard, master of the Antelope, who was making a voyage to the South Seas. We set sail from Bristol, May 4th, 1699, and our voyage at first was very prosperous.

It would not be proper, for some reasons, to trouble the reader with the particulars of our adventures in those seas; let it suffice to inform him that in our passage from thence to the East Indies we were driven by a violent storm to the north-west of Van Dieman's Land.* By an observation, we found ourselves in the latitude of 30 degrees 2 minutes south. Twelve of our crew were dead by immoderate labor and ill food; the rest were in a very weak condition. On the 5th of November, which was the beginning of summer in those parts, the weather being very hazy, the seamen spied a rock within half a cable's length of the ship; but the wind was so strong that we were driven directly upon it, and split. Six of the crew, of whom I was one, having let down the boat into the sea, made a shift to get clear of the ship and the rock. We rowed, by my computation, about three leagues, till we were able to work no longer, being already spent with labor while we were in the ship. We therefore trusted ourselves to the mercy of the waves, and in about half an hour the boat was overset by a sudden flurry from the north. What became of my companions in the boat, as well as of those who escaped

*It will be remembered how little was known of the South Pacific Ocean, or the Australian Continent, at the time when Swift wrote. The discoverer of Van Dieman's Land, in 1633— Abel Janson Tasman—gave but a very inaccurate account of the seas he traversed, and so Swift had *sea-room* enough in which to place his ideal country of Lilliput. Fortunately, while he states the latitude of the shipwreck, he avoids giving the longitude, and so we have escaped the possibility of finding the scene of his adventures among the pigmies upon the coast of Western Australia.

on the rock, or were left in the vessel, I cannot tell; but conclude they were all lost. For my own part, I swam as fortune directed me, and was pushed forward by the wind and tide. I often let my legs drop, and could feel no bottom; but when I was almost gone, and able to struggle no longer, I found myself within my depth; and by this time the storm was much abated. The declivity was so small that I walked near a mile before I got to the shore, which I conjectured was about eight o'clock in the evening. I then advanced forward near half a mile, but could not discover any sign of houses or inhabitants; at least I was in so weak a condition that I did not observe them. I was extremely tired, and with that, and the heat of the weather, and about half a pint of brandy that I drank as I left the ship, I found myself much inclined to sleep. I lay down on the grass, which was very short and soft, where I slept sounder than ever I remembered to have done in my life, and, as I reckoned, about nine hours; for when I awaked it was just daylight. I attempted to rise, but was not able to stir; for as I happened to lie on my back, I found my arms and legs were strongly fastened on each side to the ground; and my hair, which was long and thick, tied down in the same manner. I likewise felt several slender ligatures across my body, from my armpits to my thighs. I could only look upward; the sun began to grow hot, and the light offended my eyes. I heard a confused noise about me; but in the posture I lay could see nothing except the sky. In a little time I felt something alive moving on my left leg, which, advancing gently forward over my breast, came almost up to my chin; when bending my eyes downward as much as I could, I perceived it to be a human creature not six inches high,* with a bow

*Swift takes the standard of the Lilliputians to be not six inches high, which, compared with the ordinary standard of men, makes an inch of the latter equivalent to a foot of the former. This proportion will be found to be pretty accurately preserved in all the measurements, both superficial and solid. Thus we have, a little farther on, the page described as "somewhat larger than my middle finger," or about four feet and a half high.

and arrow in his hands, and a quiver at his back. In the mean time I felt at least forty more of the same kind (as I conjectured) following the first. I was in the utmost astonishment, and roared so loud that they all ran back in a fright; and some of them, as I was afterward told, were hurt with the falls they got by leaping from my sides upon the ground. However, they soon returned, and one of them, who ventured so far as to get a full sight of my face, lifting up his hands and eyes by way of admiration, cried out in a shrill but distinct voice, *Hekinah degul;* the others repeated the same words several times, but I then knew not what they meant. I lay all this while, as the reader may believe, in great uneasiness; at length, struggling to get loose, I had the fortune to break the strings, and wrench out the pegs that fastened my left arm to the ground; for by lifting it to my face, I discovered the methods they had taken to bind me; at the same time, with a violent pull, which gave me excessive pain, I a little loosened the strings that tied down my hair on the left side, so that I was just able to turn my head about two inches. But the creatures ran off a second time before I could seize them; whereupon there was a great shout in a very shrill accent, and after it ceased I heard one of them cry aloud, *Tolgo phonac;* when in an instant I felt above a hundred arrows discharged on my left hand, which pricked me like so many needles; and besides they shot another flight into the air, as we do bombs in Europe, whereof many, I suppose, fell on my body (though I felt them not), and some on my face, which I immediately covered with my left hand. When this shower of arrows was over, I fell a groaning with grief and pain, and then striving again to get loose, they discharged another volley larger than the first, and some of them attempted with spears to stick me in the sides; but by good luck I had on me a buff jerkin, which they could not pierce. I thought it the most prudent method to lie still, and my design was to continue so till night, when, my left hand being already loose, I could easily free myself; and as for the inhabitants,

I had reason to believe I might be a match for the great-est army they could bring against me, if they were all of the same size with him that I saw. But fortune disposed otherwise of me. When the people observed I was quiet, they discharged no more arrows; but by the noise I heard, I knew their numbers increased; and about four yards from me, over against my right ear, I heard a knocking for above an hour, like that of people at work; when turning my head that way, as well as the pegs and strings would permit me, I saw a stage erected about a foot and a half from the ground, capable of holding four of the inhabitants, with two or three ladders to mount it; from whence one of them, who seemed to be a person of quality, made me a long speech, whereof I understood not one syllable. But I should have mentioned that before the principal person began his oration, he cried out three times, *Langro dehul san* (these words and the former were afterward repeated and explained to me). Whereupon, immediately about fifty of the inhabitants came and cut the strings that fas-tened the left side of my head, which gave me the liberty of turning it to the right, and of observing the person and gesture of him that was to speak. He appeared to be of a middle age, and taller than any of the other three who attended him, whereof one was a page that held up his train, and seemed to be somewhat longer than my middle finger; the other two stood one on each side to support him. He acted every part of an orator,* and I could ob-

* There is something intensely ludicrous in representing the pigmy orator perched upon a stage three times the height of himself, squandering all the resources of elocution upon one who could not understand "one syllable of his long speech." Moore, in his "Ode to Sir Hudson Lowe," alludes very humor-ously to this incident:

"And how the doughty manikins
    Amused themselves with sticking pins
        And needless in the great man's breeches;
    And how some *very* little things
    That passed for lords, on scaffoldings,
        Got up and worried him with speeches."

serve many periods of threatenings, and others of promises, pity, and kindness. I answered in a few words, but in the most submissive manner, lifting up my left hand and both eyes to the sun, as calling him for a witness; and being almost famished with hunger, having not eaten a morsel for some hours before I left the ship, I found the demands of nature so strong upon me that I could not forbear showing my impatience (perhaps against the strict rules of decency) by putting my finger frequently to my mouth to signify that I wanted food. The *hurgo* (for so they call a great lord, as I afterward learned) understood me very well. He descended from the stage, and commanded that several ladders should be applied to my sides, on which above a hundred of the inhabitants mounted, and walked toward my mouth, laden with baskets full of meat, which had been provided and sent thither by the king's orders, upon the first intelligence he received of me. I observed there was the flesh of several animals, but I could not distinguish them by the taste. There were shoulders, legs, and loins, shaped like those of mutton, and very well dressed, but smaller than the wings of a lark. I ate them by two or three at a mouthful, and took three loaves at a time, about the bigness of musket-bullets. They supplied me as fast as they could, showing a thousand marks of wonder and astonishment at my bulk and appetite. I then made another sign that I wanted drink. They found by my eating that a small quantity would not suffice me; and being a most ingenious people, they slung up, with great dexterity, one of their largest hogsheads, then rolled it toward my hand, and beat out the top; I drank it off at a draught, which I might well do, for it did not hold half a pint,* and tasted like a small wine of Burgundy, but much more delicious. They brought me a second hogshead, which I drank in the same manner, and made signs for

* The Lilliputian liquid measure will, according to the standard already laid down, be (12 x 12 x 12) 1728 times less than our own; consequently the half-pint hogshead which Gulliver drank off at a draught contained nearly 108 Lilliputian gallons.

more, but they had none to give me. When I had performed these wonders, they shouted for joy, and danced upon my breast, repeating several times, as they did at first, *Hekinah degul*. They made me a sign that I should throw down the two hogsheads, but first warning the people below to stand out of the way, crying aloud, *Borach mevolah;* and when they saw the vessels in the air there was a universal shout of *Hekinah degul*. I confess I was often tempted, while they were passing backward and forward on my body, to seize forty or fifty of the first that came in my reach, and dash them against the ground. But the remembrance of what I had felt, which probably might not be the worst they could do, and the promise of honor I made them, for so I interpreted my submissive behavior, soon drove out these imaginations. Besides, I now considered myself as bound by the laws of hospitality to a people who had treated me with so much expense and magnificence. However, in my thoughts I could not sufficiently wonder at the intrepidity of these diminutive mortals, who durst venture to mount and walk upon my body, while one of my hands was at liberty, without trembling at the very sight of so prodigious a creature as I must appear to them. After some time, when they observed that I made no more demands for meat, there appeared before me a person of high rank from his imperial majesty. His excellency having mounted on the small of my right leg, advanced forward up to my face, with about a dozen of his retinue,* and pro-

---

* How thoroughly ludicrous is the image thus presented to us! The pomp of the manikin *hurgo,* with his dozen followers, traversing the body of Gulliver, from one end to the other, poking his credentials into the eyes of the giant, and being clement enough to address him "without any signs of anger."

> "They tied him down—these little men did,
> And having valiantly ascended
> Upon the mighty man's protuberance,
> They did so strut! Upon my soul,
> It must have been extremely droll
> To see their pigmy pride's exuberance!"
> *Moore's "Ode to Sir Hudson Lowe."*

ducing his credentials under the signet royal, which he applied close to my eyes, spoke about ten minutes without
any signs of anger, but with a kind of determinate resolution; often pointing forward, which, as I afterward found,
was toward the capital city, about half a mile distant,
whither it was agreed by his majesty, in council, that I
must be conveyed. I answered in few words, but to no purpose, and made a sign with my hand that was loose, putting
it to the other (but over his excellency's head, for fear of
hurting him or his train), and then to my own head and
body, to signify that I desired my liberty. It appeared
that he understood me well enough, for he shook his head
by way of disapprobation, and held his hand in a posture
to show that I must be carried as a prisoner. However, he
made other signs to let me understand that I should have
meat and drink enough, and very good treatment. Whereupon I once more thought of attempting to break my
bonds; but again, when I felt the smart of their arrows
upon my face and hands, which were all in blisters, and
many of the darts still sticking in them, and observing likewise that the number of my enemies increased, I gave
tokens to let them know that they might do with me what
they pleased. Upon this the *hurgo* and his train withdrew,
with much civility and cheerful countenances. Soon after
I heard a general shout, with frequent repetitions of the
words, *Peplom selan,* and I felt great numbers of people on
my left side relaxing the cords to such a degree that I was
able to turn upon my right side. But before this they had
daubed my face and both my hands with a sort of ointment,
very pleasant to the smell, which, in a few minutes, removed
all the smart of their arrows. These circumstances, added
to the refreshment I had received by their victuals and
drink, which were very nourishing, disposed me to sleep.
I slept about eight hours, as I was afterward assured; and
it was no wonder, for the physicians, by the emperor's
order, had mingled a sleepy potion in the hogsheads of
wine.

It seems that upon the first moment I was discovered

sleeping on the ground, after my landing, the emperor had early notice of it by an express; and determined, in council, that I should be tied in the manner I have related (which was done in the night while I slept); that plenty of meat and drink should be sent me, and a machine prepared to carry me to the capital city.

This resolution, perhaps, may appear very bold and dangerous, and I am confident would not be imitated by any prince in Europe on the like occasion. However, in my opinion, it was extremely prudent, as well as generous: for, supposing these people had endeavored to kill me with their spears and arrows while I was asleep, I should certainly have awaked with the first sense of smart, which might so far have roused my rage and strength as to have enabled me to break the strings wherewith I was tied; after which, as they were not able to make resistance, so they could expect no mercy.

These people are most excellent mathematicians,* and arrived to a great perfection in mechanics by the countenance and encouragement of the emperor, who is a renowned patron of learning. This prince has several machines fixed on wheels, for the carriage of trees and other great weights. He often builds his largest men-of-war, whereof some are nine feet long, in the woods where the timber grows, and has them carried on these engines three or four hundred yards to the sea. Five hundred carpenters and engineers were immediately set at work to prepare the greatest engine they had. It was a frame of wood, raised three inches from the ground, about seven feet long, and four wide, moving upon twenty-two wheels. The shout I heard was

* This is probably a sneer at mathematics, for which and its professors Swift had no great reverence. Like Goldsmith, he thought that proficiency in mathematics did not require the highest order of intellect; nor did he believe, with King James I., that they were altogether beyond human comprehension; for we learn from Sheridan that, on one occasion, Swift solved a very difficult problem in a very short time. The description of the process by which Gulliver is raised is not only amusing, but very ingenious and correct.

upon the arrival of this engine, which it seems set out in four hours after my landing. It was brought parallel to me as I lay. But the principal difficulty was to raise and place me in this vehicle. Eighty poles, each of one foot high, were erected for this purpose, and very strong cords, of the bigness of packthread, were fastened by hooks to many bandages, which the workmen had girt round my neck, my hands, my body, and my legs. Nine hundred of the strongest men were employed to draw up these cords, by many pulleys fastened on the poles; and thus, in less than three hours, I was raised and slung into the engine, and there tied fast. All this I was told; for, while the operation was performing, I lay in a profound sleep, by the force of that soporiferous medicine infused into my liquor. Fifteen hundred of the emperor's largest horses, each about four inches and a half high, were employed to draw me toward the metropolis, which, as I said, was half a mile distant.

About four hours after we began our journey, I awaked by a very ridiculous accident; for the carriage being stopped awhile, to adjust something that was out of order, two or three of the young natives had the curiosity to see how I looked when I was asleep: they climbed up into the engine, and advancing very softly to my face, one of them, an officer in the guards, put the sharp end of his half-pike a good way up into my left nostril, which tickled my nose like a straw, and made me sneeze violently; whereupon they stole off unperceived, and it was three weeks before I knew the cause of my waking so suddenly. We made a long march the remaining part of the day, and rested at night, with five hundred guards on each side of me, half with torches, and half with bows and arrows, ready to shoot me if I should offer to stir. The next morning, at sunrise, we continued our march, and arrived within two hundred yards of the city gates about noon. The emperor and all his court came out to meet us; but his great officers would by no means suffer his majesty to endanger his person by mounting on my body.

At the place where the carriage stopped there stood an

ancient temple esteemed to be the largest in the whole kingdom; which, having been polluted some years before by an unnatural murder, was, according to the zeal of those people, looked upon as profane, and therefore had been applied to common use, and all the ornaments and furniture carried away. In this edifice it was determined I should lodge. The great gate fronting to the north was about four feet high and almost two feet wide, through which I could easily creep. On each side of the gate was a small window, not above six inches from the ground; into that on the left side, the king's smith conveyed fourscore and eleven chains, like those that hang to a lady's watch in Europe, and almost as large, which were locked to my left leg with six-and-thirty padlocks. Over against this temple, on the other side of the great highway, at twenty feet distance, there was a turret, at least five feet high. Here the emperor ascended, with many principal lords of his court, to have an opportunity of viewing me, as I was told, for I could not see them. It was reckoned that above a hundred thousand inhabitants came out of the town upon the same errand; and, in spite of my guards, I believe there could not be fewer than ten thousand, at several times, who mounted my body, by the help of ladders. But a proclamation was soon issued to forbid it, upon pain of death. When the workmen found it was impossible for me to break loose, they cut all the strings that bound me; whereupon I rose up, with as melancholy a disposition as ever I had in my life. But the noise and astonishment of the people, at seeing me rise and walk are not to be expressed. The chain that held my left leg was about two yards long, and gave me not only the liberty of walking backward and forward in a semicircle, but being fixed within four inches of the gate, allowed me to creep in, and lie at my full length in the temple.

CHAPTER II

The Emperor of Lilliput, Attended by Several of the Nobility, Comes to See the Author in His Confinement—The Emperor's Person and Habit Described—Learned Men Appointed to Teach the Author Their Language—He Gains Favor by His Mild Disposition—His Pockets Are Searched, and His Sword and Pistols Taken from Him.

WHEN I found myself on my feet, I looked about me, and must confess I never beheld a more entertaining prospect. The country around appeared like a continued garden, and the inclosed fields, which were generally forty feet square, resembled so many beds of flowers. These fields were intermingled with woods of half a *stang*,* and the tallest trees, as I could judge, appeared to be seven feet high. I viewed the town on my left hand, which looked like the painted scenes of a city in a theatre.

I soon came out of my house, having occasion for fresh air. The emperor was already descended from the tower, and advancing on horseback toward me, which had like to have cost him dear; for the beast, though very well trained, yet wholly unused to such a sight, which appeared as if a mountain moved before him, reared up on his hinder feet; but that prince, who is an excellent horseman, kept his seat till his attendants ran in, and held the bridle, while his majesty had time to dismount. When he alighted, he surveyed me round with great admiration; but kept beyond the length of my chain. He ordered his cooks and butlers, who were already prepared, to give me victuals and drink, which they pushed forward in a sort of vehicle upon wheels,

* A stang is a pole or perch, sixteen feet and a half in length.

till I could reach them. I took these vehicles, and soon
emptied them all; twenty of them were filled with meat,
and ten with liquor; each of the former afforded me two or
three good mouthfuls; and I emptied the liquor of ten
vessels, which was contained in earthen vials, into one
vehicle, drinking it off at a draught; and so I did with the
rest. The empress and young princes of the blood of both
sexes, attended by many ladies, sat at some distance in their
chairs; but upon the accident that happened to the emperor's horse, they alighted, and came near his person,
which I am now going to describe. He is taller, by almost
the breadth of my nail, than any of his court; which alone
is enough to strike an awe into the beholders. His features
are strong and masculine, with an Austrian lip and arched
nose, his complexion olive, his countenance erect, his body
and limbs well proportioned, all his motions graceful, and
his deportment majestic. He was then past his prime,
being twenty-eight years and three quarters old, of which
he had reigned about seven in great felicity, and generally
victorious. For the better convenience of beholding him,
I lay on my side, so that my face was parallel to his, and
he stood but three yards off: however, I have had him since
many times in my hand, and therefore cannot be deceived
in the description. His dress was very plain and simple,
and the fashion of it between the Asiatic and the European;
but he had on his head a light helmet of gold, adorned with
jewels, and a plume on the crest. He held his sword drawn
in his hand to defend himself, if I should happen to break
loose; it was almost three inches long; the hilt and scabbard
were gold, enriched with diamonds. His voice was shrill,
but very clear and articulate; and I could distinctly hear
it when I stood up. The ladies and courtiers were all most
magnificently clad: so that the spot they stood upon seemed
to resemble a petticoat spread on the ground, embroidered
with figures of gold and silver.* His imperial majesty spoke

* Perhaps at no period was the dress of the upper classes
carried to a higher pitch of extravagance than in the early part
of the eighteenth century: and Swift here takes a fling at the

often to me, and I returned answers; but neither of us could understand a syllable. There were several of his priests and lawyers present (as I conjectured by their habits), who were commanded to address themselves to me; and I spoke to them in as many languages as I had the least smattering of, which were High and Low Dutch, Latin, French, Spanish, Italian, and Lingua Franca, but all to no purpose. After about two hours the court retired, and I was left with a strong guard, to prevent the impertinence, and probably the malice, of the rabble, who were very impatient to crowd about me as near as they durst; and some of them had the impudence to shoot their arrows at me, as I sat on the ground by the door of my house, whereof one very narrowly missed my left eye. But the colonel ordered six of the ring-leaders to be seized, and thought no punishment so proper as to deliver them bound into my hands; which some of his soldiers accordingly did, pushing them forward with the butt-ends of their pikes into my reach. I took them all in my right hand, put five of them into my coat-pocket, and as to the sixth, I made a countenance as if I would eat him alive. The poor man squalled terribly, and the colonel and his officers were in much pain, especially when they saw me take out my penknife; but I soon put them out of fear, for looking mildly, and immediately cutting the strings he was bound with, I set him gently on the ground, and away he ran. I treated the rest in the same manner, taking them one by one out of my pocket; and I observed both the soldiers and the people were highly delighted at this mark

---

excess. The pictures of Hogarth, and the pens of Addison and Steele, have handed down to us lively pictures of the beaux and belles, the courtiers and the "pretty fellows" of the day. Baron de Pollnitz, writing of this period, says: "The ladies and gentle-men always appear in rich dresses; for the English, who, twenty years ago, did not wear gold lace but in their army, are now embroidered and bedaubed as much as the French. I speak of persons of quality; for the citizen still contents himself with a suit of fine cloth, a good hat and wig, and fine linen. Everybody is well clothed here; and even the beggars don't make so ragged an appearance as they do elsewhere."

of my clemency, which was represented very much to my advantage at court.*

Toward night I got with some difficulty into my house, where I lay on the ground, and continued to do so about a fortnight; during which time the emperor gave orders to have a bed prepared for me. Six hundred beds of the common measure were brought in carriages, and worked up in my house; a hundred and fifty of their beds, sewn together, made up the breadth and length; and these were four double; which, however, kept me but very indifferently from the hardness of the floor, that was of smooth stone.† By the same computation, they provided me with sheets, blankets, and coverlets, tolerable enough for one who had been so long inured to hardships.

As the news of my arrival spread through the kingdom, it brought prodigious numbers—rich, idle, and curious people—to see me; so that the villages were almost emptied, and great neglect of tillage and household affairs must have ensued, if his imperial majesty had not provided, by several proclamations and orders of state, against this inconveniency. He directed that those who had already beheld me should return home, and not presume to come within fifty

* Swift was one of the first who adopted a punishment for libelers more expedient and more effective, namely, retaliation, which he administered unsparingly in the *Examiner* against his political opponents, with the almost avowed countenance of his own government.

† "Lemuel Gulliver," says Lord Orrery, in his remarks on the life and writings of Swift, "has observed great exactness in the just proportion and appearances of the several objects thus lessened and magnified." Here we have an illustration of this remark. No fewer than 144 Lilliputian beds would have been enough to form one sufficiently long and broad for the man-mountain. He was, however, but scantily supplied in the depth, having been given four instead of twelve deep. Here we see the king's parsimony in curtailing his guest to the amount of some 1200 additional beds, to say nothing of putting him to lie on the stones for want of a bedstead. Accordingly, while Gulliver seems contented with the length and breadth of his accommodation, he complains, with some justice of its shallowness.

yards of my house, without license from the court; whereby the secretary of state got considerable fees.

In the mean time the emperor held frequent councils, to debate what course should be taken with me; and I was afterward assured, by a particular friend, a person of great quality, who was as much in the secret as any, that the court was under many difficulties concerning me. They apprehended my breaking loose; that my diet would be very expensive, and might cause a famine. Sometimes they determined to starve me, or at least shoot me in the face and hands with poisonous arrows, which would soon dispatch me; but again they considered that the stench of so large a carcass might produce a plague in the metropolis, and probably spread through the whole kingdom. In the midst of these consultations, several officers of the army went to the door of the great council-chamber, and two of them being admitted, gave an account of my behavior to the six criminals above mentioned; which made so favorable an impression in the breast of his majesty, and the whole board, in my behalf, that an imperial commission was issued out, obliging all the villagers, nine hundred yards round the city, to deliver in every morning six beeves, forty sheep, and other victuals, for my sustenance; together with a proportionable quantity of bread, and wine and other liquors; for the due payment of which his majesty gave assignments upon his treasury: for this prince lives chiefly upon his own demesnes; seldom, except upon great occasions, raising any subsidies upon his subjects, who are bound to attend him in his wars at their own expense. An establishment was also made of six hundred persons to be my domestics, who had board-wages allowed for their maintenance, and tents built for them, very conveniently, on each side of my door. It was likewise ordered, that three hundred tailors should make me a suit of clothes, after the fashion of the country; that six of his majesty's greatest scholars should be employed to instruct me in their language; and lastly, that the emperor's horses, and those of the nobility and troops of guards, should be frequently exercised in my sight, to accustom themselves to me. All these orders were duly put in execution; and in about three weeks I made a great progress in learning their language; during which time the emperor frequently honored me with his visits, and was pleased to assist my masters in teaching me. We began already to converse together in some sort; and the first words I learnt were to express my desire "that he would be pleased to give me my liberty;" which I every day repeated on my knees. His answer, as I could apprehend it, was "that this must be a work of time, not to be thought on without the advice of his council, and that first I must *lumos kelmin pesso desmar lon emposa;*" that is, swear a peace with him and his kingdom. However, that I should be used with all kindness. And he advised me to "acquire by my patience and discreet behavior the good opinion of himself and his subjects." He desired, "I would not take it ill if he gave orders to certain proper officers to search me; for probably I might carry about me several weapons, which must needs be dangerous things, if they answered the bulk of so prodigious a person." I said, "His majesty should be satisfied; for I was ready to strip myself, and turn out my pockets before him." This I delivered, part in words, and part in signs. He replied, "that by the laws of the kingdom, I must be searched by two of his officers; that he knew this could not be done without my consent and assistance; and he had so good an opinion of my generosity and justice, as to trust their persons in my hands; that whatever they took from me should be returned when I left the country, or paid for, at the rate which I would set upon them." I took up the two officers in my hands, put them first into my coat pockets, and then into every other pocket about me, except my two fobs, and another secret pocket, which I had no mind should be searched, wherein I had some little necessaries that were of no consequence to any but myself. In one of my fobs there was a silver watch, and in the other a small quantity of gold in a purse. These gentlemen, having pens, ink, and paper about them, made an exact inventory of everything they saw; and when they had done, desired I would set them down, that they might deliver it to the emperor. This inventory I afterward translated into English, and is word for word as follows:

Imprimis, In the right coat-pocket of the great man-mountain (for so I interpret the words *quinbus flestrin*), after the strictest search, we found only one great piece of coarse cloth, large enough to be a foot cloth for your majesty's chief room of state. In the left pocket we saw a huge silver chest, with a cover of the same metal, which we, the searchers, were not able to lift. We desired it should be opened, and one of us stepping into it, found himself up to the mid-leg in a sort of dust, some part whereof flying up to our faces, set us both a-sneezing for several times together. In his right waistcoat-pocket we found a prodigious bundle of white thin substance, folded one over another, about the bigness of three men, tied with a strong cable, and marked with black figures; which we humbly conceive to be writings, every letter almost half as large as the palm of our hands. In the left there was a sort of engine, from the back of which were extended twenty long poles, resembling the palisadoes before your majesty's court: wherewith we conjecture the man-mountain combs his head; for we did not always trouble him with questions, because we found it a great difficulty to make him understand us. In the large pocket, on the right side of his middle cover (so I translate the word *ranfu-lo,* by which they meant my breeches), we saw a hollow pillar of iron, about the length of a man, fastened to a strong piece of timber larger than the pillar; and upon one side of the pillar were huge pieces of iron sticking out, cut into strange figures, which we knew not what to make of. In the left pocket, another engine of the same kind. In the smaller pocket on the right side, were several round flat pieces of white and red metal, of different bulk; some of the white, which seemed to be silver, were so large and heavy that my comrade and I could hardly lift them. In the left pocket were two black pillars irregularly shaped: we could not, without difficulty, reach the top of them, as we stood at the bottom of his pocket. One of them was covered, and seemed all of a piece: but at the upper end of the other there appeared a white round substance, about twice the bigness of our heads. Within each of these was inclosed a prodigious plate of steel; which, by our orders, we obliged him to show us, because we apprehended they might be dangerous engines. He took them out of their cases, and told us, that in his own country his practice was to shave his beard with one of these, and cut his meat with the other. There were two pockets which we could not enter: these he called his fobs; they were two large slits, cut into the tops of his middle cover, but squeezed close by the pressure of his body. Out of the right fob hung a great silver chain, with a wonderful kind of engine at the bottom. We directed him to draw out whatever was at the end of that chain; which appeared to be a globe, half silver, and half of some transparent metal; for, on the transparent side, we saw certain strange figures circularly drawn, and thought we could touch them, till we found our fingers stopped by that lucid substance. He put this engine to our ears, which made an incessant noise, like that of a water-mill; and we conjecture it is either some unknown animal, or the god that he worships; but we are more inclined to the latter opinion, because he assured us (if we understand him right, for he expressed himself very imperfectly), that he seldom did anything without consulting it. He called it his oracle, and said it pointed out the time for every action of his life. From the left fob he took out a net almost large enough for a fisherman, but contrived to open and shut like a purse, and served him for the same use; we found therein several massy pieces of yellow metal, which, if they be real gold, must be of immense value.

Having thus, in obedience to your majesty's commands, diligently searched all his pockets, we observed a girdle about his waist made of the hide of some prodigious animal, from which, on the left side, hung a sword of the length of five men; and on the right, a bag or pouch divided into two cells, each cell capable of holding three of your majesty's subjects. In one of these cells were several globes or balls, of a most ponderous metal, about the bigness of our heads, and required a strong hand to lift them: the other cell contained a heap of certain black grains, but of no great bulk or weight, for we could hold about fifty of them in the palms of our hands.

This is an exact inventory* of what we found about the body of the man-mountain, who used us with great civility, and due respect to your majesty's commission. Signed and sealed on the fourth day of the eighty-ninth moon of your majesty's auspicious reign.

CLEFRIN FRELOCK.
MARSI FRELOCK.

* How exquisitely ludicrous is this conception of these wise manikins searching Gulliver's pockets, and gravely noting things, most trivial and ordinary in our estimation, as of the weightiest moment, and of suspicious, if not alarming character! Johnson, who was rarely favorable to Swift, "allowed," says Boswell, "very great merit to the inventory of the articles found in the pocket of the 'man-mountain,' particularly the description of his watch."

When this inventory was read over to the emperor, he directed me, although in very gentle terms, to deliver up the several particulars. He first called for my scimitar, which I took out, scabbard and all. In the mean time, he ordered three thousand of the choicest troops (who then attended him), to surround me at a distance, with their bows and arrows just ready to discharge; but I did not observe it, for mine eyes were wholly fixed on his majesty. He then desired me to draw my scimitar, which, although it had got some rust by the sea-water, was in most parts exceedingly bright. I did so, and immediately all the troops gave a shout between terror and surprise; for the sun shone clear, and the reflection dazzled their eyes, as I waved the scimitar to and fro in my hand. His majesty, who is a most magnanimous prince, was less daunted than i could expect; he ordered me to return it into the scabbard and cast it on the ground as gently as I could, about six feet from the end of my chain. The next thing he demanded was one of the hollow iron pillars; by which he meant my pocket pistols. I drew it out, and at his desire, as well as I could, expressed to him the use of it; and charging it only with powder, which, by the closeness of my pouch, happened to escape wetting in the sea (an inconvenience against which all prudent mariners take special care to provide), I first cautioned the emperor not to be afraid, and then I let it off in the air. The astonishment here was much greater than at the sight of the scimitar. Hundreds fell down as if they had been struck dead; and even the emperor, although he stood his ground, could not recover himself for some time. I delivered up both my pistols in the same manner as I had done my scimitar, and then my pouch of powder and bullets; begging him that the former might be kept from fire, for it would kindle with the smallest spark, and blow up his imperial palace into the air. I likewise delivered up my watch, which the emperor was very curious to see, and commanded two of his tallest yeomen of the guards to bear it on a pole upon their shoulders, as draymen in England do a barrel of ale. He was amazed at the continual noise it made, and the motion of the minute-hand, which he could easily discern; for their sight is much more acute than ours. He asked the opinions of his learned men about it, which were various and remote, as the reader may well imagine without my repeating; although, indeed, I could not very perfectly understand them. I then gave up my silver and copper money, my purse, with nine large pieces cf gold, and some smaller ones; my knife and razor, my comb and silver snuff-box, my handkerchief and journal-book. My scimitar, pistols, and pouch were conveyed in carriages to his majesty's stores; but the rest of my goods were returned me.*

I had, as I before observed, one private pocket, which escaped their search, wherein there was a pair of spectacles (which I sometimes use for the weakness of mine eyes), a pocket perspective, and some other little conveniences; which, being of no consequence to the emperor, I did not think myself bound in honor to discover, and I apprehended they might be lost or spoiled, if I ventured them out of my possession.

* Every reader of history is acquainted with the rigid, and often unjustifiable searches which were, for a considerable period after the accession of the house of Hanover, instituted by the Whigs in the houses of their political opponents wherever they suspected, or affected to suspect, the owners to be favorable to the house of Stuart, or to be Papists, or harborers of Papists. It is these inquisitorial proceedings that are here the objects of Swift's irony.

CHAPTER III

*The Author Diverts the Emperor, and His Nobility of Both
Sexes, in a Very Uncommon Manner—The Diversions of
the Court of Lilliput Described—The Author Has His
Liberty Granted Him Upon Certain Conditions.*

My gentleness and good behavior had gained so far on the
emperor and his court, and indeed upon the army and people in general, that I began to conceive hopes of getting my
liberty in a short time. I took all possible methods to cultivate this favorable disposition. The natives came, by degrees, to be less apprehensive of any danger from me; I
would sometimes lie down, and let five or six of them dance
on my head; and at last the boys and girls would venture
to come and play at hide and seek in my hair. I had now
made a good progress in understanding and speaking their
language. The emperor had a mind one day to entertain
me with several of the country shows, wherein they exceeded all nations I have known, both for dexterity and
magnificence. I was diverted with none so much as that of
the rope dancers, performed upon a slender white thread
extended about two feet, and twelve inches from the
ground; upon which I shall desire liberty, with the reader's
patience, to enlarge a little.

This diversion is only practiced by those persons who are
candidates for great employments, and high favor at court.
They are trained in this art from their youth, and are not
always of noble birth, or liberal education. When a great
office is vacant, either by death or disgrace (which often
happens), five or six of those candidates petition the emperor to entertain his majesty and the court with a dance
on the rope; and whoever jumps the highest, without falling, succeeds in the office. Very often the chief ministers

23

themselves are commanded to show their skill, and to con-
vince the emperor that they have not lost their faculty.
Flimnap,* the treasurer, is allowed to cut a caper on the
straight rope, at least an inch higher than any other lord
in the whole empire. I have seen him do the somerset† several times together, upon a trencher fixed on a rope which
is no thicker than a common packthread in England. My
friend Reldresal, principal secretary for private affairs, is,
in my opinion, if I am not partial, the second after the
treasurer: the rest of the great officers are much upon a
par.

These diversions are often attended with fatal accidents,
whereof great numbers are on record. I myself have seen
two or three candidates break a limb. But the danger is
much greater when the ministers themselves are commanded
to show their dexterity; for, by contending to excel themselves and their fellows, they strain so far that there is
hardly one of them who has not received a fall, and some
of them two or three. I was assured that, a year or two
before my arrival, Flimnap would infallibly have broken
his neck, if one of the king's cushions, that accidentally lay
on the ground, had not weakened the force of his fall.

There is likewise another diversion, which is only shown
before the emperor and empress, and first minister, upon
particular occasions. The emperor lays on the table three
fine silken threads of six inches long; one is blue, the other
red, and the third green. These threads are proposed as
prizes for those persons whom the emperor has a mind to
distinguish by a peculiar mark of his favor. The ceremony
is performed in his majesty's great chamber of state, where
the candidates are to undergo a trial of dexterity, very different from the former, and such as I have not observed the

* Under the name of Flimnap, Swift designed to hold up Sir
Robert Walpole to odium and ridicule, as he had all his life
pursued him with the bitterest enmity and the most savage
satire both in prose and verse.

† *Somerset* or *summersault,* a gambol of a tumbler, in which
he springs up, turns heels over head in the air, and comes down
upon his feet.—*Orig.*

least resemblance of in any other country of the New or Old World. The emperor holds a stick in his hands, both ends parallel to the horizon, while the candidates advancing, one by one, sometimes leap over the stick, sometimes creep under it, backward and forward, several times, according as the stick is advanced or depressed. Sometimes the emperor holds one end of the stick, and his first minister the other; sometimes the minister has it entirely to himself. Whoever performs his part with most agility, and holds out the longest in leaping and creeping, is rewarded with the blue-colored silk; the red is given to the next, and the green to the third, which they all wear girt twice round about the middle; and you see few great persons about this court who are not adorned with one of these girdles.*

The horses of the army, and those of the royal stables, having been daily led before me, were no longer shy, but would come up to my very feet without starting. The riders would leap them over my hand, as I held it on the ground; and one of the emperor's huntsmen, upon a large courser, took my foot, shoe and all; which was indeed a prodigious leap. I had the good fortune to divert the emperor one day after a very extraordinary manner. I desired he would order several sticks of two feet high, and the thickness of an ordinary cane, to be brought me; whereupon his majesty commanded the master of his woods to give directions accordingly; and the next morning six woodmen arrived with as many carriages drawn by eight horses to each. I took nine of these sticks, and fixing them firmly in the ground in a quadrangular figure, two feet and a half square, I took four other sticks, and tied them parallel at each corner about two feet from the ground; then I fastened my handkerchief to the nine sticks that stood erect, and extended it on all sides, till it was tight as the top of a drum; and the four parallel sticks, rising about five inches higher than the handkerchief, served as ledges on each side.

* These decorations are obviously the three orders of knighthood—the blue being the "Garter," the red the "Bath," and the green the "Thistle."

When I had finished my work, I desired the emperor to let a troop of his best horses, twenty-four in number, come and exercise upon this plain. His majesty approved of the proposal, and I took them up, one by one, in my hands, ready mounted and armed with the proper officers to exercise them. As soon as they got into order, they divided into two parties, performed mock skirmishes, discharged blunt arrows, drew their swords, fled and pursued, attacked and retired, and, in short, discovered the best military discipline I ever beheld. The parallel sticks secured them and their horses from falling over the stage; and the emperor was so much delighted that he ordered this entertainment to be repeated several days, and once was pleased to be lifted up, and give the word of command; and, with great difficulty, persuaded even the empress herself to let me hold her in her close chair within two yards of the stage, when she was able to take a full view of the whole performance. It was my good fortune that no ill accident happened in these entertainments; only once, a fiery horse that belonged to one of the captains, pawing with his hoof, struck a hole in my handkerchief, and his foot slipping, he overthrew his rider and himself; but I immediately relieved them both, and covering the hole with one hand, I set down the troop with the other, in the same manner as I took them up. The horse that fell was strained in the left shoulder, but the rider got no hurt, and I repaired my handkerchief as well as I could; however, I would not trust the strength of it any more, in such dangerous enterprises.

About two or three days before I was set at liberty, as I was entertaining the court with this kind of feats, there arrived an express to inform his majesty that some of his subjects, riding near the place where I was first taken up, had seen a great black substance lying on the ground, very oddly shaped, extending its edges round, as wide as his majesty's bedchamber, and rising up in the middle as high as a man; that it was no living creature, as they at first apprehended, for it lay on the grass without motion; and some of them had walked round it several times; that, by mounting upon each other's shoulders, they had got to the top, which was flat and even, and stamping upon it, they found that it was hollow within; that they humbly conceived it might be something belonging to the man-mountain; and if his majesty pleased, they would undertake to bring it with only five horses. I presently knew what they meant, and was glad at heart to receive this intelligence. It seems, upon my reaching the shore, after our shipwreck, I was in such confusion, that before I came to the place where I went to sleep, my hat, which I had fastened with a string to my head while I was rowing, and had stuck on all the time I was swimming, fell off after I came to land; the string, as I conjecture, breaking by some accident, which I never observed, but thought my hat had been lost at sea. I entreated his imperial majesty to give orders it might be brought to me as soon as possible, describing to him the use and nature of it; and the next day the wagoners arrived with it, but not in a very good condition; they had bored two holes in the brim, within an inch and a half of the edge, and fastened two hooks in the holes; these hooks were tied by a long cord to the harness, and thus my hat was dragged along for above half an English mile; but, the ground in that country being extremely smooth and level, it received less damage than I expected.

Two days after this adventure, the emperor, having ordered that part of his army which quarters in and about his metropolis to be in readiness, took a fancy of diverting himself in a very singular manner. He desired I would stand like a Colossus, with my legs as far asunder as I conveniently could. He then commanded his general (who was an old experienced leader and a great patron of mine), to draw up the troops in close order, and march them under me; the foot by twenty-four abreast, and the horse by sixteen,* with drums beating, colors flying, and pikes advanced.

* The incident was naturally suggested by what is related of the celebrated brazen statue, 105 feet high, placed at the entrance of the harbor of Rhodes, with a foot on each mole, under which the largest ships, with all their sails set, were able to pass

This body consisted of three thousand foot, and a thousand horse. His majesty gave orders, upon pain of death, that every soldier in his march should observe the strictest propriety.

I had sent so many memorials and petitions for my liberty, that his majesty at length mentioned the matter, first in the cabinet, and then in a full council; where it was opposed by none, except Skyresh Bolgolam, who was pleased, without any provocation, to be my mortal enemy. But it was carried against him by the whole board, and confirmed by the emperor. That minister was *galbet*, or admiral of the realm, very much in his master's confidence, and a person well versed in affairs, but of a morose and sour complexion. However, he was at length persuaded to comply; but prevailed that the articles and conditions upon which I should be set free, and to which I must swear, should be drawn up by himself. These articles were brought to me by Skyresh Bolgolam in person, attended by two under-secretaries, and several persons of distinction. After they were read, I was demanded to swear to the performance of them: first in the manner of my own country, and afterward in the method prescribed by their laws; which was, to hold my right foot in my left hand, and to place the middle finger of my right hand on the crown of my head, and my thumb on the tip of my right ear. But because the reader may be curious to have some idea of the style and manner of expression peculiar to that people, as well as to know the articles upon which I recovered my liberty, I have made a translation of the whole instrument, word for word, as near as I was able, which I here offer to the public:

GOLBASTO MOMAREM EVLAME GURDILO SHEFIN MULLY ULLY GUE, most mighty Emperor of Lilliput, delight and terror of the universe, whose dominions extend five thousand *blustrugs* (about twelve miles in circumference) to the extremities of the globe; monarch of all monarchs, taller than the sons of men; whose feet press down to the center, and whose head strikes against the sun; at whose nod the princes of the earth shake their knees; pleasant as the spring, comfortable as the summer, fruitful as autumn, dreadful as the winter. His most sublime majesty proposes to the man-mountain, lately arrived at our celestial dominions, the following articles, which, by a solemn oath, he shall be obliged to perform:

I. The man-mountain shall not depart from our dominions, without our license under our great seal.

II. He shall not presume to come into our metropolis, without our express order; at which time the inhabitants shall have two hours' warning to keep within doors.

III. The said man-mountain shall confine his walks to our principal high-roads, and not offer to walk, or lie down, in a meadow or field of corn.

IV. As he walks the said roads he shall take the utmost care not to trample upon the bodies of any of our loving subjects, their horses or carriages, nor take any of our subjects into his hands, without their own consent.

V. If any express requires extraordinary dispatch, the man-mountain shall be obliged to carry, in his pocket, the messenger and horse a six days' journey, once in every moon, and return the said messenger back (if so required) safe to our imperial presence.

VI. He shall be our ally against our enemies in the island of Blefuscu,* and do his utmost to destroy their fleet, which is now preparing to invade us.

VII. That the said man-mountain shall, at his time of leisure, be aiding and assisting to our workmen, in helping to raise certain great stones, toward covering the wall of the principal park, and other our royal buildings.

VIII. That the said man-mountain shall, in two moons' time, deliver in an exact survey of the circumference of our dominions, by a computation of his own paces round the coast.

Lastly, That, upon his solemn oath to observe all the above articles, the said man-mountain shall have a daily allowance of meat and drink sufficient for the support of 1728 of our subjects, with free access to our royal person, and other marks of our favor. Given at our palace at Belfaborac, the twelfth day of the ninety-first moon of our reign.

* Lord Orrery says: "In Swift's description of Lilliput he seems to have had England more immediately in view; in his description of Blefuscu he seems to intend the people and kingdom of France; yet the allegory between these nations is frequently interrupted, and scarce anywhere complete." Scott truly remarks, the parallel is intentionally qualified by changing the relative description of the two countries, making Lilliput the continent, and Blefuscu the island.

I swore and subscribed to these articles with great cheerfulness and content, although some of them were not so honorable as I could have wished; which proceeded wholly from the malice of Skyresh Bolgolam, the high-admiral; whereupon my chains were immediately unlocked, and I was at full liberty. The emperor himself, in person, did me the honor to be by at the whole ceremony. I made my acknowledgments by prostrating myself at his majesty's feet; but he commanded me to rise; and after many gracious expressions, which, to avoid the censure of vanity, I shall not repeat, he added, "that he hoped I should prove a useful servant, and well deserve all the favors he had already conferred upon me, or might do for the future."

The reader may please to observe that, in the last article of the recovery of my liberty, the emperor stipulates to allow me a quantity of meat and drink sufficient for the support of 1728 Lilliputians. Some time after, asking a friend at court how they came to fix on that determinate number, he told me that his majesty's mathematicians, having taken the height of my body by the help of a quadrant, and finding it to exceed theirs in proportion of twelve to one, they concluded, from the similarity of their bodies, that mine must contain at least 1728 of theirs, and consequently would require as much food as was necessary to support that number of Lilliputians. By which the reader may conceive an idea of the ingenuity of this people, as well as the prudent and exact economy of so great a prince.

CHAPTER IV

*Mildendo, the Metropolis of Lilliput, Described, Together
With the Emperor's Palace—A Conversation Between the
Author and the Principal Secretary, Concerning the Af-
fairs of that Empire—The Author Offers to Serve the
Emperor in His Wars.*

THE first request I made, after I had obtained my liberty,
was, that I might have license to see Mildendo, the metropolis; which the emperor easily granted me, but with a special charge to do no hurt either to the inhabitants or their
houses. The people had notice, by proclamation, of my
design to visit the town. The wall which encompassed it is
two feet and a half high, and at least eleven inches broad,
so that a coach and horses may be driven very safely round
it; and it is flanked with strong towers at ten feet distance.
I stepped over the great western gate, and passed very
gently and sideling through the two principal streets, only
in my short waistcoat, for fear of damaging the roofs and
eaves of the houses with the skirts of my coat. I walked
with the utmost circumspection, to avoid treading on any
stragglers who might remain in the streets; although the
orders were very strict, that all people should keep in their
houses, at their own peril. The garret windows and tops of
houses were so crowded with spectators that I thought in
all my travels I had not seen a more populous place. The
city is an exact square, each side of the wall being five hundred feet long. The two great streets, which run across and
divide it into four quarters, are five feet wide. The lanes
and alleys, which I could not enter, but only viewed them
as I passed, are from twelve to eighteen inches. The town
is capable of holding five hundred thousand souls; the

houses are from three to five stories; the shops and markets
well provided.

The emperor's palace is in the center of the city, where
the two great streets meet. It is inclosed by a wall of two
feet high, and twenty feet distant from the building. I had
his majesty's permission to step over this wall; and the
space being so wide between that and the palace, I could
easily view it on every side. The outward court is a square
of forty feet, and includes two other courts: in the inmost
are the royal apartments, which I was very desirous to see,
but found it extremely difficult; for the great gates, from
one square into another, were but eighteen inches high, and
seven inches wide. Now the buildings of the outer court
were at least five feet high, and it was impossible for me to
stride over them without infinite damage to the pile, though
the walls were strongly built of hewn stone, and four inches
thick. At the same time, the emperor had a great desire
that I should see the magnificence of his palace; but this I
was not able to do till three days after, which I spent in
cutting down, with my knife, some of the largest trees in
the royal park, about a hundred yards' distance from the
city. Of these trees I made two stools, each about three
feet high, and strong enough to bear my weight. The people having received notice a second time, I went again
through the city to the palace, with my two stools in my
hands. When I came to the side of the outer court I stood
upon one stool, and took the other in my hand; this I
lifted over the roof, and gently set it down on the space
between the first and second court, which was eight feet
wide. I then stepped over the building very conveniently
from one stool to the other, and drew up the first after me
with a hooked stick. By this contrivance I got into the
inner court; and lying down upon my side, I applied my
face to the windows of the middle stories, which were left
open on purpose, and discovered the most splendid apartments that could be imagined. There I saw the empress
and the young princes, in their several lodgings, with their
chief attendants about them. Her imperial majesty was

pleased to smile very graciously upon me, and gave me out of the window her hand to kiss.*

But I shall not anticipate the reader with further descriptions of this kind, because I reserve them for a greater work, which is now almost ready for the press; containing a general description of this empire, from its first erection, through a long series of princes; with a particular account of their wars and politics, laws, learning and religion; their plants and animals; their peculiar manners and customs, with other matters very curious and useful: my chief design at present being only to relate such events and transactions as happened to the public or to myself during a residence of about nine months in that empire.

One morning, about a fortnight after I had obtained my liberty, Reldresal, principal secretary (as they style him) for private affairs, came to my house, attended only by one servant. He ordered his coach to wait at a distance, and desired I would give him an hour's audience; which I readily consented to, on account of his quality and personal merits, as well as of the many good offices he had done me during my solicitations at court. I offered to lie down, that he might the more conveniently reach my ear; but he chose rather to let me hold him in my hand during our conversation. He began with compliments on my liberty, said "he might pretend to some merit in it;" but, however, added, "that if it had not been for the present situation of things at court, perhaps I might not have obtained it so soon. For," said he, "as flourishing a condition as we may appear to be in to foreigners, we labor under two mighty evils—a violent faction at home, and the danger of an invasion by a most potent enemy from abroad. As to the first, you are to understand, that for above seventy moons past there have been two struggling parties in this empire,

---

* The Empress of Lilliput is designed to represent Queen Anne, though the character is not brought out with much distinctness. The graciousness of the reception is in accordance with the reputation of the queen, who was pronounced by Lord Dartmouth to be "the best bred person in her dominions."

under the names *Tramecksan* and *Slamecksan,* from the high and low heels of their shoes, by which they distinguish themselves. It is alleged, indeed, that the high heels are most agreeable to our ancient constitution; but, however this be, his majesty has determined to make use only of low heels in the administration of the government, and all offices in the gift of the crown, as you cannot but observe; and particularly that his majesty's imperial heels are lower by at least a *drurr* than any of his court (*drurr* is a measure about the fourteenth part of an inch). The animosities between these two parties run so high that they will neither eat, nor drink, nor talk with each other. We compute the *Tramecksan* or high heels, to exceed us in number; but the power is wholly on our side. We apprehend his imperial highness, the heir to the crown, to have some tendency toward the high heels; at least we can plainly discover that one of his heels is higher than the other, which gives him a hobble in his gait. Now, in the midst of these intestine disquiets, we are threatened with an invasion from the island of Blefuscu, which is the other great empire of the universe, almost as large and powerful as this of his majesty. For as to what we have heard you affirm, that there are other kingdoms and states in the world inhabited by human creatures as large as yourself, our philosophers are in much doubt, and would rather conjecture that you dropped from the moon, or one of the stars; because it is certain that a hundred mortals of your bulk would in a short time destroy all the fruits and cattle of his majesty's dominions; besides, our histories of six thousand moons make no mention of any other regions than the two great empires of Lilliput and Blefuscu, which two mighty powers have, as I was going to tell you, been engaged in a most obstinate war for six-and-thirty moons past. It began upon the following occasion: it is allowed on all hands that the primitive mode of breaking eggs, before we eat them, was upon the larger end, but his majesty's grandfather, while he was a boy, going to eat an egg, and breaking it according to the ancient practice, happened to cut one of his fingers; whereupon the emperor, his father, published an edict, commanding all his subjects, upon great penalties, to break the smaller end of their eggs. The people so highly resented this law, that our histories tell us, there have been six rebellions raised on that account; wherein one emperor lost his life, and another his crown. These civil commotions were constantly fomented by the monarchs of Blefuscu; and when they were quelled, the exiles always fled for refuge to that empire. It is computed that eleven thousand persons have at several times suffered death rather than submit to break their eggs at the smaller end. Many hundred large volumes have been published upon this controversy; but the books of the Big Endians have been long forbidden, and the whole party rendered incapable by law of holding employments. During the course of these troubles, the emperors of Blefuscu did frequently expostulate by their ambassadors, accusing us of making a schism in religion, by offending against a fundamental doctrine of our great prophet Lustrog, in the fifty-fourth chapter of the Blundecral, which is their Alcoran. This, however, is thought to be a mere strain upon the text; for the words are these: that all true believers break their eggs at the convenient end; and which is the convenient end seems, in my humble opinion, to be left to every man's conscience, or at least in the power of the chief magistrate to determine.* Now, the Big Endian exiles have found so much credit in the Emperor of Blefuscu's court, and so much private assistance and encouragement from their private party here at home, that a bloody war has been carried on between the two empires

* The application of the several details in relation to this controversy of the egg-breaking is very obvious. The emperor who lost his crown is James II. We have allusion to the religious persecutions under Elizabeth and Mary; the intrigues of the Court of France, and the endeavor to place Mary Queen of Scots on the English throne, and extirpate the Protestant religion; the support given to the Pretender; and finally, the penal enactments and political disabilities imposed on the Catholics. Swift intimates that the great points of controversy should be left to each man's conscience.

for six-and-thirty moons, with varied success; during which time we have lost forty capital ships, and a much greater number of smaller vessels, together with thirty thousand of our best seamen and soldiers; and the damage received by the enemy is reckoned to be somewhat greater than ours. However, they have now equipped a numerous fleet, and are just preparing to make a descent upon us; and his imperial majesty, placing great confidence in your valor and strength, has commanded me to lay this account of his affairs before you."

I desired the secretary to present my humble duty to the emperor; and to let him know, "that I thought it would not become me, who was a foreigner, to interfere with parties; but I was ready, with the hazard of my life, to defend his person and state against all invaders."

CHAPTER V

The Author, By An Extraordinary Stratagem, Prevents An Invasion—A High Title of Honor Is Conferred Upon Him—Ambassadors Arrive from the Emperor of Blefuscu, and Sue for Peace.

THE empire of Blefuscu is an island situated to the north-east of Lilliput, from which it is parted only by a channel of eight hundred yards wide. I had not yet seen it, and upon this notice of an intended invasion, I avoided appearing on that side of the coast, for fear of being discovered by some of the enemy's ships, who had received no intelligence of me; all intercourse between the two empires having been strictly forbidden during the war, upon pain of death, and an embargo laid by our emperor upon all vessels whatsoever. I communicated to his majesty a project I had formed of seizing the enemy's whole fleet; which, as our scouts assured us, lay at anchor in the harbor, ready to sail with the first fair wind. I consulted the most experienced seamen upon the depth of the channel, which they had often plumbed; who told me, that in the middle at high water it was seventy *glumgluffs* deep, which is about six feet of European measure; and the rest of it fifty *glumgluffs* at most. I walked toward the north-east coast, over against Blefuscu; where, lying down behind a hillock, I took out my small perspective glass, and viewed the enemy's fleet at anchor, consisting of about fifty men-of-war, and a great number of transports. I then came back to my house, and gave orders (for which I had a warrant) for a great quantity of the strongest cable and bars of iron. The cable was about as thick as packthread, and the bars of the length and size of a knitting-needle. I trebled the cable to make it stronger, and for the same reason I twisted three

of the iron bars together, bending the extremities into a
hook. Having thus fixed fifty hooks to as many cables, I
went back to the north-east coast, and putting off my coat,
shoes, and stockings, walked into the sea, in my leathern
jerkin, about half an hour before high water. I waded with
what haste I could, and swam in the middle about thirty
yards, till I felt ground. I arrived at the fleet in less than
half an hour. The enemy were so frightened when they
saw me, that they leaped out of their ships and swam to
shore, where there could not be fewer than thirty thousand
souls: I then took my tackling, and fastening a hook to the
hole at the prow of each, I tied all the cords together at the
end. While I was thus employed, the enemy discharged
several thousand arrows, many of which stuck in my hands
and face; and, besides the excessive smart, gave me much
disturbance in my work. My greatest apprehension was
for mine eyes, which I should have infallibly lost, if I had
not suddenly thought of an expedient. I kept, among other
little necessaries, a pair of spectacles, in a private pocket
which, as I observed before, had escaped the emperor's
searchers. These I took out, and fastened as strongly as I
could upon my nose, and thus armed, went on boldly with
my work, in spite of the enemy's arrows, many of which
struck against the glasses of my spectacles, but without any
other effect than a little to discompose them. I had now
fastened all the hooks, and taking the knot in my hand,
began to pull; but not a ship would stir, for they were all
too fast held by their anchors; so that the boldest part of
my enterprise remained. I therefore let go the cord, and
leaving the hooks fixed to the ships, I resolutely cut with
my knife the cables that fastened the anchors, receiving
about two hundred shots in my face and hands; then I
took up the knotted end of the cables, to which my hooks
were tied, and with the greatest ease drew fifty of the
enemy's largest men-of-war after me.

The Blefuscudians, who had not the least imagination of
what I intended, were at first confounded with astonishment. They had seen me cut the cables, and thought my

design was only to let the ships run adrift, or fall foul of each other; but when they perceived the whole fleet moving in order, and saw me pulling at the end, they set up such a scream of grief and despair as it is almost impossible to describe or conceive. When I had got out of danger, I stopped awhile to pick out the arrows that stuck in my hands and face; and rubbed on some of the same ointment that was given me on my first arrival, as I have formerly mentioned. I then took off my spectacles, and waiting about an hour, till the tide was a little fallen, I waded through the middle with my cargo, and arrived safe at the royal port of Lilliput.

The emperor and his whole court stood on the shore, expecting the issue of this great adventure. They saw the ships move forward in a large half-moon, but could not discern me, who was up to my breast in water. When I advanced to the middle of the channel, they were yet in pain, because I was under water to my neck.* The emperor concluded me to be drowned, and that the enemy's fleet was approaching in a hostile manner; but he was soon eased of his fears; for the channel growing shallower every step I made, I came in a short time within hearing, and holding up the end of the cable, by which the fleet was fastened, I cried in a loud voice, "Long live the most

* "If there be a point," observes Professor De Morgan, "in which Swift has overdrawn the monster, it is when he makes him drag after him fifty line-of-battle ships, which had held 30,000 men. Swift, therefore, supposes that a man up to his neck in water could drag by a rope a mass equal to 50/1728 of a line-of-battle ship of his own time. Or put it thus: the 30,000 men who jumped out of their ships would amount in weight and bulk to a little more than seventeen men of our size. Could a man, up to his neck in water, drag the boat which would hold seventeen men not closely packed? Probably not; and still less could Gulliver have dragged the ships." The proposition may be put even still more simply: Could thirty-five average able-bodied men, up to their necks in water, move a line-of-battle ship? Does this, after all, seem so improbable a feat? In the capture of the Blefuscudian fleet we have an allusion to the increase of the maritime power of England over France, gained by the treaty of Utrecht, in 1713.

puissant King of Lilliput!" This great prince received me at my landing with all possible encomiums, and created me a *nardac* on the spot, which is the highest title of honor among them.

His majesty desired I would take some other opportunity of bringing all the rest of his enemy's ships into his ports. And so immeasurable is the ambition of princes, that he seemed to think of nothing less than reducing the whole empire of Blefuscu into a province, and governing it by a viceroy; of destroying the Big Endian exiles, and compelling that people to break the smaller end of their eggs, by which he would remain the sole monarch of the whole world. But I endeavored to divert him from this design, by many arguments drawn from the topics of policy as well as justice; and I plainly protested, "that I would never be an instrument of bringing a free and brave people into slavery;" and, when the matter was debated in council, the wisest part of the Ministry were of my opinion.

This open, bold declaration of mine was so opposite to the schemes and politics of his imperial majesty, that he could never forgive me. He mentioned it in a very artful manner at council, where I was told that some of the wisest appeared, at least by their silence, to be of my opinion; but others, who were my enemies, could not forbear some expressions which by a side wind reflected on me; and from this time began an intrigue between his majesty and a junto of ministers, maliciously bent against me, which broke out in less than two months, and had like to have ended in my utter destruction. Of so little weight are the greatest services to princes, when put into the balance with a refusal to gratify their passions.

About three weeks after this exploit, there arrived a solemn embassy from Blefuscu, with humble offers of a peace; which was soon concluded upon conditions very advantageous to our emperor, wherewith I shall not trouble the reader. There were six ambassadors, with a train of about five hundred persons: and their entry was very magnificent, suitable to the grandeur of their master, and the importance of their business. When their treaty was finished, wherein I did them several good offices by the credit I now had, or at least appeared to have, at court, their excellencies, who were privately told how much I had been their friend, made me a visit in form. They began with many compliments upon my valor and generosity, invited me to that kingdom, in the emperor their master's name, and desired me to show them some proofs of my prodigious strength, of which they had heard so many wonders; wherein I readily obliged them, but shall not trouble the reader with the particulars.

When I had for some time entertained their excellencies, to their infinite satisfaction and surprise, I desired they would do me the honor to present my most humble respects to the emperor their master, the renown of whose virtues had so justly filled the whole world with admiration, and whose royal person I resolved to attend, before I returned to my own country. Accordingly, the next time I had the honor to see the emperor, I desired his general license to wait on the Blefuscudian monarch, which he was pleased to grant me, as I could perceive, in a very cold manner; but could not guess the reason, till I had a whisper from a certain person, "that Flimnap and Bolgolam had represented my intercourse with those ambassadors as a mark of disaffection;" from which I am sure my heart was wholly free. And this was the first time I began to conceive some imperfect idea of courts and ministers.

It is to be observed that these ambassadors spoke to me by an interpreter, the languages of both empires differing as much from each other as any two in Europe, and each nation priding itself upon the antiquity, beauty, and energy of their own tongue, with an avowed contempt of that of their neighbor: yet our emperor, standing upon the advantage he had got by the seizure of their fleet, obliged them to deliver their credentials, and make their speech, in the Lilliputian tongue. And it must be confessed, that from the great intercourse of trade and commerce between both realms: from the continual reception of exiles, which is mutual among them; and from the custom, in each empire, to send their young nobility and richer gentry to the other, in order to polish themselves by seeing the world, and understanding men and manners; there are few persons of distinction, or merchants, or seamen, who dwell in the maritime parts, but what can hold conversation in both tongues; as I found some weeks after, when I went to pay my respects to the Emperor of Blefuscu, which, in the midst of great misfortunes through the malice of my enemies, proved a very happy adventure to me, as I shall relate in its proper place.

CHAPTER VI

Of the Inhabitants of Lilliput—Their Learning, Laws, and Customs—The Manner of Educating Their Children— The Author's Way of Living in that Country—His Vindication of a Great Lady.

ALTHOUGH I intend to leave the description of this empire to a particular treatise, yet, in the mean time, I am content to gratify the curious reader with some general ideas. As the common size of the natives is somewhat under six inches high, so there is an exact proportion in all other animals, as well as plants and trees; for instance, the tallest horses and oxen are between four and five inches in height, the sheep an inch and a half, more or less; their geese about the bigness of a sparrow; and so the several gradations downward, till you come to the smallest, which, to my sight, were almost invisible; but Nature has adapted the eyes of the Lilliputians to all objects proper for their view; they see with great exactness, but at no great distance. And to show the sharpness of their sight toward objects that are near, I have been much pleased with observing a cook pulling a lark which was not as large as the common fly; and a young girl threading an invisible needle with invisible silk. Their tallest trees are about seven feet high; I mean some of those in the great royal park, the tops whereof I could but just reach with my fist clinched.* The other vegetables are in the same proportion; but this I leave to the reader's imagination.

* This is one of the many instances in the travels which show the manner in which the mind of the narrator seems to conform to the dimensions of everything around him, and to think of what is great and small, not according to the English standard, but that of the country in which he finds himself.

I shall say but little at present of their learning, which, for many ages, has flourished in all its branches among them; but their manner of writing is very peculiar, being neither from the left to the right, like the Europeans; nor from the right to the left, like the Arabians; nor from up to down, like the Chinese; but a slant, from one corner of the paper to the other, like ladies in England.*

There are some laws and customs in this empire very peculiar; and if they were not so directly contrary to those of my own dear country, I should be tempted to say a little in their justification. It is only to be wished they were as well executed. The first I shall mention relates to informers. All crimes against the state are punished here with the utmost severity; but, if the person accused makes his innocence plainly to appear upon his trial, the accuser is immediately put to an ignominious death; and out of his goods or lands the innocent person is quadruply recompensed for the loss of his time, for the danger he underwent, for the hardship of his imprisonment, and for all the charges he has been at in making his defense; or, if that fund be insufficient, it is largely supplied by the crown. The emperor also confers on him some public mark of his favor, and proclamation of his innocence is made throughout the whole city.

They look upon fraud as a greater crime than theft, and therefore seldom fail to punish it with death; for they allege that care and vigilance, with a very common understanding, may preserve a man's goods from thieves; but honesty has no fence against superior cunning; and since it is necessary that there should be a perpetual intercourse of buying and selling, and dealing upon credit, where fraud is permitted and connived at, or has no law to punish it, the honest dealer is always undone, and the knave gets the ad-

---

* Lord Mahon cites this passage in proof of the especial talent which Swift possessed in his manner of implying or assuming the charge he wishes to convey. Here his object is to censure the manner in which (as appears from one of his letters) English ladies then wrote.

vantage. I remember, when I was once interceding with the king for a criminal who had wronged his master of a great sum of money, which he had received by order, and ran away with; and happened to tell his majesty, by way of extenuation, that it was only a breach of trust, the emperor thought it monstrous in me to offer as a defense the greatest aggravation of the crime; and truly I had little to say in return, further than the common answer, that different nations had different customs; for, I confess, I was heartily ashamed.

Although we usually call reward and punishment the two hinges upon which all government turns, yet I could never observe this maxim to be put in practice by any nation, except that of Lilliput. Whoever can there bring sufficient proof that he has strictly observed the laws of his country for seventy-three moons, has a claim to certain privileges, according to his quality or condition in life, with a proportionate sum of money out of a fund appropriated for that use; he likewise acquires the title of *snilpall*, or legal, which is added to his name, but does not descend to his posterity. And these people thought it a prodigious defect of policy among us, when I told them that our laws were enforced only by penalties, without any mention of reward. It is upon this account that the image of Justice, in their courts of judicature, is formed with six eyes, two before, as many behind, and on each side one, to signify circumspection; with a bag of gold open in her right hand, and a sword sheathed in her left, to show she is more disposed to reward than to punish.

In choosing persons for all employments, they have more regard to good morals than to great abilities; for, since government is necessary to mankind, they believe that the common size of human understanding is fitted to some station or other; and that Providence never intended to make the management of public affairs a mystery to be comprehended only by a few persons of sublime genius, of which there are seldom three born in an age; but they suppose truth, justice, temperance, and the like, to be in every man's

power; the practice of which virtues, assisted by experience and a good intention, would qualify any man for the
service of his country, except where a course of study is required. But they thought the want of moral virtues was
so far from being supplied by superior endowments of the
mind, that employments could never be put into such dangerous hands as those of persons so qualified; and at least,
that the mistakes committed by ignorance, in a virtuous
disposition, would never be of such fatal consequence to the
public weal, as the practices of a man whose inclinations
led him to be corrupt, and who had great abilities to manage, to multiply, and defend his corruptions.

In like manner, the disbelief of a Divine Providence
renders a man incapable of holding any public station; for,
since kings avow themselves to be the deputies of Providence, the Lilliputians think nothing can be more absurd
than for a prince to employ such men as disown the authority under which he acts.

In relating these and the following laws, I would only be
understood to mean the original institutions, and not the
most scandalous corruptions into which these people are
fallen by the degenerate nature of man.

For, as to that infamous practice of acquiring great employments by dancing on the ropes, or badges of favor and
distinction by leaping over sticks and creeping under them,
the reader is to observe, that they were first introduced by
the grandfather of the emperor now reigning, and grew to
the present height by the gradual increase of party and
faction.

Ingratitude is among them a capital crime, as we read it
to have been in some other countries; for they reason thus:
that whoever makes ill return to his benefactor must needs
be a common enemy to the rest of mankind, from whom he
has received no obligation; and therefore such a man is not
fit to live.

Their notions relating to the duties of parents and children differ extremely from ours. They think that the
tenderness of parents toward their young proceeds from

natural principle: for which reason, they will never allow that a child is under any obligation to his father or his mother for bringing him into the world: which, considering the miseries of human life, was neither a benefit in itself, nor intended so by his parents.* Upon these, and the like reasonings, their opinion is that parents are the last of all others to be trusted with the education of their own children; and therefore they have in every town public nurseries, where all parents except cottagers and laborers, are obliged to send their infants of both sexes to be reared and educated, when they come to the age of twenty moons, at which time they are supposed to have some rudiments of docility. These schools are of several kinds, suited to different qualities, and both sexes. They have certain professors, well skilled in preparing children for such a condition of life as befits the rank of their parents, and their own caprices as well as inclinations.

I shall first say something of the male nurseries, and then of the female.

The nurseries for males of noble or eminent birth are provided with grave and learned professors and their several deputies. The clothes and food of the children are plain and simple. They are bred up in the principles of honor, justice, courage, modesty, clemency, religion, and love of their country; they are always employed in some business, except in the times of eating and sleeping, which are very short, and two hours for diversions, consisting of bodily exercises. They are dressed by men till four years of age, and then are obliged to dress themselves, although their quality be ever so great; and the women attendants, who are aged proportionably to ours at fifty, perform only

* "This idea," says Sir Walter Scott, "seems to be borrowed from Cyrano Bergerac's voyage to the moon, where he finds a people with whom it was the rule that the fathers obeyed their children." Swift, however, does not advocate, even in satire, so monstrous a principle. He is contented with suggesting the freedom from all moral obligation on the part of children to love or obey their parents.

the most menial offices. They are never suffered to converse with servants, but go together in smaller or greater
numbers to take their diversions, and always in the presence of a professor, or one of his deputies; whereby they
avoid those early bad impressions of folly and vice to which
our children are subject. Their parents are suffered to see
them only twice a year; the visit is to last but an hour;
they are allowed to kiss the child at meeting and parting;
but a professor, who always stands by on those occasions,
will not suffer them to whisper, or use any fondling expressions, or bring any presents of toys, sweet-meats, and the
like. The pension from each family for the education and
entertainment of a child, upon failure of due payment, is
levied by the emperor's officers.

The nurseries for children of ordinary gentlemen, merchants, traders, and handicrafts, are managed proportionably after the same manner; only those designed for trades
are put out apprentices at eleven years old: whereas, those
of persons of quality continue in their exercises till fifteen,
which answers to twenty-one with us; but the confinement
is gradually lessened for the last three years.

In the female nurseries, the young girls of quality are
educated much like the males, only they are dressed by
orderly servants of their own sex; but always in the presence of a professor or deputy, till they come to dress themselves, which is at five years old. And if it be found that
these nurses ever presume to entertain the girls with fright-
ful or foolish stories, or the common follies practiced by
chamber-maids among us, they are publicly whipped thrice
about the city, imprisoned for a year, and banished for life
to the most desolate part of the country. Thus, the young
ladies there are as much ashamed of being cowards and
fools as the men; and despise all personal ornaments, beyond decency and cleanliness; neither did I perceive any
difference in their education made by their differenc of sex
only that the exercises of the females were not altogether
so robust; and that some rules were given them relating to
domestic life, and a smaller compass of learning was en-

joined them: for their maxim is, that among people of quality, a wife should always be a reasonable and agreeable companion, because she cannot always be young. When the girls are twelve years old, which is the marriageable age, their parents or guardians take them home, with great expressions of gratitude to the professors, and seldom without the tears of the young lady and her companions.*

In the nurseries of females of the meaner sort, the children are instructed in work proper for their sex, and their several degrees; those intended for apprentices arc dismissed at seven years old; the rest are kept to eleven.

The meaner families who have children at these nurseries are obliged, beside their annual pension, which is as low as possible, to return to the steward of the nursery a small monthly share of their gettings, to be a portion for the child; and therefore all parents are limited in their expenses by the law. For the Lilliputians think nothing can be more unjust than for people, in subservience to their own appetites, to bring children into the world, and leave the burden of supporting them on the public. As to persons of quality, they give security to appropriate a certain sum for each child, suitable to their condition: and these funds are always managed with good husbandry and the most exact justice.

The cottagers and laborers keep their children at home, their business being only to till and cultivate the earth, and therefore their education is of little consequence to the public; but the old and diseased among them are supported by hospitals; for begging is a trade unknown in this empire.†

* The state of education among the people of England at the time was very defective, and engaged the attention of many writers. Swift has left us two essays on the subject: one on modern education, and the other on the education of young ladies.

† The sketch of the laws and customs of Lilliput is a covert censure upon some of the defects in English jurisprudence, and the administration of justice in Swift's day. Many of these defects have, however, been since remedied, especially by more stringent laws against fraudulent traders and breaches of trust

And here it may, perhaps, divert the curious reader to give some account of my domestics, and my manner of living in this country, during a residence of nine months and thirteen days. Having a head mechanically turned, and being likewise forced by necessity, I had made for myself a table and chair convenient enough, out of the largest trees in the royal park. Two hundred sempstresses were employed to make me shirts, and linen for my bed and table, all of the strongest and coarsest kind they could get; which, however, they were forced to quilt together in several folds, for the thickest was some degrees finer than lawn. Their linen is usually three inches wide, and three feet make a piece. The sempstresses took my measure as I lay on the ground, one standing at my neck, and another at my middle, with a strong cord extended, that each held by the end, while a third measured the length of the cord with the rule of an inch long. Then they measured my right thumb, and desired no more; for by a mathematical computation, that twice round the thumb is once round the wrist, and so on to the neck and waist, and by the help of my old shirt, which I displayed on the ground before them for a pattern, they fitted me exactly. Three hundred tailors were employed in the same manner to make me clothes; but they had another contrivance for taking my measure. I kneeled down, and they raised a ladder from the ground to my neck; upon this ladder one of them mounted, and let fall a plumb-line from my collar to the floor, which just answered the length of my coat; but my waist and arms I measured myself. When my clothes were finished, which was done in my house (for the largest of theirs would not have been able to hold them), they looked like the patchwork made by ladies in England, only that mine were all of a color.

I had three hundred cooks to dress my victuals, in little convenient huts, built about my house, where they and their families lived, and prepared two dishes apiece. I took up twenty waiters in my hand and placed them on the table; a hundred more attended below on the ground, some with dishes of meat, and some with barrels of wine and other liquors slung on their shoulders: all which the waiters above drew up, as I wanted, in a very ingenious manner, by certain cords, as we draw the bucket up a well in Europe. A dish of their meat was a good mouthful, and a barrel of their liquor a reasonable draught. Their mutton yields to ours, but their beef is excellent. I have had a sirloin so large that I have been forced to make three bites of it; but this is rare. My servants were astonished to see me eat it, bones and all, as in our country we do the leg of a lark. Their geese and turkeys I usually ate at a mouthful, and I confess they far exceed ours. Of their smaller fowl I could take up twenty or thirty at the end of my knife.

One day his imperial majesty, being informed of my way of living, desired "that himself and his royal consort, with the young princes of the blood of both sexes, might have the happiness," as he was pleased to call it, "of dining with me." They came accordingly, and I placed them in chairs of state, upon my table, just over against me, with their guards about them. Flimnap, the lord high treasurer, attended there likewise with his white staff; and I observed he often looked on me with a sour countenance, which I would not seem to regard, but ate more than usual, in honor to my dear country, as well as to fill the court with admiration. I have some private reasons to believe that this visit from his majesty gave Flimnap an opportunity of doing me ill offices to his master. That minister had always been my secret enemy, though he outwardly caressed me more than was usual to the moroseness of his nature. He represented to the emperor "the low condition of his treasury; that he was forced to take up money at a great discount; that exchequer bills would not circulate under nine per cent below par; that I had cost his majesty above a million and a half of *sprugs* (their greatest gold coin, about the bigness of a spangle); and, upon the whole, that it would be advisable in the emperor to take the first fair occasion of dismissing me."

I am here obliged to vindicate the reputation of an excellent lady, who was an innocent sufferer upon my account. The treasurer took a fancy to be jealous of his wife, from the malice of some evil tongues, who informed him that her grace had taken a violent affection for my person; and the court scandal ran for some time, that she once came privately to my lodging. This I solemnly declare to be a most infamous falsehood, without any grounds, further than that her grace was pleased to treat me with all innocent marks of freedom and friendship. I own she came often to my house, but always publicly, nor ever without three more in the coach, who were usually her sister and young daughter, and some particular acquaintance; but this was common to many other ladies of the court; and I will appeal to my servants around, whether they at any time saw a coach at my door without their knowing what persons were in it. On those occasions, when a servant had given me notice, my custom was to go immediately to the door; and, after paying my respects, to take up the coach and two horses very carefully in my hands (for, if there were six horses, the postilion always unharnessed four), and place them on a table, where I had fixed a movable rim, quite round, of five inches high, to prevent accidents; and I have often had four coaches and horses at once on my table, full of company, while I sat in my chair leaning my face toward them; and while I was engaged with one set, the coachmen would gently drive the others round my table. I have passed many an afternoon very agreeably in these conversations. But I defy the treasurer, or his two informers (I will name them, and let them make the best of it), Clustril and Drunlo, to prove that any person ever came to me *incognito*, except the secretary Reldresal, who was sent by express command of his imperial majesty, as I have before related. I should not have dwelt so long upon this particular, if it had not been a point wherein the reputation of a great lady is so nearly concerned, to say nothing of my own; though I then had the honor to be a *nardac*, which the treasurer himself is not; for all the world knows, that ne is only a *glumglum,* a title inferior by one degree, as that of a marquis is to a duke in England; yet I allow he preceded me in right of his post. These false informations, which I afterward came to the knowledge of by an accident not proper to mention, made the treasurer show his lady for some time an ill countenance, and me a worse; and although he was at last undeceived, and reconciled to her, yet I lost all credit with him, and found my interest decline very fast with the emperor himself, who was, indeed, too much governed by that favorite.*

* It would be impossible to conceive anything more exquisitely absurd, or more irresistibly comic, than the whole of this episode touching the honor of the treasurer's lady. The solemn earnestness with which Gulliver vindicates her character, the elaborate detail of proofs into which he enters to establish her innocence as well as his own, the defiance of the treasurer and his two informers to show any visits *incognito,* and his apology for dwelling so long on the subject, form the most felicitous exhibition of that sly and quiet humor of which Swift was so great a master. Whether Swift had any particular person in view can be only a matter of conjecture.

CHAPTER VII

The Author, Being Informed of a Design to Accuse Him of
High Treason, Makes His Escape to Blefuscu—His Re-
ception There.

BEFORE I proceed to give an account of my leaving this
kingdom, it may be proper to inform the reader of a private
intrigue, which had been for two months forming against
me.

I had been hitherto, all my life, a stranger to courts, for
which I was unqualified by the meanness of my condition.
I had, indeed, heard and read enough of the dispositions of
great princes and ministers; but never expected to have
found such terrible effects of them in so remote a country,
governed, as I thought, by very different maxims from
those in Europe.

While I was just preparing to pay my attendance on the
Emperor of Blefuscu, a considerable person at court (to
whom I had been very serviceable, at a time when he lay
under the highest displeasure of his imperial majesty) came
to my house very privately at night, in a close chair, and,
without sending in his name, desired admittance. The
chairmen were dismissed; I put the chair, with his lordship in it, into my coat-pocket, and, giving orders to a
trusty servant to say I was indisposed and gone to sleep,
I fastened the door of my house, placed the chair on the
table, according to my usual custom, and sat down by it.
After the common salutations were over, observing his lordship's countenance full of concern, and inquiring into the
reason, he desired I would hear him with patience, in a
matter that highly concerned my honor and my life. His
speech was to the following effect, for I took notes of it as
soon as he left me:

"You are to know," said he, "that several committees of

council have lately been called in the most private manner, on your account; and it is but two days since his majesty came to a full resolution.

"You are very sensible that Skyresh Bolgolam (*galbet* or high-admiral) has been your mortal enemy, almost ever since your arrival. His original reasons I know not; but his hatred is increased since your great success against Blefuscu, by which his glory as admiral is much obscured.

"This lord, in conjunction with Flimnap, the high-treasurer, whose enmity against you is notorious, on account of his lady; Limtoc, the general; Lalcon, the chamberlain; and Balmuff, the grand justiciary, have prepared articles of impeachment against you for treason and other capital crimes."

The preface made me so impatient, being conscious of my own merits and innocence, that I was going to interrupt him; when he entreated me to be silent, and thus proceeded:

"Out of gratitude for the favors you have done me, I procured information of the whole proceedings, and a copy of the articles; wherein I ventured my head for your service

"ARTICLES OF IMPEACHMENT AGAINST QUINBUS FLESTRIN, THE MAN-MOUNTAIN.

"ARTICLE I. That the said Quinbus Flestrin, having brought the imperial fleet of Blefuscu into the royal port, and being afterward commanded by his imperial majesty to seize all the other ships of the said empire of Blefuscu, and reduce that empire to a province, to be governed by a viceroy from hence, and to destroy and to put to death, not only all the Big Endian exiles, but likewise all the people of that empire who would not immediately forsake the Big Endian heresy; he, the said Flestrin, like a false traitor against his most auspicious, serene, imperial majesty, did petition to be excused from the said service, upon pretense of unwillingness to force the consciences or destroy the liberties and lives of an innocent people.

"ARTICLE II. That, whereas certain ambassadors arrived from the court of Blefuscu, to sue for peace in his majesty's court; he, the said Flestrin, did, like a false traitor, aid, abet, comfort, and divert the said ambassadors, although he knew them to be servants to a prince who was lately an open enemy to his imperial majesty, and in an open war against his said majesty.

"ARTICLE III. That the said Quinbus Flestrin, contrary to the duty of a faithful subject, is now preparing to make a voyage to the court and empire of Blefuscu, for which he has received only verbal license from his imperial majesty; and, under color of the said license, does falsely and traitorously intend to take the said voyage, and thereby to aid, comfort, and abet the Emperor of Blefuscu, so lately an enemy and in open war with his imperial majesty aforesaid.

"There are some other articles; but these are the most important, of which I have read you an abstract.

"In the several debates upon this impeachment, it must be confessed that his majesty gave many marks of his great lenity; often urging the services you had done him, and endeavoring to extenuate your crimes. The treasurer and admiral insisted that you should be put to the most painful and ignominious death, by setting fire to your house at night; and the general was to attend with twenty thousand men, armed with poisoned arrows, to shoot you on the face and hands. Some of your servants were to have private orders to strew a poisonous juice on your shirts and sheets, which would soon make you tear your own flesh, and die in the utmost torture. The general came into the same opinion; so that, for a long time, there was a majority against you; but his majesty resolving, if possible, to spare your life, at last bought off the chamberlain.

"Upon this incident, Reldresal, principal secretary for private affairs, who always approved himself your true friend, was commanded by the emperor to deliver his opinion, which he accordingly did; and therein justified the good thoughts you have of him. He allowed your crimes to be great, but that there was still room for mercy, the most commendable virtue in a prince, and for which his majesty was so justly celebrated. He said, the friendship between you and him was so well known to the world, that perhaps the most honorable board might think him partial; however, in obedience to the command he had received, he would freely offer his sentiments. That if his majesty, in consideration of your services, and pursuant to his own merciful disposition, would please to spare your life, and only give orders to put out both your eyes, he humbly conceived that by this expedient justice might in some measure be satisfied, and all the world would applaud the lenity of the emperor, as well as the fair and generous proceedings of those who have the honor to be his counselors. That the loss of your eyes would be no impediment to your bodily strength, by which you might still be useful to his majesty; that blindness is an addition to courage, by concealing dangers from us; that the fear you had for your eyes was the greatest difficulty in bringing over the enemy's fleet; and it would be sufficient for you to see by the eyes of the ministers, since the greatest princes do no more.

"This proposal was received with the utmost disapprobation by the whole board. Bolgolam, the admiral, could not preserve his temper; but rising up in a fury, said he wondered how the secretary durst presume to give his opinion for preserving the life of a traitor; that the services you had performed were, by all true reasons of state, the great aggravation of your crimes; the same strength which enabled you to bring over the enemy's fleet might serve, upon the first discontent, to carry it back; that he had good reasons to think that you were Big Endian in your heart; and, as treason begins in the heart before it appears in overt acts, so he accused you as a traitor on that account, and therefore insisted you should be put to death.

"The treasurer was of the same opinion; he showed to what straits his majesty's revenue was reduced, by the charge of maintaining you, which would soon grow insupportable; that the secretary's expedient of putting out your eyes was so far from being a remedy against this evil, that it would probably increase it, as is manifest from the common practice of blinding some kind of fowls, after which they fed the faster, and grew sooner fat; that his sacred majesty and the council, who are your judges, were, in their own consciences, fully convinced of your guilt, which was a sufficient argument to condemn you to death, without the formal proofs required by the strict letter of the law.

"But his imperial majesty, fully determined against capital punishment, was graciously pleased to say, that since the council thought the loss of your eyes too easy a censure, some other way may be inflicted hereafter. And your friend the secretary, humbly desiring to be heard again, in answer to what the treasurer had objected, concerning the great charge his majesty was at in maintaining you, said, that his excellency, who had the sole disposal of the emperor's revenue, might easily provide against that evil, by gradually lessening your establishment; by which, for want of sufficient food, you will grow weak and faint, and lose your appetite, and consume in a few months; neither would the stench of your carcass be then so dangerous, when it should become more than half diminished; and immediately upon your death five or six thousand of his majesty's subjects might, in two or three days, cut your flesh from your bones, take it away by cartloads, and bury it in distant parts to prevent infection, leaving the skeleton as a monument of admiration to posterity.

"Thus upon the great friendship of the secretary, the whole affair was compromised. It was strictly enjoined that the project of starving you by degrees should be kept a secret; but the sentence of putting out your eyes was entered on the books; none dissenting except Bolgolam, the admiral, who, being a creature of the empress, was perpetually instigated by her majesty to insist upon your death.

"In three days, your friend the secretary will be directed to come to your house, and read before you the articles of impeachment; and then to signify the great lenity and favor of his majesty and council, whereby you are only condemned to the loss of your eyes, which his majesty does not question you will gratefully and humbly submit to; and twenty of his majesty's surgeons will attend, to see the operation performed, by discharging very sharp-pointed arrows into the balls of your eyes, as you lie on the ground.

"I leave to your prudence what measures you will take; and to avoid suspicion, I must immediately return in as private a manner as I came."

His lordship did so; and I remained alone, under many doubts and perplexities of mind.

It was a custom introduced by this prince and his ministry (very different, as I have been assured, from the practice of former times), that after the court had decreed any cruel execution, either to gratify the monarch's resentment, or the malice of a favorite, the emperor always made a speech to his whole council, expressing his great lenity and tenderness, as qualities known and confessed by all the world. This speech was immediately published throughout the kingdom; nor did anything terrify the people so much as those encomiums on his majesty's mercy; because it was observed that the more these praises were enlarged and insisted on, the more inhuman was the punishment, and the more innocent the sufferer. Yet as to myself, I must confess, having never been designed for a courtier, either by my birth or education, I was so ill a judge of things, that I could not discover the lenity and favor of this sentence, but conceived it (perhaps erroneously) to be rather rigorous than gentle. I sometimes thought of standing my trial; for although I could not deny the facts alleged in the several articles, yet I hoped they would admit of some extenuation. But having in my life perused many state trials, which I ever observed to terminate as the judges thought fit to direct, I durst not rely on so dangerous a decision, in so critical a juncture, and against such powerful enemies.

Once I was strongly bent upon resistance: for while I had liberty the whole strength of that empire could hardly subdue me, and I might easily with stones pelt the metropolis to pieces; but I soon rejected that project with horror, by remembering the oath I had made to the emperor, the favors I received from him, and the high title of *nardac* he conferred upon me. Neither had I so soon learned the gratitude of courtiers, to persuade myself that his majesty's present severities acquitted me of all past obligations.

At last, I fixed upon a resolution, for which it is probable I may incur some censure, and not unjustly; for I

confess I owe the preserving of mine eyes, and consequently
my liberty, to my own great rashness and want of experience; because, if I had then known the nature of princes
and ministers, which I have since observed in many other
courts, and their methods of treating criminals less obnox-
ious than myself, I should, with great alacrity and readiness,
have submitted to so easy a punishment. But hurried on
by the precipitancy of youth, and having his imperial
majesty's license to pay my attendance upon the Emperor
of Blefuscu, I took this opportunity, before the three days
were elapsed, to send a letter to my friend the secretary,
signifying my resolution of setting out that morning for
Blefuscu, pursuant to the leave I had got; and, without
waiting for an answer, I went to that side of the island
where our fleet lay. I seized a large man-of-war, and tied
the cable to the prow; and, lifting up the anchors, I stripped
myself, put my clothes (together with my coverlet, which
I carried under my arm) into the vessel, and drawing it
after me, between wading and swimming arrived at the
royal port of Blefuscu, where the people had long expected
me.* They lent me two guides to direct me to the capital

---

* As Gulliver was expected in Blefuscu, so was Bolingbroke
expected in France, having carefully made all his arrangements
to escape thither. On the night of the 25th of March, 1715, he
attended the performance at Drury Lane Theatre to its close,
bespoke the particular play for the ensuing night, then proceeded
homeward, disguised himself in a large cloak and black wig, as
a servant of M. La Vigne, one of the messengers of the French
king, and proceeding to Dover, where he had a narrow escape
of detention, crossed over to Calais, where the governor's coach
awaited him on his arrival. In a letter which he wrote from
Dover, said to have been addressed to Lord Lansdowne, Bolingbroke justified his flight upon reasons similar to those given by
Gulliver for leaving Lilliput: "You will excuse me when you
know that I had certain and repeated information, from some
who are in the secret of affairs, that a resolution was taken by
those who have power to execute it, to pursue me to the scaffold.
. . . Had there been the least reason to hope for a fair and open
trial, after having been already prejudged unheard by two
Houses of Parliament, I should not have declined the strictest
examination."

city, which is of the same name: I held them in my hands, till I came within two hundred yards of the gate, and desired them "to signify my arrival to one of the secretaries, and let him know I there waited his majesty's commands." I had an answer in about an hour, "that his majesty, attended by the royal family and great officers of the court, was coming out to receive me." I advanced a hundred yards. The emperor and his train alighted from their horses, the empress and ladies from their coaches, and I did not perceive they were in any fright or concern. I lay on the ground to kiss his majesty and the empress's hands. I told his majesty, that I was come according to my promise, and with the license of the emperor, my master, to have the honor of seeing so mighty a monarch, and to offer him any service in my power, consistent with my duty to my own prince; not mentioning a word of my disgrace, because I had hitherto no regular information of it, and might suppose myself wholly ignorant of any such design; neither could I reasonably conceive that the emperor would discover the secret while I was out of his power; wherein, however, it soon appeared I was deceived.

I shall not trouble the reader with the particular account of my reception at this court, which was suitable to the generosity of so great a prince; nor of the difficulties I was in for want of a house and bed, being forced to lie on the ground, wrapped up in my coverlet.*

---

* The difficulties and privations which Gulliver suffered on his arrival in Blefuscu are probably intended to refer to the bereaved condition in which Bolingbroke found himself when he reached France. Deserted by friends and flatterers, stripped of rank, fortune, and political power, he found himself an impoverished exile in that country where, a short time before, he had been caressed by the king, courted by the nobles, and honored by the people. Indeed, the change affected his health, for he fell sick shortly after his arrival.

CHAPTER VIII

The Author, by a Lucky Accident, Finds Means to Leave Blefuscu, and, After Some Difficulties, Returns to His Native Country.

THREE days after my arrival, walking, out of curiosity, to the north-east coast of the island, I observed, about half a league off in the sea, something that looked like a boat overturned. I pulled off my shoes and stockings, and, wading two or three hundred yards, I found the object to approach nearer by force of the tide; and then plainly saw it to be a real boat, which I supposed might by some tempest have been driven from a ship; whereupon I returned immediately toward the city, and desired his imperial majesty to lend me twenty of the tallest vessels he had left, after the loss of his fleet, and three thousand seamen, under the command of his vice-admiral. This fleet sailed round while I went back the shortest way to the coast, where I first discovered the boat. I found the tide had driven it still nearer. The seamen were all provided with cordage, which I had beforehand twisted to a sufficient strength. When the ships came up, I stripped myself, and waded till I came within a hundred yards of the boat, after which I was forced to swim till I got up to it. The seamen threw me the end of the cord, which I fastened to a hole in the forepart of the boat, and the other end to a man-of-war; but I found all my labor to little purpose; for, being out of my depth, I was not able to work. In this necessity I was forced to swim behind, and push the boat forward, as often as I could, with one of my hands; and the tide favoring me, I advanced so far that I could just hold up my chin and feel the ground. I rested two or three minutes,

62

and then gave the boat another shove, and so on, till the sea was no higher than my arm-pits; and now the most laborious part being over I took out my other cables, which were stowed in one of the ships, and fastened them first to the boat, and then to nine of the vessels which attended me; the wind being favorable, the seamen towed and I shoved until we arrived within forty yards of the shore, and waiting till the tide was out, I got dry to the boat; and by the assistance of two thousand men, with ropes and engines, made a shift to turn it on its bottom, and found it was but little damaged.

I shall not trouble the reader with the difficulties I was under, by the help of certain paddles, which cost me ten days making, to get my boat into the royal port of Blefuscu, where a mighty concourse of people appeared upon my arrival, full of wonder at the sight of so prodigious a vessel. I told the emperor "that my good fortune had thrown this boat in my way, to carry me to some place whence I might return to my native country; and begged his majesty's orders for getting materials to fit it up, together with his license to depart;" which, after some kind expostulations, he was pleased to grant.

I did very much wonder, in all this time, not to have heard* of any express relating to me from our emperor to the court of Blefuscu. But I was afterward given privately to understand, that his imperial majesty, never imagining I had the least notice of his designs, believed I was only gone to Blefuscu in performance of my promise, according to the license he had given me, which was well known at our court, and would return in a few days, when the ceremony was ended. But he was at last in pain at my long

* Sheridan observes upon this sentence, that it is ungrammatical, adding that it should have been written, "I did very much wonder, in all this time, at not having heard," etc. Similar objections have been made by him to many other phrases and expressions throughout the work, which he considers as slovenly writing. I am disposed to think that Swift used such phraseology as in keeping with the character of Gulliver, and the plain provincial style in which he might be supposed to write.

absence; and, after consulting with the treasurer and the rest of that cabal, a person of quality was dispatched with the copy of the articles against me. This envoy had instructions to represent to the monarch of Blefuscu "the great lenity of his master, who was content to punish me no further than the loss of mine eyes; that I had fled from justice; and, if I did not return in two hours, I should be deprived of my title of *nardac,* and declared a traitor." The envoy further added, "that, in order to maintain the peace and amity between both empires, his master expected that his brother of Blefuscu would give orders to have me sent back to Lilliput, bound hand and foot, to be punished as a traitor."

The emperor of Blefuscu, having taken three days to consult, returned an answer consisting of many civilities and excuses. He said, "that as for sending me bound, his brother knew it was impossible; that although I had deprived him of his fleet, yet he owed great obligations to me for many good offices I had done him in making the peace. That, however, both their majesties would soon be made easy; for I had found a prodigious vessel on the shore, able to carry me on the sea, which he had given orders to fit up, with my assistance and direction; and he hoped in a few weeks both empires would be freed from so insupportable an incumbrance."

With this answer the envoy returned to Lilliput, and the monarch of Blefuscu related to me all that had passed, offering me at the same time (but under the strictest confidence) his gracious protection, if I would continue in his service; wherein, although I believed him sincere, yet I resolved nevermore to put any confidence in princes or ministers where I could possibly avoid it; and therefore, with all due acknowledgment of his favorable intentions, I humbly begged to be excused. I told him, "that since fortune, whether good or evil, had thrown a vessel in my way, I was resolved to venture myself on the ocean, rather than be an occasion of difference between two such mighty monarchs." Neither did I find the emperor at all displeased;

and I discovered, by a certain accident, that he was very glad of my resolution, and so were most of his ministers.*

These considerations moved me to hasten my departure somewhat sooner than I intended; to which the court, impatient to have me gone, very readily contributed. Five hundred workmen were employed to make two sails to my boat according to my directions, by quilting thirteen folds of their strongest linen together. I was at the pains of making ropes and cables, by twisting ten, twenty, or thirty of the thickest and strongest of theirs. A great stone that I happened to find, after a long search, by the sea-shore, served me for an anchor. I had the tallow of three hundred cows for greasing my boat and other uses. I was at incredible pains in cutting down some of the largest timber-trees for oars and masts, wherein I was, however, much assisted by his majesty's ship-carpenters, who helped me in smoothing them after I had done the rough work.

* The readiness of the monarch and ministry of Blefuscu to get rid of Gulliver denotes the desire of Louis and his Ministry to free themselves from the intrigues of Bolingbroke, whose restless mind was the cause of perpetual alarm, as likely to embroil them with the English Court. Ere we take leave of one who has been so constantly alluded to in the voyage to Lilliput, it may not be amiss to say something of so remarkable a man—one lavishly endowed with almost every intellectual and natural gift, improved by education, and adorned by wealth. As a wit, a scholar, a writer, and a speaker, he occupied the highest place; the friend of every man of letters in his day, from Dryden down to Gay. The eulogies of his contemporaries are familiar to all scholars. Swift wrote: "I think Mr. St. John the greatest young man I ever knew; wit, capacity, beauty, quickness of apprehension, good learning, and an excellent taste; the best orator in the House of Commons." And he praises his vast range of wit and fancy, and his invincible eloquence. "His address," says Lord Chesterfield, "pre-engages, his eloquence persuades, and his knowledge informs all who approach him." Pope pronounces him "the best writer of the age;" while Voltaire, who knew him as a youth, declares, *"J'ai trouvé dans cet illustre Anglais tout l'erudition de son pays et toute la politesse du notre."* Burke and Pitt made him their model for oratory, and the latter used to say that he would rather recover a speech of Bolingbroke's than any of the lost works of antiquity.

In about a month, when all was prepared, I sent to receive his majesty's commands, and to take my leave. The emperor and royal family came out of the palace; I lay down on my face to kiss his hand, which he very graciously gave me; so did the empress and the young princes of the blood. His majesty presented me with fifty purses of two hundred *sprugs* apiece, together with his picture at full length, which I put immediately into one of my gloves, to keep it from being hurt. The ceremonies at my departure were altogether too many to trouble the reader with at this time.

I stored the boat with the carcasses of a hundred oxen and three hundred sheep, with bread and drink proportionable, and as much meat ready dressed as four hundred cooks could provide. I took with me six cows and two bulls alive, with as many ewes and rams, intending to carry them into my own country, and propagate the breed; and to feed them on board, I had a good bundle of hay, and a bag of corn. I would gladly have taken a dozen of the natives, but this was a thing the emperor would by no means permit; and, besides a diligent search into my pockets, his majesty engaged my honor "not to carry away any of his subjects, although with their own consent and desire."

Having thus prepared all things as well as I was able, I set sail on the 24th day of September, 1701, at six in the morning; and when I had gone about four leagues to the northward, the wind being at the southeast, at six in the evening I descried a small island, about half a league to the north-west. I advanced forward, and cast anchor on the lee-side of the island, which seemed to be uninhabited. I then took some refreshment, and went to my rest. I slept well, as I conjecture, at least six hours, for I found the day broke in two hours after I awoke. It was a clear night. I ate my breakfast before the sun was up; and heaving anchor, the wind being favorable, I steered the same course that I had done the day before, wherein I was directed by my pocket-compass. My intention was to reach, if possible, one of those islands which I had reason to believe lay to the north-east of Van Diemen's Land. I discovered nothing all that day; but upon the next, about three in the afternoon, when I had by my computation made twenty-four leagues from Blefuscu, I descried a sail steering to the south-east; my course was due east. I hailed her, but could get no answer; yet I found that I gained upon her, for the wind slackened. I made all the sail I could, and in half an hour she spied me, then hung out her ancient, and discharged a gun. It is not easy to express the joy I was in, upon the unexpected hope of once more seeing my beloved country and the dear pledges I left in it. The ship slackened her sails, and I came up with her between five and six in the evening, September 26th; but my heart leaped within me to see her English colors. I put my cows and sheep into my coat pocket, and got on board with all my little cargo of provisions. The vessel was an English merchantman, returning from Japan by the North and South Seas; the captain, Mr. John Biddle, of Deptford, a very civil man, and an excellent sailor. We were now in the latitude 30 degrees south; there were about fifty men in the ship; and here I met an old comrade of mine, one Peter Williams, who gave me a good character to the captain. This gentleman treated me with kindness, and desired I would let him know what place I came from last, and whither I was bound; which I did in a few words, but he thought I was raving and that the dangers I had undergone had disturbed my head; whereupon I took my black cattle and sheep out of my pocket, which, after great astonishment, clearly convinced him of my veracity. I then showed him the gold given me by the emperor of Blefuscu, together with his majesty's picture at full length, and some other rarities of that country. I gave him two purses of two hundred *sprugs* each, and promised, when we arrived in England, to make him a present of a cow and a sheep.

I shall not trouble the reader with a particular account of this voyage, which was very prosperous for the most part. We arrived in the Downs on the 13th of April, 1702. I had only one misfortune, that the rats on board carried away one of my sheep; I found her bones in a hole, picked clean from the flesh. The rest of my cattle I got safe ashore, and set them a-grazing in a bowling-green at Greenwich, where the fineness of the grass made them feed very heartily, though I had always feared the contrary; neither could I possibly have preserved them in so long a voyage, if the captain had not allowed me some of his best biscuit, which, rubbed to powder and mingled with water, was their constant food.* The short time I continued in England, I made a considerable profit by showing my cattle to many persons of quality and others; and before I began my second voyage I sold them for six hundred pounds. Since my last return I find the breed is considerably increased, especially the sheep, which I hope will prove much to the advantage of the woolen manufacture, by the fineness of their fleeces.

I stayed but two months with my wife and family, for my insatiable desire of seeing foreign countries would suffer me to continue no longer. I left fifteen hundred pounds with my wife, and fixed her in a good house at Redriff. My remaining stock I carried with me, part in money and part in goods, in hopes to improve my fortunes. My eldest uncle, John, had left me an estate in land, near Epping, of about thirty pounds a year; and I had a long lease of the "Black Bull" in Fetter Lane, which yielded me as

---

* The consistency with which Swift sustains his fiction is everywhere visible. A less careful writer would have put the cattle in a pasture, where the inequalities of the ground and the coarseness and length of the grass would have made it impossible for them to live. Gulliver puts them in the short, fine grass of a smooth bowling-green, after having fed them through the voyage on finely-powdered biscuit. Nor does he forget to comment on the fineness of the fleeces, as calculated to improve the woolen manufacture, a subject which, at the time, occupied the Legislature a good deal.

much more; so that I was not in any danger of leaving my family upon the parish. My son Johnny, named so after his uncle, was at the grammar-school, and a towardly child. My daughter Betty (who is now well married, and has children) was then at her needle-work. I took leave of my wife, and boy and girl, with tears on both sides, and went on board the Adventure, a merchant-ship of three hundred tons, bound for Surat; Captain John Nicholas, of Liverpool, commander. But my account of this voyage must be referred to the second part of my travels.*

* A discussion, of little practical value, has arisen as to the origin of the name of Gulliver. Mr. Henry T. Riley says: "It appears to me by no means improbable that 'Gulliver' is a hybrid word, coined in the sarcastic corner of Swift's brain, and that its components are the words *gull in verity;* it being his meaning that he gulled the world in telling them the truth." This hypothesis is more ingenious than probable. The account given by another writer is more natural: "The names of Gulliver and Gulliford are quiet common in parts of Somerset. . . . Many years ago, I remember passing a cart, in that neighborhood, with the name of Gulliver on it, and remarked to my father, with whom I was walking, that it was the same name as the hero of Swift's book. Upon which my father told me Swift had met with the name precisely in the same manner; that he was, when contemplating his intended work, much in want of a name, and that, when out walking or riding one day, I know not where, a cart passed him with 'Gulliver' on it, which he at once decided should be the name of his hero, as it was quite uncommon. For the same reason, my father informed me, he also chose, 'Lemuel.' I do not know my father's authority for this little history."

[After the first edition of the "Travels" had appeared, Gay wrote a Lilliputian ode, addressed to Quinbus Flestrin, by Titty Tit, poet-laureate to His Majesty of Lilliput. Pope thus refers to it in a letter to Swift, March 8th, 1726–7: "You received, I hope, some commendatory verses from a horse, and a Lilliputian, to Gulliver; and an heroic epistle to Mrs. Gulliver. The bookseller would fain have printed them before the second edition of the book, but I would not permit it without your approbation; nor do I much like them." We concur in the last observation. The ode of the Lilliputian laureate is rather ingenious than clever; the lines, except the last of each stanza, being trisyllabic, to represent the pigmy proportions of Lilliputian poetry. We subjoin the ode.]

TO QUINBUS FLESTRIN, THE MAN-MOUNTAIN

An Ode

BY TITTY TIT, ESQ.,

POET-LAUREATE TO HIS MAJESTY OF LILLIPUT

Translated into English

In amaze,
Lost, I gaze!
Can our eyes
Reach thy size?
May my lays
Swell with praise
Worthy thee!
Worthy me!
Muse, inspire
All thy fire!
Bards of old
Of him told,
When they said
Atlas' head
Propp'd the skies:
See, and believe
   your eyes.

See him stride
Valleys wide,
Over woods,
Over floods.
When he treads,
Mountains' heads
Groan and shake:
Armies quake,
Lest his spurn
Overturn
Man and steed:
Troops, take heed.
Left and right,
Speed your flight!
Lest an host
Beneath his foot
   be lost.

Turn'd aside
From his hide,
Safe from wound
Darts rebound;
From his nose
Clouds he blows;
When he speaks,
Thunder breaks!
When he eats,
Famine threats;
When he drinks,
Neptune shrinks!
Nigh thy ear,
In mid-air,
On thy hand
Let me stand,
So shall I,
Lofty poet, **touch**
   the sky.

A VOYAGE TO
BROBDINGNAG

A Voyage To Brobdingnag*

CHAPTER I

A Great Storm Descried—The Long-boat Sent to Fetch Water—The Author Goes With It to Discover the Country—He Is Left on Shore, Is Seized by One of the Natives, and Carried to a Farmer's House—His Reception, with Several Accidents that Happened There—A Description of the Inhabitants.

HAVING been condemned, by nature and fortune, to an active and restless life, in two months after my return I again left my native country, and took shipping in the Downs, on the 20th day of June, 1702, in the Adventure— Captain John Nicholas, a Cornishman, commander—bound for Surat. We had a prosperous gale, till we arrived at the Cape of Good Hope, where we landed for fresh water; but

* Hitherto we have been inspecting humanity, as it were, through a telescope reversed, in which every object appears diminished; we are now to use the instrument the other way, and looking through the smaller end, see all things magnified. Or, to use the metaphor of Lord Orrery, "the inhabitants of Lilliput are represented as if reflected from a convex mirror, by which every object is reduced to a despicable minuteness; the inhabitants of Brobdingnag, by a contrary mirror, are enlarged to a shocking deformity. In Lilliput we behold a set of puny insects, or animalcules, in human shape, ridiculously engaged in affairs of importance; in Brobdingnag the monsters of enormous size are employed in trifles." Perhaps a more novel, happy, and ingenious idea never occurred to the mind of any author, than this sudden transposition of the condition of the beholder and of the objects beheld. It comes upon one with a surprise that is absolutely startling, each fiction intensifying the other by the charm and effect of contrast, like those optical

discovering a leak, we unshipped our goods, and wintered there; for the captain falling sick of an ague, we could not leave the Cape till the end of March. We then set sail, and had a good voyage till we passed the Straits of Madagascar; but having got northward of that island, and to about five degrees south latitude, the winds, which in those seas are observed to blow a constant equal gale between the north and west, from the beginning of December to the beginning of May, on the 19th of April began to blow with much greater violence, and more westerly than usual, continuing so for twenty days together; during which time we were driven a little to the east of the Molucca Islands, and about three degrees northward of the line, as our captain found by an observation he took the 2d of May, at which time the wind ceased, and it was a perfect calm, whereat I was not a little rejoiced. But he, being a man well experienced in the navigation of those seas, bid us all prepare against a storm, which accordingly happened the

---

toys by which the eye, after gazing a long time on one color, is suddenly filled with its complementary. There is another striking contrast between the first and second voyages. We pass from personal satire against individuals to general satire against institutions. "In the Voyage to Brobdingnag," observes Scott, "the satire is of a more general character; nor is it easy to trace any particular reference to the political events or statesmen of the period. It merely exhibits human actions and sentiments as they might appear in the apprehension of beings of immense strength, and, at the same time, of a cold, reflecting, and philosophical character. The monarch of these sons of Anak is designed to embody Swift's ideas of a patriot king, indifferent to what was curious, and cold to what was beautiful, feeling only interest in that which was connected with general utility and the public weal. To such a prince the intrigues, scandals, and stratagems of a European court are represented as equally odious in their origin, and contemptible in their progress." Throughout the "Voyage to Brobdingnag," as throughout that to Lilliput, we have the same wonderful power of making fiction appear like truth, by the minute attention to consistency, the little incidental details of unimportant affairs, and the liveliness and graphic force of narration; we have, too, the bitter invective, the trenchant sarcasm, and the stinging jest which Swift knew how to use with such terrible power.

day following; for the southern wind, called the southern monsoon, began to set in.

Finding it was likely to overblow, we took in our sprit-sail, and stood by to hand the fore-sail; but, making foul weather, we looked the guns were all fast, and handed the mizzen. The ship lay very broad off, so we thought it better spooning before the sea, than trying or hulling. We reefed the fore-sail, and set him, and hauled aft the fore-sheet; the helm was hard a-weather. The ship wore bravely. We belayed the fore down-haul; but the sail was split, and we hauled down the yard, and got the sail into the ship, and unbound all the things clear of it. It was a very fierce storm; the sea broke strange and dangerous. We hauled off upon the lanyards of the whip-staff, and helped the man at the helm. We would not get down our topmast, but let all stand, because she scudded before the sea very well, and we knew that the topmast being aloft, the ship was the wholesomer, and made better way through the sea, seeing we had sea-room. When the storm was over, we set fore-sail and main-sail, and brought the ship to. Then we set the mizzen, main-top-sail, and the fore-top-sail. Our course was east-north-east, the wind was at south-west. We got the starboard tacks aboard; we cast off the weather-bowlings, weather-braces, and lifts; we set in the lee-braces, and hauled them tight, and belayed them; and hauled over the mizzen and hauled forward by tack to windward, and kept her full and by as near as she would lie.*

* One cannot but admire the ingenuity of Swift in this account of the management and working of the good ship, the "Adventure, Captain John Nicholas," during the storm. The manner in which the nautical phrases are used gives a wonderful air of reaiity to the whole, and must remind the reader of the tedious minuteness with which the old navigators described their voyages, and which Swift probably meant to satirize. So accurate, indeed, is the imitation of the technicalities, that Scott informs us seamen have been known to work hard in order to attain a perfect understanding of those details. There is nothing in the fictions of De Foe that surpasses this description for vividness and verisimilitv.

During this storm, which was followed by a strong wind
west-south-west, we were carried, by my computation, about
five hundred leagues to the east, so that the oldest sailor on
board could not tell in what part of the world we were.
Our provisions held out well; our ship was stanch, and
our crew all in good health; but we lay in the utmost distress for water. We thought it best to hold on the same
course, rather than turn more northerly, which might have
brought us to the north-west part of Great Tartary, and
into the Frozen Sea.

On the 16th day of June, 1703, a boy on the topmast
discovered land. On the 17th, we came in full view of a
great island or continent (for we knew not whether); on
the south side whereof was a small neck of land jutting out
into the sea, and a creek too shallow to hold a ship of
above one hundred tons. We cast anchor within a league
of this creek, and our captain sent a dozen of his men well
armed in the long-boat, with vessels for water, if any could
be found. I desired his leave to go with them, that I might
see the country, and make what discoveries I could. When
we came to land, we saw no river or spring, nor any sign
of inhabitants. Our men therefore wandered on the shore
to find out some fresh water near the sea, and I walked
alone about a mile on the other side, where I observed the
country all barren and rocky. I now began to be weary,
and seeing nothing to entertain my curiosity, I returned
gently down toward the creek; and the sea being full in
my view, I saw our men already got into the boat, and rowing for life to the ship. I was going to holloa after them,
although it had been to little purpose, when I observed a
huge creature walking after them in the sea, as fast as he
could; he waded not much deeper than his knees, and took
prodigious strides; but our men had the start of him half
a league, and the sea thereabout being full of sharp-pointed
rocks, the monster was not able to overtake the boat.*

* The belief in giants, as a race, and not merely as excep-
tional individuals of the species, was very generally entertained
in ancient times; and, even when Swift wrote, the accounts of

This I was afterward told, for I durst not stay to see the issue of the adventure; but ran as fast as I could the way I first went, and then climbed up a steep hill, which gave me some prospect of the country. I found it fully cultivated; but that which first surprised me was the length of the grass, which, in those grounds that seemed to be kept for hay, was about twenty feet high.

I fell into a high road, for so I took it to be, though it

---

the enormous size of the Patagonians and the Indians of Virginia were not wholly discredited. That mankind was at first of gigantic dimensions is a tradition that obtains in almost all nations. The Mohammedans say that their prophet affirmed that Adam was as tall as a high palm tree, and that Eve was of such enormous size that when her head lay on one hill, her knees rested on two others in the plain, about two musket-shots asunder. Some of the Rabbins pretend that the stature of Adam was so gigantic that it reached even to the heavens, and extended from one end of the world to the other; and that it was reduced after the transgression—first, to the measure of 100 ells; and as others say to 1000 to 900 cubits, which was done at the request of the angels, who were terrified at his enormous stature, or who were envious and jealous on this account (see Sale's "Koran," pt. viii., chap. 2, and notes). In the Island of Ceylon, near Caltura, is a remarkable mountain, called Pico de Adam, or Adam's Peak, on the summit of which is a natural hollow, exhibiting the rude outline of a human foot about five feet long, and of proportionate breadth, called the Sri Pada, or Sacred Footstep. The Mohammedan tradition is, that when Adam and Eve were cast down from Paradise, Adam fell on the Isle of Ceylon, or Serendib, and Eve near Jeddah (the port of Mecca), in Arabia; and that when Adam set one foot on the top of the hill, he had the other in the sea. A very interesting account of the Pico de Adam will be found in Sir Emerson Tennent's learned work on Ceylon. In the year 1817, M. Nicolas Henrion presented to the Academie Royale des Inscriptions et Belles Lettres "un echelle Chronologique de la difference des tailles humaines depuis la Creation du Monde jusqu'a Jesus Christ." In this scale he assigns to Adam the height of 123 feet 9 inches, and to Eve 118 feet 9¾ inches, from which he deduces the relative proportion of the height of the sexes as 25 to 24, which is pretty near the truth. Noah he makes 20 feet less than Adam, Abraham is reduced to between 27 and 28 feet, Moses to 13 feet, Hercules to 10 feet, and Alexander to 6 feet (see Eloge de M. Henrion "Hist. d'l'Acad. des Inscrps. et Belles Lettres." tom. v., ꝑ. 382).

served to the inhabitants only as a foot-path through a field of barley. Here I walked on for some time, but could see little on either side, it being now near harvest, and the corn rising at least forty feet. I was an hour walking to the end of this field, which was fenced in with a hedge of at least one hundred and twenty feet high, and the trees so lofty that I could make no computation of their altitude. There was a stile to pass from this field into the next. It had four steps, and a stone to cross over when you came to the uppermost. It was impossible for me to climb this stile, because every step was six feet high, and the upper stone about twenty. I was endeavoring to find some gap in the hedge, when I discovered one of the inhabitants in the next field, advancing toward the stile, of the same size with him whom I saw in the sea pursuing our boat. He appeared as tall as an ordinary spire steeple, and took about ten yards at every stride,* as near as I could guess. I was struck with the utmost fear and astonishment, and ran to hide myself in the corn, whence I saw him at the top of the stile looking back into the next field on the right hand, and heard him call in a voice many degrees louder than a speaking-trumpet; but the noise was so high in the air that at first I certainly thought it was thunder. Whereupon seven monsters, like himself, came toward him, with reaping-hooks in their hands, each hook about the largeness of six scythes. These people were not so well clad as the first, whose servants or laborers they seemed to be; for, upon some words he spoke, they went to reap the corn in the field where I lay. I kept from them at as great a dis-

* A definite idea of the stature of the people of Brobdingnag is here for the first time conveyed by our author, and in a very skillful manner, by a comparison which leaves it to the reader to infer the height from the length of the step. Professor de Morgan justly observes that "Swift has masked with so much art the arithmetical questions that arise, that the interest of the reader is well preserved. The first definite indication of the Brobdingnaggian stature is conveyed in the description of a monster 'who took about ten yards at every stride.' The average human step is thirty inches, the twelfth of ten yards."

tance as I could, but was forced to move with extreme difficulty, for the stalks of the corn were sometimes not above a foot distant, so that I could hardly squeeze my body betwixt them. However, I made a shift to go forward, till I came to a part of the field where the corn had been laid by the rain and wind. Here it was impossible for me to advance a step; for the stalks were so interwoven that I could not creep through, and the beards of the fallen ears so strong and pointed, that they pierced through my clothes into my flesh. At the same time I heard the reapers not above a hundred yards behind me. Being quite dispirited with toil, and wholly overcome by grief and despair, I lay down between two ridges, and heartily wished I might there end my days. I bemoaned my desolate widow and fatherless children. I lamented my own folly and willfulness, in attempting a second voyage, against the advice of all my friends and relations. In this terrible agitation of mind, I could not forbear thinking of Lilliput, whose inhabitants looked upon me as the greatest prodigy that ever appeared in the world; where I was able to draw an imperial fleet in my hand, and perform those other actions which will be recorded forever in the chronicles of that empire; while posterity shall hardly believe them, although attested by millions. I reflected what a mortification it must prove to me to appear as inconsiderable in this nation as one single Lilliputian would be among us. But this I conceived was to be the least of my misfortunes; for, as human creatures are observed to be more savage and cruel in proportion to their bulk, what could I expect but to be a morsel in the mouth of the first among these enormous barbarians who should happen to seize me? Undoubtedly philosophers are in the right, when they tell us nothing is great or little otherwise than by comparison. It might have pleased Fortune to have let the Lilliputians find some nation where the people were as diminutive with respect to them as they were to me. And who knows but that even this prodigious race of mortals might be equally overmatched in some distant part of the world, whereof we have yet no discovery?

Scared and confounded as I was, I could not forbear going on with these reflections, when one of the reapers approaching within ten yards of the ridge where I lay, made me apprehend that with the next step I should be squashed to death under his foot, or cut in two with his reaping-hook. And, therefore, when he was again about to move, I screamed as loud as fear could make me; whereupon the huge creature trod short, and looking round about under him for some time, at last espied me as I lay on the ground. He considered awhile with the caution of one who endeavors to lay hold on a small, dangerous animal, in such a manner that it shall not be able either to scratch or bite him, as I myself had sometimes done with a weasel in England. At length he ventured to take me behind, by the middle, between his forefinger and thumb, and brought me within three yards of his eyes, that he might behold my shape more perfectly. I guessed his meaning, and my good fortune gave me so much presence of mind, that I resolved not to struggle in the least as he held me in the air, above sixty feet from the ground, although he grievously pinched my sides, for fear I should slip through his fingers. All I ventured was to raise mine eyes toward the sun, and place my hands together in a supplicating posture, and to speak some words in a humble, melancholy tone, suitable to the condition I then was in: for I apprehended every moment that he would dash me against the ground, as we usually do any little hateful animal which we have a mind to destroy. But my good star would have it, that he appeared pleased with my voice and gestures, and began to look upon me as a curiosity, much wondering to hear me pronounce articulate words, although he could not understand them. In the mean time I was not able to forbear groaning and shedding tears, and turning my head toward my sides; letting him know, as well as I could, how cruelly I was hurt by the pressure of his thumb and finger. He seemed to apprehend my meaning; for, lifting up the lappet of his coat, he put me gently into it, and immediately ran along with me to his master, who was a substantial farmer, and the same person I had first seen in the field.

The farmer having (as I supposed by their talk) received such an account of me as his servant could give him, took a piece of a small straw, about the size of a walking-staff, and therewith lifted up the lappets of my coat; which it seems he thought to be some kind of covering that nature had given me. He blew my hair aside, to take a better view of my face. He called his hinds about him, and asked them, as I afterward learned, whether they had ever seen in the fields any little creature that resembled me. He then placed me softly on the ground upon all fours, but I got immediately up and walked slowly backward and forward, to let those people see I had no intent to run away. They all sat down in a circle about me, the better to observe my motions. I pulled off my hat, and made a low bow toward the farmer. I fell on my knees, and lifted up my hands and eyes, and spoke several words as loud as I could; I took a purse of gold out of my pocket, and humbly presented it to him. He received it on the palm of his hand, then applied it close to his eye to see what it was, and afterward turned it several times with the point of a pin (which he took out of his sleeve), but could make nothing of it. Whereupon I made a sign that he should place his hand on the ground. I then took the purse, and opening it, poured all the gold into his palm. There were six Spanish pieces of four pistoles each, beside twenty or thirty smaller coins. I saw him wet the tip of his little finger upon his tongue, and take up one of my largest pieces, and then another; but he seemed to be wholly ignorant what they were. He made me a sign to put them again into my purse, and the purse again into my pocket, which, after offering it to him several times, I thought it best to do.

The farmer, by this time, was convinced I must be a rational creature. He spoke often to me; but the sound of his voice pierced my ears like that of a watermill, yet his words were articulate enough. I answered as loud as I could in several languages, and he often laid his ear within two yards of me; but all in vain, for we were wholly unintelligible to each other. He then sent his servants to their work, and taking his handkerchief out of his pocket, he doubled and spread it on his left hand, which he placed flat on the ground with the palm upward, making me a sign to step into it, as I could easily do, for it was not above a foot in thickness. I thought it my part to obey, and, for fear of falling, laid myself at full length upon the handkerchief, with the remainder of which he wrapped me up to the head for further security; and in this manner carried me home to his house. There he called his wife, and showed me to her; but she screamed and ran back, as women in England do at the sight of a toad or a spider. However, when she had awhile seen my behavior, and how well I observed the signs her husband made, she was soon reconciled, and by degrees grew extremely tender of me.

It was about twelve at noon, and a servant brought in dinner. It was only one substantial dish of meat (fit for the plain condition of a husbandman), in a dish of about four-and-twenty feet diameter. The company were, the farmer and his wife, three children, and an old grandmother. When they were sat down, the farmer placed me at some distance from him on the table, which was thirty feet high from the floor. I was in a terrible fright, and kept as far as I could from the edge, for fear of falling. The wife minced a bit of meat, then crumbled some bread on a trencher, and placed it before me. I made her a low bow, took out my knife and fork, and fell to eating, which gave them exceeding delight. The mistress sent her maid for a small dram cup, which held about two gallons, and filled it with drink; I took up the vessel with much difficulty in both hands, and in a most respectful manner drank to her ladyship's health, expressing the words as loud as I could in English, which made the company laugh so heartily, that I was almost deafened with the noise. This liquor tasted like a small cider, and was not unpleasant. Then the master made me a sign to come to his trencher side; but as I walked on the table, being in great surprise

ʟai the time, as the indulgent reader will easily conceive and
excuse, I happened to stumble against a crust, and fell flat
on my face, but received no hurt. I got up immediately,
and observing the good people to be in much concern, I
took my hat (which I held under my arm out of good
manners), and waving it over my head, made three huzzas,
to show I had got no mischief by my fall.* But advancing
forward toward my master (as I shall henceforth call him),
his youngest son, who sat next to him, an arch boy of about
ten years old, took me up by the legs, and held me so high
in the air that I trembled in every limb: but his father
snatched me from him, and at the same time gave him such
a box on the left ear as would have felled a European troop
of horse to the earth, ordering him to be taken from the
table. But being afraid this boy might owe me a spite,
and well remembering how mischievous all children among
us naturally are to sparrows, rabbits, young kittens, and
puppy dogs, I fell on my knees, and pointing to the boy,
made my master to understand as well as I could that I
desired his son might be pardoned. The father complied,
and the lad took his seat again, whereupon I went to him
and kissed his hand, which my master took, and made him
stroke me gently with it.†

In the midst of dinner, my mistress's favorite cat leaped
into her lap. I heard a noise behind me like that of a
dozen stocking-weavers at work; and turning my head, I
found it proceeded from the purring of that animal, who

* The conduct of the Brobdingnaggian farmer is very pleasantly described—poking Gulliver with a straw, blowing aside his
hair, and placing him on the ground "on all fours." How ludicrous is the idea of Gulliver presenting the farmer with a purse
of gold! and how just the satire upon the vanity of trusting to
riches as a panacea for all the ills of life, conveyed by Swift
when he makes the farmer motion to Gulliver to put up his
money again in his purse!

† This incident of the young giant urchin, seizing Gulliver
by the legs, is but too true to nature, and conveys a just rebuke
to many, both young and old, who—some through thoughtless-
ness, some from a cruelty of disposition—worry or injure small
animals.

seemed to be three times larger than an ox, as I computed by the view of her head and one of her paws, while her mistress was feeding and stroking her. The fierceness of this creature's countenance altogether discomposed me; though I stood at the further end of the table, above fifty feet off, and though my mistress held her fast, for fear she might give a spring, and seize me in her talons. But it happened there was no danger, for the cat took not the least notice of me, when my master placed me within three yards of her. And as I have been always told, and found true by experience in my travels, that flying or discovering fear before a fierce animal, is a certain way to make it pursue or attack you, so I resolved, in this dangerous juncture, to show no manner of concern. I walked with intrepidity five or six times before the very head of the cat, and came within half a yard of her; whereupon she drew herself back, as if she were more afraid of me. I had less apprehension concerning the dogs, whereof three or four came into the room, as it is usual in farmers' houses; one of which was a mastiff, equal in bulk to four elephants, and a greyhound, somewhat taller than the mastiff, but no so large.

When dinner was almost done, the nurse came in with a child of a year old in her arms, who immediately spied me, and began to squall that you might have heard from London Bridge to Chelsea, after the usual oratory of infants, to get me for a plaything. The mother, out of pure indulgence, took me up, and put me toward the child, who presently seized me by the middle, and got my head into his mouth,* where I roared so loud that the urchin was frighted, and let me drop; and I should infallibly have broke my neck if the mother had not held her apron under me. The nurse, to quiet her babe, made use of a rattle, which was a kind of hollow vessel, filled with great stones, and fastened by a cable to the child's waist; but all in vain; she was forced to apply the last remedy by giving it drink.

* This incident is, no doubt, intended as a censure on mothers who often indulge their children at the expense of their fellow-creatures or of other animals.

The strange appearance of the spots, pimples, and freckles on this woman's skin made me reflect upon the fair skins of our English ladies, who appear so beautiful to us, only because they are of our own size, and their defects not to be seen but through a magnifying-glass; where we find by experiment that the smoothest and whitest skins look rough, and coarse, and ill-colored.

I remember, when I was at Lilliput, the complexions of those diminutive people appeared to me the fairest in the world; and talking upon this subject with a person of learning there, who was an intimate friend of mine, he said that my face appeared much fairer and smoother when he looked on me from the ground than it did upon a nearer view, when I took him up in my hand, and brought him close, which he confessed was at first a very shocking sight. He said he could discover great holes in my skin; that the stumps of my beard were ten times stronger than the bristles on a boar; and my complexion made up of several colors altogether disagreeable: although I must beg leave to say for myself, that I am as fair as most of my sex and country, and very little sunburnt by all my travels. On the other side, discoursing of the ladies in that emperor's court, he used to tell me, "one had freckles, another too large a mouth, a third too large a nose!" nothing of which I was able to distinguish. I confess this reflection was obvious enough; which, however, I could not forbear, lest the reader might think those vast creatures were actually deformed: for I must do them the justice to say, they are a comely race of people; particularly the features of my master's countenance, although he was but a farmer, when I beheld him from a height of sixty feet, appeared well proportioned.

When dinner was done, my master went out to his laborers, and, as I could discover by his voice and gesture, gave his wife a strict charge to take care of me. I was very much tired, and disposed to sleep, which my mistress perceiving, she put me on her own bed, and covered me with a clean white handkerchief, but larger and coarser than the mainsail of a man-of-war.

I slept about two hours, and dreamt I was at home with my wife and children, which aggravated my sorrows, when I awaked, and found myself alone in a vast room, between two and three hundred feet wide, and about two hundred high, lying in a bed twenty yards wide. My mistress was gone about her household affairs, and had locked me in. The bed was eight yards from the floor. Although wishing to get down, I durst not presume to call; and if I had, it would have been in vain, with such a voice as mine, at so great a distance as from the room where I lay to the kitchen where the family kept. While I was under these circumstances, two rats crept up the curtains, and ran smelling backward and forward on my bed. One of them came up almost to my face, whereupon I rose in a fright, and drew out my hanger to defend myself. These horrible animals had the boldness to attack me on both sides, and one of them held his fore-feet at my collar; but I had the good fortune to rip up his belly before he could do me any mischief. He fell down at my feet; and the other, seeing the fate of his comrade, made his escape, but not without one good wound on the back, which I gave him as he fled, and made the blood run trickling from him. After this exploit, I walked gently to and fro on the bed, to recover my breath and loss of spirits. These creatures were of the size of a large mastiff, but infinitely more nimble and fierce; so that if I had taken off my belt before I went to sleep I must have infallibly been torn to pieces and devoured. I measured the tail of the dead rat, and found it to be two yards long, wanting an inch; but it went against my stomach to draw the carcass off the bed, where it lay still bleeding. I observed it had yet some life, but with a strong slash across the neck, I thoroughly dispatched it.

Soon after my mistress came into the room, who, seeing me all bloody, ran and took me up in her hand. I pointed to the dead rat, smiling and making other signs to show I was not hurt; whereat she was extremely rejoiced, calling the maid to take up the dead rat with a pair of tongs, and throw it out of the window. Then she set me on a table where I showed her my hanger all bloody, and wiping it on the lappet of my coat, returned it to the scabbard. I was anxious to wash and dress myself, and therefore endeavored to make my mistress understand that I desired to be set down on the floor; which after she had done, my bashfulness would not suffer me to express myself further than by pointing at the door, and bowing several times. The good woman, with much difficulty, at last perceived what I would be at, and left me to myself for a short time.

I hope the gentle reader will excuse me for dwelling on these and the like particulars, which, however insignificant they may appear to groveling, vulgar minds, yet will certainly help a philosopher to enlarge his thoughts and imagination, and apply them to the benefit of public as well as private life, which was my sole design in presenting this and other accounts of my travels to the world; wherein I have been chiefly studious of truth, without affecting any ornaments of learning or of style. But the whole scene of this voyage made so strong an impression on my mind, and is so deeply fixed in memory, that in committing it to paper I did not omit one material circumstance; however, upon a strict review, I blotted out several passages of less moment, which were in my first copy, for fear of being censured as tedious and trifling, whereof travelers are often, perhaps not without justice, accused.*

* Swift takes occasion, in this passage, to censure openly, as he had before covertly ridiculed, the tediousness and self-conceit exhibited so frequently in books of travel.

CHAPTER II

A Description of the Farmer's Daughter—The Author Carried to a Market Town, and Then to the Metropolis— The Particulars of His Journey.

MY MISTRESS had a daughter of nine years old, a child of towardly parts for her age, very dexterous at her needle, and skillful in dressing her baby. Her mother and she contrived to fit up the baby's cradle for me against night; the cradle was put into a small drawer of a cabinet, and the drawer placed upon a hanging shelf, for fear of the rats. This was my bed all the time I stayed with those people, though made more convenient by degrees, as I began to learn their language, and make my wants known. This young girl was so handy, that after I had once or twice pulled off my clothes before her, she was able to dress or undress me, though I never gave her that trouble when she would let me do either myself. She made me seven shirts, and some other linen, of as fine cloth as could be got, which indeed was coarser than sackcloth; and these she constantly washed for me with her own hands. She was likewise my school-mistress, to teach me the language; when I pointed to any thing, she told me the name of it in her own tongue, so that in a few days I was able to call for whatever I had a mind to. She was very good-natured, and not above forty feet high, being little of her age. She gave me the name of *grildrig*, which the family took up, and afterward the whole kingdom. The word imports what the Latins call *homunculus*; the Italians, *homunceletion*; and the English, *manikin*. To her I chiefly owe my preservation in that country; we never parted while I was there; I called her my *glumdalclitch*, or little nurse; and should be guilty of great ingratitude if I omitted this honorable mention of her

88

care and affection toward me, which I heartily wish it lay
in my power to requite as she deserves, instead of being the
innocent but unhappy instrument of her disgrace, as I have
too much reason to fear.

It now began to be known and talked of in the neighbor-
hod, that my master had found a strange animal in the field,
about the bigness of a *splacnuck*, but exactly shaped in
every part like a human creature; which it likewise imitated in all its actions; seemed to speak in a little language
of its own, had already learnt several words of theirs, went
erect upon two legs, was tame and gentle, would come when
it was called, do whatever it was bid, had the finest limbs
in the world, and a complexion fairer than a nobleman's
daughter of three years old. Another farmer, who lived
hard by, and was a particular friend of my master, came
on a visit on purpose to inquire into the truth of this story.
I was immediately produced and placed upon a table,
where I walked as I was commanded, drew my hanger, put
it up again, made my reverence to my master's guest, asked
him in his own language how he did, and told him he was
welcome, just as my little nurse had instructed me. This
man, who was old and dim-sighted, put on his spectacles
to behold me better; at which I could not forbear laughing
very heartily, for his eyes appeared like the full moon shining into a chamber at two windows. Our people, who discovered the cause of my mirth, bore me company in laughing, at which the old fellow was fool enough to be angry,
and out of countenance. He had the character of a great
miser; and, to my misfortune, he well deserved it, by the
bad advice he gave my master, to show me as a sight upon
a market-day in the next town, which was half an hour's
riding, about two-and-twenty miles from our house. I
guessed there was some mischief abroad contriving, when
I observed my master and his friend whispering long together, sometimes pointing at me; and my fears made me
fancy that I overheard and understood some of their words.
But the next morning Glumdalclitch, my little nurse, told
me the whole matter, which she had cunningly picked out

from her mother. The poor girl laid me on her bosom, and
fell weeping with shame and grief. She apprehended some
mischief would happen to me from rude, vulgar folks, who
might squeeze me to death, or break one of my limbs by
taking me in their hands. She had also observed how
modest I was in my nature, how nicely I regarded my
honor, and what an indignity I should conceive it to be exposed for money, as a public spectacle, to the meanest of
the people. She said her papa and mamma had promised
that Grildrig should be hers; but now she found they meant
to serve her as they did last year, when they pretended to
give her a lamb, and yet, as soon as it was fat, sold it to
a butcher. For my own part, I may truly affirm, that I
was less concerned than my nurse. I had a strong hope,
which never left me, that I should one day recover my
liberty; and as to the ignominy of being carried about for
a monster, I considered myself to be a perfect stranger in
the country, and that such a misfortune could never be
charged upon me as a reproach, if ever I should return to
England; since the king of Great Britain himself, in my
condition, must have undergone the same distress.

My master, pursuant to the advice of his friend, carried
me in a box, the next market-day, to the neighboring town,
and took along with him his little daughter, my nurse, upon
a pillion behind him. The box was close on every side, with
a little door for me to go in and out, and a few gimlet-holes
to let in air. The girl had been so careful as to put the
quilt of her baby's bed into it, for me to lie down on.
However, I was terribly shaken and discomposed in this
journey, though it were but of half an hour; for the horse
went about forty feet at every step, and trotted so high,
that the agitation was equal to the rising and falling of a
ship in a great storm, but much more frequent. Our journey was somewhat farther than from London to St. Al-
ban's. My master alighted at an inn which he used to
frequent; and after consulting awhile with the innkeeper,
and making some necessary preparations, he hired the *grul-
tred,* or crier, to give notice through the town of a strange

creature to be seen at the sign of the Green Eagle, not so big as a *splacnuck* (an animal in that country very finely shaped), about six feet long, and in every part of the body resembling a human creature, which could speak several words, and perform a hundred diverting tricks.

I was placed upon a table in the largest room of the inn, which might be near three hundred feet square. My little nurse stood on a low stool close to the table, to take care of me, and direct what I should do. My master, to avoid a crowd, would suffer only thirty people at a time to see me. I walked about on the table as the girl commanded: she asked me questions, as far as she knew my understanding of the language reached, and I answered them as loud as I could. I turned about several times to the company, paid my humble respects, said they were welcome, and used some other speeches I had been taught. I took up a thimble filled with liquor, which Glumdalclitch had given me for a cup, and drank their health. I drew out my hanger, and flourished with it after the manner of fencers in England. My nurse gave me a part of a straw, which I exercised as a pike, having learnt the art in my youth. I was that day shown to twelve sets of company, and as often forced to act over again the same fopperies, till I was half dead with weariness and vexation; for those who had seen me made such wonderful reports, that the people were ready to break down the doors to come in.* My master for his own interest, would not suffer any one to touch me except my nurse; and to prevent danger, benches were set round the table at such a distance as put me out of everybody's reach. However, an unlucky school-boy aimed a hazel-nut at my head, which very narrowly missed me; otherwise it came with so much violence, that it would have infallibly knocked out my brains, for it was almost as large as a small pumpkin; but I had the satisfaction to

* Swift's description of the exhibition of Gulliver to the Brobdingnaggian rustics, and the anxiety of the crowds to see him, is a correct representation of the passion for sight-seeing that prevailed in England in his day.

see the young rogue well beaten and turned out of the room.

My master gave public notice that he would show me again the next market-day; and in the mean time he prepared a more convenient vehicle for me, which he had reason enough to do; for I was so tired with my first journey, and with entertaining compny for eight hours together, that I could hardly stand upon my legs or speak a word. It was at least three days before I recovered my strength; and that I might have no rest at home, all the neighboring gentlemen from a hundred miles round, hearing of my fame, came to see me at my master's own house. There could not be fewer than thirty persons, with their wives and children (for the country is very populous); and my master demanded the rate of a full room whenever he showed me at home, although it were only to a single family; so that for some time I had but little ease every day of the week (except Wednesday, which is their Sabbath), although I were not carried to the town.

My master, finding how profitable I was likely to be, resolved to carry me to the most considerable cities in the kingdom. Having therefore provided himself with all things necessary for a long journey, and settled his affairs at home, he took leave of his wife, and on the 17th of August, 1703, about two months after my arrival, we set out for the metropolis, situate near the middle of that empire, and about three thousand miles' distance from our house. My master made his daughter, Glumdalclitch, ride behind him. She carried me on her lap, in a box tied about her waist. The girl had lined it on all sides with the softest cloth she could get, well quilted underneath, furnished it with her baby's bed, provided me with linen and other necessaries, and made everything as convenient as she could. We had no other company but a boy of the house, who rode after us with the luggage.

My master's design was to show me in all the towns by the way, and to step out of the road, for fifty or a hundred miles, to any village or person of quality's house, where he might expect custom. We made easy journeys, of

not above seven or eight score miles a day: for Glumdalclitch, on purpose to spare me, complained she was tired
with the trotting of the horse. She often took me out of
my box at my desire, to give me air, and show me the
country, but always held me fast by a leading-string. We
passed over five or six rivers, many degrees broader and
deeper than the Ganges: and there was hardly a rivulet so
small as the Thames at London Bridge.* We were ten
weeks in our journey, and I was shown in eighteen large
towns, besides many villages and private families.

On the 26th day of October, we arrived at the metropolis,
called in their language *Lorbrulgrud*, or Pride of the Universe. My master took a lodging in the principal street of
the city, not far from the royal palace, and put out bills in
the usual form, containing an exact description of my person and parts. He hired a large room, between three and
four hundred feet wide. He provided a table sixty feet
in diameter, upon which I was to act my part, and pali-
sadoed it round three feet from the edge, and as many
high, to prevent my falling over. I was shown ten times
a day, to the wonder and satisfaction of all people. I could
now speak the language tolerably well, and perfectly understood every word that was spoken to me. Besides, I had
learnt their alphabet, and could make a shift to explain a
sentence, here and there: for Glumdalclitch had been my
instructor while we were at home, and at leisure hours during our journey. She carried a little book in her pocket,
not much larger than Sanson's Atlas; it was a common
treatise for the use of young girls, giving a short account
of their religion; out of this she taught me my letters, and
interpreted the words.

* According to the Brobdingnaggian scale, as compared with
that of England, we find Swift still keeping within reasonable
bounds. Assuming that the sea-coast where Gulliver was cast
ashore was at the extremity of the kingdom, we have the metropolis (stated to be situate in the middle) at a distance
equivalent to about 250 miles with us. The journeys would be
from about twelve to fourteen miles a day, and the deviations
from the direct course would scarcely exceed nine miles at most.

CHAPTER III

*The Author Sent for to Court—The Queen Buys Him of
His Master, the Farmer, and Presents Him to the King—
He Disputes with His Majesty's Great Scholars—An
Apartment at Court Provided for the Author—He Is in
High Favor with the Queen—He Stands up for the Honor
of His Own Country—His Quarrels with the Queen's
Dwarf.*

THE frequent labors I underwent every day made, in a few
weeks, a very considerable change in my health; the more
my master got by me, the more insatiable he grew; I had
quite lost my stomach, and was almost reduced to a skeleton. The farmer observing it, and concluding I must soon
die, resolved to make as good a hand of me as he could.
While he was thus reasoning and resolving within himself,
a *sardral*, or gentleman-usher, came from court, commanding my master to carry me immediately thither, for the
diversion of the queen and her ladies. Some of the latter
had already been to see me, and reported strange things of
my beauty, behavior, and good sense. Her majesty, and
those who attended her, were beyond measure delighted
with my demeanor. I fell on my knees, and begged the
honor of kissing her imperial foot; but this gracious princess
held out her little finger toward me, after I was set on the
table, which I embraced in both my arms, and put the tip
of it with the utmost respect to my lip. She asked me some
general questions about my country and my travels, which
I answered as distinctly and in as few words as I could.
She asked whether I could be content to live at court. I
bowed down to the board of the table, and humbly answered, that I was my master's slave; but if I were at my
own disposal, I should be proud to devote my life to her

majesty's service. She then asked my master whether he was willing to sell me at a good price. He, who apprehended that I could not live a month, was ready enough to part with me, and demanded a thousand pieces of gold, which were ordered him on the spot, each piece being about the bigness of eight hundred moidores; but allowing for the proportion of all things between that country and Europe, and the high price of gold among them, this was hardly so great a sum as a thousand guineas would be in England. I then said to the queen, since I was now her majesty's most humble creature and vassal, I must beg the favor that Glumdalclitch, who had always tended me with so much care and kindness, and knew how to do it so well, might be admitted into the service, and continue to be my nurse and instructor.

Her majesty agreed to my petition, and easily got the farmer's consent, who was glad enough to have his daughter preferred at court, and the poor girl herself was not able to hide her joy. My late master withdrew, bidding me farewell, and saying he had left me in a good service; to which I replied not a word, only making him a slight bow.

The queen observed my coldness; and when the farmer was gone out of the apartment, asked me the reason. I made bold to tell her majesty that I owed no other obligation to my late master than his not dashing out the brains of a poor harmless creature found by chance in his fields, which obligation was amply recompensed by the gain he had made in showing me through half the kingdom, and the price he had now sold me for. That the life I had since led was laborious enough to kill an animal of ten times my strength. That my health was much impaired by the continual drudgery of entertaining the rabble every hour of the day; and that if my master had not thought my life in danger, her majesty would not have got so cheap a bargain. But as I was out of all fear of being ill-treated under the protection of so great and good an empress, the ornament of nature, the darling of the world, the delight of her subjects, the phœnix of the creation, so I hoped my late master's apprehensions would appear to be groundless; for I had already found my spirits revived by the influence of her most august presence.*

This was the sum of my speech, delivered with great improprieties and hesitation. The latter part was altogether framed in the style peculiar to that people, whereof I learned some phrases from Glumdalclitch, while she was carrying me to court.

The queen, giving great allowance for my defectiveness in speaking, was, however, surprised at so much wit and good sense in so diminutive an animal. She took me in her own hand, and carried me to the king, who was then retired to his cabinet. His majesty, a prince of much gravity and austere countenance, not well observing my shape at first view, asked the queen, after a cold manner, how long it was since she grew fond of a *splacnuck?* for such, it seems, he took me to be, as I lay upon my breast in her majesty's right hand. But this princess, who has an infinite deal of wit and humor, set me gently on my feet upon the scrutoire, and commanded me to give his majesty an account of myself, which I did in a very few words: and Glumdalclitch, who attended at the cabinet door, and could not endure I should be out of her sight, being admitted, confirmed all that had passed from my arrival at her father's house.

The king, although he is as learned a person as any in his dominions, having been educated in the study of philosophy, and particularly mathematics, yet when he observed my shape exactly, and saw me walk erect, before I began to speak, conceived I might be a piece of clock-work (which has in that country arrived to a very great perfection), contrived by some ingenious artist. But when he

* Sir Walter Scott observes that the portrait of the queen of the Brobdingnags, who is represented as amiable and inquisitive—the protectress of the pigmy stranger—is unquestionably designed as a compliment to the Princess of Wales, whom Swift was then desirous to gratify, though he afterward seems to have transferred his allegiance to Mrs. Howard.

heard my voice, and found what I delivered to be regular and rational, he could not conceal his astonishment. He was by no means satisfied with the relation I gave him of the manner I came into his kingdom, but thought it a story concerted between Glumdalclitch and her father, who had taught me a set of words, to make me sell at a better price. Upon this imagination he put several other questions to me, and still received rational answers: no otherwise defective than by a foreign accent and an imperfect knowledge of the language, with some rustic phrases which I had learned at the farmer's house, and did not suit the polite style of a court.

His majesty sent for three great scholars, who were then in the weekly waiting, according to the custom in that country. These gentlemen, after they had examined my shape with much nicety, were of different opinions concerning me. They all agreed that I could not be produced according to the regular laws of nature, because I was not framed with a capacity of preserving my life, either by swiftness, or climbing of trees, or digging holes in the earth. They observed by my teeth, which they viewed with great exactness, that I was a carnivorous animal, yet most quadrupeds being an overmatch for me, and field-mice, with some others, too nimble, they could not imagine how I should be able to support myself, unless I fed upon snails and other insects, which they offered, by many learned arguments, to evince that I could not possibly do. One of these virtuosi seemed to think that I might be an embryo or abortive birth. But this opinion was rejected by the other two, who observed my limbs to be perfect and finished; and that I had lived several years, as it was manifest from my beard, the stumps whereof they plainly discovered through a magnifying-glass. They would not allow me to be a dwarf, because my littleness was beyond all degrees of comparison; for the queen's favorite dwarf, the smallest ever known in the kingdom, was nearly thirty feet high. After much debate, they concluded unanimously that I was only *relplum scalcath*, which is, interpreted literally,

lusus naturæ;* a determination exactly agreeable to the
modern philosophy of Europe, whose professors, disdaining
the old evasion of occult causes, whereby the followers of
Aristotle endeavored in vain to disguise their ignorance,
have invented this wonderful solution of all difficulties, to
the unspeakable advancement of human knowledge.

After this decisive conclusion, I entreated to be heard a
word or two. I applied myself to the king, and assured
his majesty that I came from a country which abounded
with several millions of both sexes, and of my own stature;
where the animals, trees, and houses were all in proportion,
and where, by consequence, I might be as able to defend
myself, and to find sustenance, as any of his majesty's subjects could do here; which I took for a full answer to those
gentlemen's arguments. To this they only replied by a
smile of contempt, saying that the farmer had instructed
me very well in my lesson. The king, who had a much better understanding, dismissing his learned men, sent for the
farmer, who, by good fortune, was not yet gone out of the
town. Having therefore first examined him privately, and
then confronted him with me and the young girl, his majesty began to think that what we told him might possibly
be true. He desired the queen to order that a particular
care should be taken of me; and was of opinion that Glumdalclitch should still continue in her office of tending me,
because he observed we had great affection for each other.
A convenient apartment was provided for her at court;

* In this serio-comic discussion of the three learned philosophers, the author no doubt ridicules the speculations of some of
the naturalists of his own day, and, not improbably, has in view
some of the members of the Royal Society, for whom he did
not entertain very great reverence. The arguments used by these
sages are a just censure on the pride and presumption of those
persons who, in every age, are found to put forward their own
crude hypotheses and speculative theories, and who would assail
the truths of Revelation, and arraign the wisdom of Providence
in the creation and government of the world. The device of the
lusus naturæ, in which these pundits finally take refuge, to conceal their ignorance, is a stroke of satire as happy as it is severe.

she had a sort of governess appointed to take care of her education, a maid to dress her, and two other servants for menial offices; but the care of me was wholly appropriated to herself. The queen commanded her own cabinet-maker to contrive a box, that might serve me for a bed-chamber, after the model that Glumdalclitch and I should agree upon. This man was a most ingenious artist; and according to my direction, in three weeks finished for me a wooden chamber of sixteen feet square and twelve high, with sash-windows, a door, and two closets, like a London bed-chamber. The board that made the ceiling was to be lifted up and down by two hinges, to put in a bed ready furnished by her majesty's upholsterer, which Glumdalclitch took out every day to air, made it with her own hands, and letting it down at night, locked up the roof over me. A nice workman, who was famous for little curiosities, undertook to make me two chairs, with backs and frames, of a substance not unlike ivory, and two tables, with a cabinet to put my things in. The room was quilted on all sides, as well as the floor and ceiling, to prevent any accident from the carelessness of those who carried me, and to break the force of a jolt, when I went in a coach. I desired a lock for my door, to prevent rats and mice from coming in. The smith, after several attempts, made the smallest that ever was seen among them, for I have known a larger at the gate of a gentleman's house in England. I made a shift to keep the key in a pocket of my own, fearing Glumdalclitch might lose it. The queen likewise ordered the thinnest silks that could be gotten, to make me clothes, not much thicker than an English blanket, very cumbrous till I was accustomed to them. They were after the fashion of the kingdom, partly resembling the Persian and partly the Chinese, and are a very grave and decent habit.

The queen became so fond of my company, that she could not dine without me. I had a table placed upon the same at which her majesty ate, just at her elbow, and a chair to sit on. Glumdalclitch stood on a stool on the floor, near my table, to assist and take care of me. I had an entire set of silver dishes and plates, and other necessaries, which, in proportion to those of the queen, were not much bigger than what I have seen in a London toy-shop, for the furniture of a baby house; these my little nurse kept in her pocket in a silver box, and gave me at meals as I wanted them, always cleaning them herself. No person dined with the queen but the two princesses royal, the eldest sixteen years old, and the younger at that time thirteen and a month. Her majesty used to put a bit of meat upon one of my dishes, out of which I carved for myself, and her diversion was to see me eat in miniature; for the queen (who had indeed but a weak stomach) took up, at a mouthful, as much as a dozen English farmers could eat at a meal, which to me was for some time a very nauseous sight. She would craunch the wing of a lark, bones and all, between her teeth, although it were nine times as large as that of a full-grown turkey; and put a bit of bread in her mouth as big as two twelve-penny loaves. She drank, out of a golden cup, above a hogshead at a draught. Her knives were twice as long as a scythe, set straight upon the handle. The spoons, forks, and other instruments were all in the same proportion. I remember, when Glumdalclitch carried me, out of curiosity, to see some of the tables at court, where ten or a dozen of those enormous knives and forks were lifted up together, I thought I had never till then beheld so terrible a sight.

It is the custom, that every Wednesday (which, as I have observed, is their Sabbath) the king and queen, with the royal issue of both sexes, dine together in the apartment of his majesty, to whom I was now become a great favorite; and at these times my little chair and table were placed at his left hand, before one of the salt-cellars. This prince took a pleasure in conversing with me, inquiring into the manners, religion, laws, government, and learning of Europe; wherein I gave him the best account I was able. His apprehension was so clear and his judgment so exact, that he made very wise reflections and observations upon all I said. But I confess, that after I had been a little too

copious in talking of my own beloved country, of our trade
and wars by sea and land, of our schisms in religion and
parties in the state, the prejudices of his education prevailed so far that he could not forbear taking me up in his
right hand, and, stroking me gently with the other, after
a hearty fit of laughing, asked me whether I was a Whig or
a Tory? Then turning to his first minister, who waited
behind him with a white staff nearly as tall as the mainmast
of the Royal Sovereign, he observed how contemptible a
thing was human grandeur, which could be mimicked by
such diminutive insects as I: "and yet," says he, "I dare
engage these creatures have their titles and distinctions of
honor; they contrive little nests, and burrows, that they
call houses and cities; they make a figure and dress in
equipage; they love, they fight, they dispute, they cheat,
they betray." * And thus he continued, while my color
came and went several times, with indignation, to hear our
noble country—the mistress of arts and arms; the scourge
of France; the arbitress of Europe; the seat of virtue,
piety, honor, and truth; the pride and envy of the world—
so contemptuously treated.

But as I was not in a condition to resent injuries, so,
upon mature thoughts, I began to doubt whether I was
injured or no. For, after having been accustomed several
months to the sight and converse of this people, and observed every object upon which I cast mine eyes to be of
proportionable magnitude, the horror I had at first conceived from their bulk and aspect was so far worn off, that
if I had then beheld a company of English lords and ladies
in their finery and birthday clothes, acting their several
parts in the most courtly manner of strutting, and bowing,
and prating, to say the truth, I should have been strongly
tempted to laugh as much at them as the king and his
grandees did at me. Neither, indeed, could I forbear smiling at myself when the queen used to place me upon her

* What an admirable satire on the vanity and worthlessness
of many of those things which mankind set store by is conveyed
in these reflections of the king!

hand toward a looking-glass, by which both our persons appeared before me in full view together; and there could be nothing more ridiculous than the comparison; so that I really began to imagine myself dwindled many degrees below my usual size.

Nothing angered and mortified me so much as the queen's dwarf; who, being of the lowest stature that was ever in that country (for I verily think he was not full thirty feet high), became so insolent at seeing a creature so much beneath him, that he would always affect to swagger and look big as he passed by me in the queen's antechamber, while I was standing on some table talking with the lords or ladies of the court, and he seldom failed of a smart word or two upon my littleness; against which I could only revenge myself by calling him "brother," challenging him to wrestle, and such repartees as are usually in the mouths of court pages. One day at dinner, this malicious little cub was so nettled with something I had said to him, that, raising himself upon the frame of her majesty's chair, he took me up by the middle, as I was sitting down, not thinking any harm, and let me drop into a large silver bowl of cream, and then ran away as fast as he could. I fell over head and ears, and, if I had not been a good swimmer, it might have gone very hard with me; for Glumdalclitch at that instant happened to be at the other end of the room, and the queen was in such a fright that she wanted presence of mind to assist me. But my little nurse ran to my relief, and took me out, after I had swallowed above a quart of cream. I was put to bed; however, I received no other damage than the loss of a suit of clothes, which were utterly spoiled. The dwarf was soundly whipped, and, as a further punishment, forced to drink up the bowl of cream into which he had thrown me, neither was he ever restored to favor; for soon after the queen bestowed him on a lady of high quality, so that I saw him no more, to my very great satisfaction; for I could not tell to what extremity such a malicious urchin might have carried his resentment.

He had before served me a scurvy trick, which set the

queen a-laughing, although at the same time she was heartily vexed, and would have immediately cashiered him if I
had not been so generous as to intercede. Her majesty had
taken a marrow-bone upon her plate, and, after knocking
out the marrow, placed the bone again on the dish erect,
as it stood before; the dwarf, watching his opportunity
when Glumdalclitch was gone to the sideboard, mounted the
stool that she stood on to take care of me at meals, took
me up in both hands, and, squeezing my legs together,
wedged them into the marrow-bone above my waist, where
I stuck for some time, and made a very ridiculous figure.
I believe it was near a minute before any one knew what
was become of me; for I thought it below me to cry out.*
But as princes seldom get their meat hot, my legs were not
scalded, only my stockings and breeches were in a sad condition. The dwarf, at my entreaty, had no other punishment than a sound whipping.

I was frequently rallied by the queen upon account of
my fearfulness; and she used to ask me whether the people
of my country were as great cowards as myself. The occasion was this: the kingdom is much pestered with flies in
summer; and these odious insects, each of them as big as a
Dunstable lark, hardly gave me any rest while I sat at
dinner, with their continual humming and buzzing about
mine ears. They would sometimes alight upon my victuals,

* This ludicrous incident was probably suggested to the mind
of Swift by an anecdote that is related of a somewhat similar
treatment of the celebrated dwarf, Jeffrey Hudson. Shortly
after the marriage of Charles I., the Duke of Buckingham, in
whose service Jeffrey then was, gave an entertainment to the
king and queen, at his mansion at Burleigh-on-the-Hill. The
duchess had the little dwarf, who was then young and only
eighteen inches high, put into a pie-dish and served up as a cold
pie to the queen, who was so much taken with the pleasantry
that she promoted Jeffrey to her own service. Hudson had a
large soul in his little body, and was as valiant as a giant. He
did battle, it is said, on one occasion, with a turkey-cock—an
achievement which was celebrated by the poet-laureate, Sir
William Davenant, in a poem entitled "Jeffreidos," and which,
not improbably, suggested Gulliver's encounter with the wasps.

and they would fix upon my nose or forehead, where they stung me to the quick, smelling very offensively; and I could easily trace that viscous matter which, our naturalists tell us, enables those creatures to walk with their feet upward upon a ceiling.* I had much ado to defend myself against these detestable animals, and could not forbear starting when they came on my face. It was the common practice of the dwarf to catch a number of these insects in his hand, as school-boys do among us, and let them out suddenly under my nose, on purpose to frighten me and divert the queen. My remedy was to cut them in pieces with my knife, as they flew in the air, wherein my dexterity was much admired.

I remember, one morning, when Glumdalclitch had set me in a box upon a window, as she usually did in fair days, to give me air (for I durst not venture to let the box be hung on a nail out of the window, as we do with cages in England), after I had lifted up one of my sashes, and sat down at my table to eat a piece of sweet cake for my breakfast, above twenty wasps, allured by the smell, came flying into the room, humming louder than the drones of as many

---

* Though the naturalists in Swift's day were of opinion that some viscous matter exuded from flies enabled them to walk upon the ceiling, what enables them so to walk is, nevertheless, to this hour an unsettled question. Not long before Swift wrote these travels, Dr. Hooke for the first time broached the theory that the phenomenon was produced by small bristles or tenters, like the wire teeth of a wool-card, with which the soles of the insect's feet were furnished. Then came the learned Dr. Derham, in Swift's own day, with a new theory. "Flies," said he, "besides their sharp-hooked nails, have also skinny palms to their feet, to enable them to stick on glass and other smooth bodies by the pressure of the atmosphere;" and he illustrates the process by a common practice of boys, who lift stones by a wet piece of leather applied to their top. Some fifty years ago, however, Mr. Blackwell took to experimenting upon flies, and he found that they could walk up the sides of an exhausted receiver just as freely as if the air had been admitted; and so he denied the correctness of the vacuum hypothesis, and went back to Dr. Hooke's view in part, and in part to the older hypothesis of the viscous fluid.

bagpipes. Some of them seized my cake, and carried it piecemeal away; others flew about my head and face, confounding me with their noise, and putting me in the utmost terror of their stings. However, I had the courage to rise and draw my hanger, and attack them in the air. I dispatched four of them, but the rest got away, and I presently shut my window. These insects are as large as partridges; I took out their stings, and found them an inch and a half long, and as sharp as needles. I carefully preserved them all; and having since shown them, with other curiosities, in several parts of Europe, upon my return to England, I gave three to Gresham College, and kept the fourth for myself.

CHAPTER IV

*The Country Described—A Proposal for Correcting Modern
Maps—The King's Palace, and Some Account of the
Metropolis—The Author's Way of Traveling—The Chief
Temple Described.*

I now intend to give the reader a short description of this
country, as far as I traveled in it, which was not above two
thousand miles round Lorbrulgrud, the metropolis. For
the queen, whom I always attended, never went farther
when she accompanied the king in his progresses, and there
stayed till his majesty returned from viewing his frontiers.
The whole extent of this prince's dominions reaches about
six thousand miles in length, and from three to five in
breadth; whence I cannot but conclude that our geographers of Europe are in a great error by supposing nothing
but sea between Japan and California; for it was ever my
opinion that there must be a balance of earth to counter-
poise the great continent of Tartary; and therefore they
ought to correct their maps and charts by joining this vast
tract of land to the north-west parts of America, wherein
I shall be ready to lend them my assistance.*

The kingdom is a peninsula, terminating to the north-east
of a ridge of mountains thirty miles high, which are altogether impassable, by reason of the volcanoes upon the
tops; neither do the most learned know what sort of mortals

* The description here given of the country is quite in the
style of the works of travel which Swift imitates so admirably.
A reference to the chart which he has given of his ideal kingdom
of Brobdingnag will show that he projected it westward from
the mainland of America, as a vast peninsula. The notion that
land in any part of the globe was counterpoised by land in the
opposite part of the same hemisphere was a favorite theory of
the old geographers.

inhabit beyond those mountains, or whether they be inhabited at all. On the three other sides it is bounded by the ocean. There is not one seaport in the whole kingdom; and those parts of the coast into which the rivers issue are so full of pointed rocks, and the sea generally so rough, that there is no venturing with the smallest of their boats; so that these people are wholly excluded from any commerce with the rest of the world. But the large rivers are full of vessels, and abound with excellent fish; for they seldom get any from the sea, because the sea-fish are of the same size with those in Europe, and consequently not worth catching; whereby it is manifest that nature, in the production of plants and animals of so extraordinary a bulk, is wholly confined to this continent, of which I leave the reasons to be determined by philosophers. However, now and then they take a whale that happens to be dashed against the rocks, which the common people feed on heartily. These whales I have known so large that a man could hardly carry one upon his shoulders; and sometimes, for curiosity, they are brought in hampers to Lorbrulgrud: I saw one of them in a dish at the king's table, which passed for a rarity, but I did not observe he was fond of it; for I think, indeed, the bigness disgusted him, although I have seen one somewhat larger in Greenland.

The country is well inhabited, for it contains fifty-one cities, near a hundred walled towns, and a great number of villages. To satisfy my curious reader, it may be sufficient to describe Lorbrulgrud. The city stands upon almost two equal parts, on each side the river that passes through. It contains about eighty thousand houses, and about six hundred thousand inhabitants. It is in length three *glomglungs* (which make about fifty-four English miles), and two and a half in breadth; as I measured it myself in the royal map made by the king's order, which was laid on the ground on purpose for me, and extended a hundred feet: I paced the diameter and circumference several times barefoot, and, computing by the scale, measured it pretty exactly.

The king's palace is no regular edifice, but a heap of

buildings, about seven miles round; the chief rooms are generally two hundred and forty feet high, and broad and long in proportion. A coach was allowed to Glumdalclitch and me, wherein her governess frequently took her out to see the town, or go among the shops; and I was always of the party, carried in my box; although the girl, at my own desire, would often take me out, and hold me in her hand, that I might more conveniently view the houses and the people, as we passed along the streets. I reckoned our coach to be about the square of Westminster Hall, but not altogether so high; however, I cannot be very exact. One day the governess ordered the coachman to stop at several shops, where the beggars, watching their opportunity, crowded to the sides of the coach, and gave me the most horrible spectacle that ever a European eye beheld. There was a fellow with a wen in his neck, larger than five wool-packs; and another with a couple of wooden legs, each about twenty feet high. But the most hateful sight of all was the insects crawling on their clothes.

Besides the large box in which I was usually carried, the queen ordered a smaller one to be made for me, of about twelve feet square and ten high, for the convenience of traveling; because the other was somewhat too large for Glumdalclitch's lap, and cumbersome in the coach; it was made by the same artist, whom I directed in the whole contrivance. This traveling-closet was an exact square, with a window in the middle of three of the squares, and each window was latticed with iron wire on the outside, to prevent accidents in long journeys. On the fourth side, which had no window, two strong staples were fixed, through which the person who carried me, when I had a mind to be on horseback, put a leathern belt, and buckled it about his waist. This was always the office of some grave and trusty servant, in whom I could confide, whether I attended the king and queen in their progresses, or were disposed to see the gardens, or pay a visit to some great lady or minister of state in the court, when Glumdalclitch happened to be out of order; for I soon began to be known and esteemed among the greatest officers, I suppose more upon account of their majesties' favor than any merit of my own. In journeys, when I was weary of the coach, a servant on horseback would buckle on my box, and place it upon a cushion before him; and there I had a full prospect of their country on three sides, from my three windows. I had, in this closet, a field-bed and a hammock hung from the ceiling, two chairs and a table, neatly screwed to the floor, to prevent being tossed about by the agitation of the horse or the coach. And having been long used to sea voyages, those motions, although sometimes very violent, did not much discompose me.

Whenever I had a mind to see the town, it was always in my traveling-closet; which Glumdalclitch held in her lap in a kind of open sedan, after the fashion of the country, borne by four men, and attended by two others in the queen's livery. The people, who had often heard of me, were very curious to crowd about the sedan; and the girl was complaisant enough to make the bearers stop, and to take me in her hand, that I might be more conveniently seen.

I was very desirous to see the chief temple, and particularly the tower belonging to it, which is reckoned the highest in the kingdom. Accordingly, one day my nurse carried me thither, but I may truly say I came back disappointed; for the height is not above three thousand feet, reckoning from the ground to the highest pinnacle top; which, allowing for the difference between the size of those people and us in Europe, is no great matter for admiration, not at all equal in proportion (if I rightly remember) to Salisbury steeple. But, not to detract from a nation to which, during my life, I shall acknowledge myself extremely obliged, it must be allowed, that whatever this famous tower wants in height is amply made up in beauty and strength; for the walls are near a hundred feet thick, built of hewn stone, whereof each is about forty feet square, and adorned on all sides with statues of gods and emperors, cut in marble, larger than life, placed in their several niches.

I measured a little finger which had fallen down from one of these statues, and lay unperceived among some rubbish, and found it exactly four feet and an inch in length. Glumdalclitch wrapped it up in her handkerchief, and carried it home in her pocket, to keep among her trinkets, of which the girl was very fond, as children at her age usually are.*

The king's kitchen is indeed a noble building, vaulted at top, and about six hundred feet high. The great oven is not so wide, by ten paces, as the cupola at St. Paul's; for I measured the latter on purpose, after my return. But if I should describe the kitchen grate, the prodigious pots and kettles, the joints of meat turned on the spits, with many other particulars, perhaps I should be hardly believed: at least, a severe critic would be apt to think I enlarged a little, as travelers are often suspected to do. To avoid which censure, I fear I have run too much into the other extreme; and that if this treatise should happen to be translated into the language of Brobdingnag (which is the general name of that kingdom), and transmitted thither, the king and his people would have reason to complain that I had done them an injury by a false and diminutive representation.

His majesty seldom keeps above six hundred horses in his stables; they are generally from fifty-four to sixty feet high. But when he goes abroad on solemn days, he is attended, for state, by a militia guard of five hundred horse, which, indeed, I thought was the most splendid sight that could be ever beheld, till I saw part of his army in battalia, whereof I shall find another occasion to speak.

* The gigantic figures, both of men and other animals, which have been described by travelers in Egypt surpass the description that our author here gives us of the statues of Brobdingnag. The famous colossal figure at Rhodes, to which Swift himself alludes in his "Voyage to Lilliput," must have represented a man nearly 120 feet high; consequently the little finger would have been about six feet long—far longer than that which Gulliver found among the rubbish in the temple.

CHAPTER V

Several Adventures that Happened to the Author—The Execution of a Criminal—The Author Shows His Skill in Navigation.

I sʜᴏᴜʟᴅ have lived happy enough in that country if my littleness had not exposed me to several ridiculous and troublesome accidents: some of which I shall venture to relate. Glumdalclitch often carried me into the gardens of the court in my smaller box, and would sometimes take me out of it, and hold me in her hand, or set me down to walk. I remember, before the dwarf left the queen, he followed us one day into those gardens, and my nurse having set me down, he and I being close together, near some dwarf apple-trees, I must needs show my wit by a silly allusion between him and the trees, which happens to hold in their language as it does in ours. Whereupon, the malicious rogue, watching his opportunity, when I was walking under one of them, shook it directly over my head, by which a dozen apples, each of them near as large as a Bristol barrel, came tumbling about my ears; one of them hit me on the back as I chanced to stoop, and knocked me down flat on my face; but I received no other hurt, and the dwarf was pardoned at my desire, because I had given the provocation.*

Another day, Glumdalclitch left me on a smooth grass-plot to divert myself, while she walked at some distance with her governess. In the mean time there suddenly fell such a violent shower of hail that I was immediately, by

---

* When once we realize the diminutive dimensions of Gulliver, as compared with those of the people and things around him, we are prepared for the accidents which would continually befall him, narrated so pleasantly and so naturally by our author.

the force of it, struck to the ground; and when I was down, the hailstones gave me such cruel bangs all over the body, as if I had been pelted with tennis-balls; however, I made a shift to creep on all fours, and shelter myself, by lying flat on my face, on the lee-side of a border of lemon-thyme, but so bruised from head to foot that I could not go abroad for ten days. Neither is this at all to be wondered at, because Nature, in that country, observing the same proportion through all her operations, a hailstone is near eighteen hundred times as large as one in Europe;* which I can assert upon experience, having been so curious as to weigh and measure them.

But a more dangerous accident happened to me in the same garden, where my little nurse, believing she had put me in a secure place (which I often entreated her to do, that I might enjoy my own thoughts), and having left the box at home, to avoid the trouble of carrying it, went to another part of the garden with her governess and some ladies of her acquaintance. While she was absent, and out of hearing, a small white spaniel that belonged to one of the chief gardeners, having got by accident into the garden, happened to range near the place where I lay; the dog, following the scent, came directly up, and taking me in his mouth, ran straight to his master, wagging his tail, and set me gently on the ground. By good fortune he had been so well taught that I was carried between his teeth without the least hurt, or even tearing my clothes. But the poor gardener, who knew me well, and had a great kindness for me, was in a terrible fright; he gently took me up in both his hands, and asked me how I did; but I was so amazed

* This is another instance of the many to be found throughout these travels, of Swift's minute attention to the proportions which he has once established between Gulliver and those among whom he is cast, whether they be Lilliputians or Brobdingnagians. Taking the latter to be twelve times as large as an ordinary man, and everything in the country on the same scale, we shall, of course, have the hailstones greater than those of England by the cube of 12, that is—1728, or, as Swift says, "near eighteen hundred times."

and out of breath that I could not speak a word. In a few minutes I came to myself, and he carried me safe to my little nurse, who, by this time, had returned to the place where she left me, and was in cruel agonies when I did not appear, nor answer when she called. She severely reprimanded the gardener on account of his dog. But the thing was hushed up, and never known at court, for the girl was afraid of the queen's anger; and truly, as to myself, I thought it would not be for my reputation that such a story should go about.

This accident determined Glumdalclitch never to trust me abroad, for the future, out of her sight. I had been long afraid of this resolution, and therefore concealed from her some little unlucky adventures that happened in those times when I was left by myself. Once a kite, hovering over the garden, made a stoop at me, and if I had not resolutely drawn my hanger, and run under a thick espalier, he would have certainly carried me away in his talons. Another time, walking to the top of a fresh mole-hill, I fell to my neck in the hole through which that animal had cast up the earth, and coined a reason, not worth remembering, to excuse myself for spoiling my clothes. I likewise broke my right shin against the shell of a snail, which I happened to stumble over, as I was walking along and thinking on poor England.

I cannot tell whether I was more pleased or mortified to observe, in these solitary walks, that the smaller birds did not appear to be at all afraid of me, but would hop about within a yard's distance, looking for worms and other food, with as much indifference and security as if no creature at all were near them. I remember a thrush had the confidence to snatch out of my hand, with his bill, a piece of cake that Glumdalclitch had just given me for my breakfast. When I attempted to catch any of these birds, they would boldly turn against me, endeavoring to peck my fingers, which I durst not venture within their reach; and then they would hop back unconcerned, to hunt for worms or snails, as they did before. But one day I took a thick

cudgel, and threw it with all my strength, so luckily, at a
linnet, that I knocked him down, and seizing him by the
neck with both my hands, ran with him in triumph to my
nurse. However, the bird, who had been only stunned, recovering himself, gave me so many boxes with his wings, on
both sides of my head and body, though I held him at
arm's length, and was out of the reach of his claws, that I
was twenty times thinking to let him go. But I was soon
relieved by one of our servants, who wrung off the bird's
neck, and I had him next day for dinner, by the queen's
command. This linnet, as near as I can remember, seemed
to be somewhat larger than an English swan.

The maids of honor* often invited Glumdalclitch to their
apartments, and desired she would bring me along with her,
on purpose to have the pleasure of seeing and touching me.
To me their endearments were very disgusting, which I do
not mention or intend to the disadvantage of those excellent
ladies, for whom I have all manner of respect; but I conceive that my sense was more acute in proportion to my
littleness, and that those illustrious persons were no more
disagreeable to their lovers, or to each other, than people of
the same quality are with us in England. And after all, I
found the natural odor of their skin was much more sup-
portable than when they used perfumes, under which I
immediately swooned away. I cannot forget that an intimate friend of mine in Lilliput took the freedom, in a warm
day, when I had used a good deal of exercise, to complain
of a strong smell about me, although I am as little faulty
that way as most of my sex; but I suppose his faculty of
smelling was as nice with regard to me as mine was to that
of this people. Upon this point, I cannot forbear doing
justice to the queen, my mistress, and Glumdalclitch, my
nurse, whose persons were as sweet as those of any lady in
England.

One day, a young gentleman, who was nephew to my
nurse's governess, came and pressed them both to see an

* It is very certain that the maids of honor of the English
court found but little favor in the eyes of Swift.

execution. It was of a man who had murdered one of that gentleman's intimate acquaintance. Glumdalclitch was prevailed on to be of the company, very much against her inclination, for she was naturally tender-hearted; and as for myself, although I abhorred such kind of spectacles, yet my curiosity tempted me to see something that I thought must be extraordinary. The malefactor was fixed in a chair upon a scaffold erected for that purpose, and his head cut off at one blow, with a sword of forty feet long. The veins and arteries spouted up such a prodigious quantity of blood, and so high in the air, that the great *jet d'eau* at Versailles was not equal, for the time it lasted; and the head, when it fell upon the scaffold-floor, gave such a bounce as made me start, although I was at least half an English mile distant.

The queen, who often used to hear me talk of sea-voyages, and took all occasions to divert me when I was melancholy, asked me whether I understood how to handle a sail or an oar, and whether a little exercise of rowing might not be convenient for my health. I answered that I understood both very well; for although my proper employment had been to be surgeon or doctor to the ship, yet often, upon a pinch, I was forced to work like a common mariner. But I could not see how this could be done in their country, where the smallest wherry was equal to a first-rate man-of-war among us; and such a boat as I could manage would never live in any of their rivers. Her majesty said, if I would contrive a boat, her own joiner should make it, and she would provide a place for me to sail in. The fellow was an ingenious workman, and, by my instructions, in ten days finished a pleasure-boat, with all its tackling, able conveniently to hold eight Europeans. When it was finished, the queen was so delighted that she ran with it in her lap to the king, who ordered it to be put in a cistern full of water, with me in it, by the way of trial; where I could not manage my two sculls or little oars for want of room. But the queen had before contrived another project. She ordered the joiner to make a wooden trough of three hundred feet long, fifty broad, and eight deep; which being well pitched, to prevent leaking, was placed on the floor along the wall, in an outer room of the palace. It had a tap near the bottom to let out the water when it began to grow stale, and two servants could easily fill it in half an hour. Here I often used to row for my own diversion, as well as that of the queen and her ladies, who thought themselves well entertained with my skill and agility. Sometimes I would put up my sail, and then my business was only to steer, while the ladies gave me a gale with their fans; and when they were weary, some of their pages would blow my sail forward with their breath, while I showed my art by steering starboard or larboard as I pleased. When I had done, Glumdalclitch always carried back my boat into her closet, and hung it on a nail to dry.

In this exercise I once met with an accident, which had like to have cost me my life; for one of the pages having put my boat into the trough, the governess who attended Glumdalclitch very officiously lifted me up, to place me in the boat; but I happened to slip through her fingers, and should infallibly have fallen down forty feet upon the floor, if, by the luckiest chance in the world, I had not been stopped by a corking-pin that stuck in the good gentlewoman's stomacher; the head of the pin passed between my shirt and the waistband of my breeches, and thus I was held by the middle in the air till Glumdalclitch ran to my relief.

Another time, one of the servants, whose office it was to fill my trough every third day with fresh water, was so careless as to let a huge frog (not perceiving it) slip out of his pail. The frog lay concealed till I was put into my boat, but then, seeing a resting-place, climbed up, and made it lean so much on one side that I was forced to balance it with all my weight on the other, to prevent overturning. When the frog was got in, it hopped at once half the length of the boat, and then over my head, backward and forward, daubing my face and clothes with its odious slime. The largeness of its features made it appear the most deformed animal that can be conceived. However, I desired Glumdalclitch to let me deal with it alone. I banged it a good while with one of my sculls, and at last forced it to leap out of the boat.

But the greatest danger I ever underwent in that kingdom was from a monkey, who belonged to one of the clerks of the kitchen. Glumdalclitch had locked me up in her closet while she went somewhere upon business, or a visit. The weather being very warm, the closet window was left open, as well as the windows and the door of my bigger box, in which I usually lived, because of its largeness and conveniency. As I sat quietly meditating at my table, I heard something bounce in at the closet window, and skip about from one side to the other; whereat, although I was much alarmed, yet I ventured to look out, but not stirring from my seat; and then I saw this frolicsome animal frisking and leaping up and down, till at last he came to my box, which he seemed to view with great pleasure and curiosity, peeping in at the door and every window. I retreated to the farther corner of my room, or box; but the monkey, looking in at every side, put me into such a fright that I wanted presence of mind to conceal myself under the bed, as I might easily have done. After some time spent in peeping, grinning, and chattering, he at last espied me; and reaching one of his paws in at the door, as a cat does when she plays with a mouse, although I often shifted place to avoid him, he at length seized the lappet of my coat (which, being made of that country's silk, was very thick and strong), and dragged me out. He took me up in his right fore-foot and held me as a nurse does a child she is going to suckle, just as I have seen the same sort of creature do with a kitten in Europe; and when I offered to struggle, he squeezed me so hard that I thought it more prudent to submit. I have good reason to believe that he took me for a young one of his own species, by his often stroking my face very gently with his other paw. In these diversions he was interrupted by a noise at the closet-door, as if somebody was opening it; whereupon he suddenly leaped up to the window, at which he had come in, and thence upon the leads and gutters, walking upon three legs, and holding me in the fourth, till he clambered up a roof next to ours. I heard Glumdalclitch give a shriek at the moment he was carrying me out. The poor girl was almost distracted; that quarter of the palace was all in an uproar; the servants ran for ladders; the monkey was seen by hundreds in the court, sitting upon the ridge of a building, holding me like a baby in one of his fore-paws, and feeding me with the other, by cramming into my mouth some victuals he had squeezed out of the bag on one side of his chaps, and patting me when I would not eat; whereat many of the rabble below could not forbear laughing: neither do I think they justly ought to be blamed, for, without question, the sight was ridiculous enough to everybody but myself. Some of the people threw up stones, hoping to drive the monkey down: but this was strictly forbidden, or else, very probably, my brains had been dashed out.

The ladders were now applied, and mounted by several men; which the monkey observing, and finding himself almost encompassed, not being able to make speed enough with his three legs, let me drop on a ridge tile, and made his escape. Here I sat for some time, five hundred yards from the ground, expecting every moment to be blown down by the wind, or to fall by my own giddiness, and come tumbling over and over from the ridge to the eaves: but an honest lad, one of my nurse's footmen, climbed up, and putting me into his breeches-pocket, brought me down safe.

I was almost choked with the filthy stuff the monkey crammed down my throat; but my dear little nurse picked it out of my mouth with a small needle, and then I fell a-vomiting, which gave me great relief. Yet I was so weak and bruised in the sides with the squeezes given me by this odious animal, that I was forced to keep my bed a fortnight. The king, queen, and all the court sent every day to inquire after my health; and her majesty made me several visits during my sickness. The monkey was killed, and an order made that no such animal should be kept about the palace.

When I attended the king after my recovery, to return him thanks for his favors, he was pleased to rally me a good deal upon this adventure. He asked me what my thoughts and speculations were while I lay in the monkey's paw; how I liked the victuals he gave me; his manner of feeding; and whether the fresh air on the roof had sharpened my stomach. He desired to know what I would have done upon such an occasion in my own country. I told his majesty that in Europe we had no monkeys, except such as were brought as curiosities from other places, and so small that I could deal with a dozen of them together, if they presumed to attack me. And as for that monstrous animal with whom I was so lately engaged (it was, indeed, as large as an elephant), if my fears had suffered me to think so far as to make use of my hanger (looking fiercely, and clapping my hand upon the hilt as I spoke), when he poked his paw into my chamber, perhaps I should have given him such a wound as would have made him glad to withdraw it with more haste than he put it in. This I delivered in a firm tone, like a person who was jealous lest his courage should be called in question. However, my speech produced nothing else besides a loud laughter, which all the respect due to his majesty from those about him could not make them contain. This made me reflect how vain an attempt it is for a man to endeavor to do himself honor among those who are out of all degrees of equality or comparison with him. And yet I have seen the moral of my own behavior very frequent in England since my return; where a little contemptible varlet, without the least title to birth, person, wit, or common-sense, shall presume to look with importance, and put himself upon a footing with the greatest person of the kingdom.

I was every day furnishing the court with some ridiculous story, and Glumdalclitch, although she loved me to excess, yet was arch enough to inform the queen whenever I committed any folly that she thought would be diverting to her majesty. The girl who had been out of order was carried by her governess to take the air about an hour's distance or thirty miles from town. They alighted out of the coach near a small footpath in a field, and Glumdalclitch setting down my traveling-box, I went out of it to walk. There was a small heap of dirt in the path, and I must needs try my activity by attempting to leap over it. I took a run, but unfortunately jumped short, and found myself just in the middle, up to my knees. I waded through with some difficulty, and one of the footmen wiped me as clean as he could with his handkerchief, for I was filthily bemired; and my nurse confined me to my box till we returned home, when the queen was soon informed of what had passed, and the footman spread it about the court; so that all the mirth for some days was at my expense.

CHAPTER VI *

Several Contrivances of the Author to Please the King and Queen—He Shows His Skill in Music—The King Inquires Into the State of England, which the Author Relates to Him—The King's Observations Thereon.

I USED to attend the king's levee once or twice a week, and had often seen him under the barber's hand, which indeed was at first very terrible to behold, for the razor was almost twice as long as an ordinary scythe.

His majesty, according to the custom of the country, was only shaved twice a week. I once prevailed on the barber to give me some of the suds or lather, out of which I picked forty or fifty of the strongest stumps of hair. I then took a piece of fine wood, and cut it like the back of a comb, making several holes in it at equal distances with as small a needle as I could get from Glumdalclitch. I fixed in the stumps so artificially, scraping and sloping them with my knife toward the points, that I made a very tolerable comb; which was a seasonable supply, my own being so much broken in the teeth that it was almost useless: neither did I know any artist in that country so nice and exact as would undertake to make me another.

And this puts me in mind of an amusement wherein I spent many of my leisure hours. I desired the queen's woman to save for me the combings of her majesty's hair, whereof in time I got a good quantity; and consulting with my friend the cabinet-maker, who had received general orders to do little jobs for me, I directed him to make two chair-frames, no larger than those I had in my box, and to

* In this chapter Swift reviews the political condition of England, and gives his views upon the state of its government and institutions.

bore little holes with a fine awl round those parts where I
designed the backs and seats; through these holes I wove
the strongest hairs I could pick out, just after the manner
of the cane-chairs in England. When they were finished, I
made a present of them to her majesty, who kept them in
her cabinet, and used to show them for curiosities, as, indeed, they were the wonder of every one that beheld them.
The queen would have had me sit upon one of these chairs,
but I absolutely refused to obey her, protesting I would
rather die a thousand deaths than sit contemptuously upon
those precious hairs that once adorned her majesty's head.
Of these hairs (as I had always a mechanical genius) I likewise made a neat little purse, about five feet long, with her
majesty's name deciphered in gold letters, which I gave to
Glumdalclitch by the queen's consent. To say the truth,
it was more for show than use, being not of strength to bear
the weight of the larger coins, and therefore she kept nothing in it but some little toys that girls are fond of.

The king, who delighted in music, had frequent concerts
at court, to which I was sometimes carried, and set in my
box on the table to hear them; but the noise was so great
that I could hardly distinguish the tunes. I am confident
that all the drums and trumpets of a royal army, beating
and sounding together, just at your ears, could not equal it.
My practice was to have my box removed from the place
where the performers sat, as far as I could; then to shut
the doors and windows of it, and draw the window curtains;
after which I found their music not disagreeable.

I had learned in my youth to play a little upon the
spinet. Glumdalclitch kept one in her chamber, and a
master attended twice a week to teach her: I called it a
spinet, because it somewhat resembled that instrument, and
was played upon in the same manner. A fancy came into
my head that I would entertain the king and queen with an
English tune upon this instrument. But this appeared extremely difficult; for the spinet was near sixty feet long,
each key being almost a foot wide, so that with my arms
extended I could not reach to above five keys; and to press

them down required a good smart stroke with my fist, which would be too great a labor, and to no purpose. The method I contrived was this: I prepared two round sticks, about the bigness of common cudgels; they were thicker at one end than the other, and I covered the thicker ends with pieces of a mouse's skin, that by rapping on them I might neither damage the tops of the keys nor interrupt the sound. Before the spinet a bench was placed, about four feet below the keys, and I was put upon the bench. I ran sidling upon it, that way and this, as fast as I could, banging the proper keys with my two sticks, and made a shift to play a jig, to the great satisfaction of both their majesties; but it was the most violent exercise that I ever underwent; and yet I could not strike above sixteen keys, nor consequently play the bass and treble together, as other artists do; which was a great disadvantage to my performance.

The king who, as I before observed, was a prince of excellent understanding, would frequently order that I should be brought in my box, and set upon the table in his closet: he would then command me to bring one of my chairs out of my box, and sit down within three yards' distance upon the top of the cabinet, which brought me almost to a level with his face. In this manner I had several conversations with him. I one day took the freedom to tell his majesty that the contempt he discovered toward Europe and the rest of the world did not seem answerable to those excellent qualities of mind that he was master of; that reason did not extend itself with the bulk of the body; on the contrary, we observed in our country that the tallest persons were usually the least provided with it; that among other animals, bees and ants had the reputation of more industry, art, and sagacity than many of the larger kinds; and that, as inconsiderable as he took me to be, I hoped I might live to do his majesty some signal service. The king heard me with attention, and began to conceive a much better opinion of me than he had ever before. He desired I would give him as exact an account of the government of England as

I possibly could; because, as fond as princes commonly are of their own customs (for so he conjectured of other monarchs by my former discourses), he should be glad to hear of anything that might deserve imitation.

Imagine with thyself, courteous reader, how often I then wished for the tongue of Demosthenes or Cicero, that might have enabled me to celebrate the praise of my own dear native country, in a style equal to its merits and felicity.

I began my discourse by informing his majesty that our dominions consisted of two islands, which comprised three mighty kingdoms, under one sovereign, besides our plantations in America. I dwelt long upon the fertility of our soil, and the temperature of our climate. I then spoke at large upon the constitution of an English Parliament; partly made up of an illustrious body, called the House of Peers—persons of the noblest blood and of the most ancient and ample patrimonies. I described that extraordinary care was always taken of their education in arts and arms, to qualify them for being counselors both to the king and kingdom; to have a share in the legislature; to be members of the highest court of judicature, whence there can be no appeal; and to be champions always ready for the defense of their prince and country, by their valor, conduct, and fidelity. That these were the ornament and bulwark of the kingdom, worthy followers of their most renowned ancestors, whose honor had been the reward of their virtue, from which their posterity were never once known to degenerate. To these were joined several holy persons, as part of that assembly, under the title of bishops, whose peculiar business is to take care of religion and of those who instruct the people therein. These were searched and sought out through the whole nation, by the prince and his wisest counselors, among such of the priesthood as were most deservedly distinguished by the sanctity of their life and the depth of their erudition; who were, indeed, the spiritual fathers of the clergy and the people.

That the other part of the Parliament consisted of an assembly, called the House of Commons, who were all principal gentlemen, freely picked and culled out by the people themselves, by their great abilities and love of their country, to represent the wisdom of the whole nation. And that these two bodies made up the most august assembly in Europe, to whom, in conjunction with the prince, the whole legislature is committed.

I then descended to the courts of justice; over which the judges, those venerable sages and interpreters of the law, presided, for determining the disputed rights and properties of men, as well as for the punishment of vice and protection of innocence. I mentioned the prudent management of our treasury; the valor and achievements of our forces, by sea and land. I computed the number of our people, by reckoning how many millions there might be of each religious sect or political party among us. I did not omit even our sports and pastimes, or any other particular which I thought might redound to the honor of my country. And I finished all with a brief historical account of affairs and events in England for about a hundred years past.

This conversation was not ended under five audiences, each of several hours; and the king heard the whole with great attention, frequently taking notes of what I spoke, as well as memorandums of what questions he intended to ask me.

When I had put an end to these long discourses, his majesty, in a sixth audience, consulted his notes, proposed many doubts, queries, and objections upon every article. He asked what methods were used to cultivate the minds and bodies of our young nobility, and in what kind of business they commonly spent the first and most teachable part of their lives; what course was taken to supply that assembly when any noble family became extinct; what qualifications were necessary in those who are to be created new lords—whether the humor of the prince, a sum of money to a court lady, or a design of strengthening a party opposite to the public interest, ever happened to be the motive in those advancements; what share of knowledge these lords had in the laws of their country, and how they came by it, so as to enable them to decide the properties of their fellow-subjects, in the last resort; whether they were always so free from avarice, partialities, or want, that a bribe, or some other sinister view, could have no place among them; whether those holy lords I spoke of were always promoted to that rank on account of their knowledge in religious matters, and the sanctity of their lives—had never been compliers with the times while they were common priests, or slavish, prostitute chaplains to some nobleman, whose opinions they continued servilely to follow after they were admitted into that assembly.

He then desired to know what arts were practiced in electing those whom I called commoners—whether a stranger, with a strong purse, might not influence the vulgar voters to choose him before their own landlord, or the most considerable gentleman in the neighborhood; how it came to pass that people were so violently bent upon getting into this assembly, which I allowed to be a great trouble and expense, often to the ruin of their families, without any salary or pension—because this appeared such an exalted strain of virtue and public spirit, that his majesty seemed to doubt it might possibly not be always sincere. And he desired to know whether such zealous gentlemen could have any views of refunding themselves for the charges and trouble they were at, by sacrificing the public good to the designs of a weak and vicious prince, in conjunction with a corrupted ministry. He multiplied his questions, and sifted me thoroughly upon every part of this head, proposing numberless inquiries and objections, which I think it not prudent or convenient to repeat.*

Upon what I said in relation to our courts of justice, his majesty desired to be satisfied in several points; and this I was the better able to do, having been formerly almost

* The pertinent questions which Swift puts into the mouth of the sovereign of Brobdingnag are meant as severe strictures upon the corrupt practices of the ministers in securing the return of their own partisans to Parliament.

ruined by a long suit in Chancery, which was decreed for me with costs. He asked what time was usually spent in determining between right and wrong, and what degree of expense; whether advocates and orators had liberty to plead in causes manifestly known to be unjust, vexatious, or oppressive; whether party, in religion or politics, was observed to be of any weight in the scale of justice; whether those pleading orators were persons educated in the general knowledge of equity, or only in provincial, national, and other local customs; whether they or their judges had any part in penning those laws, which they assumed the liberty of interpreting, and glossing upon at their pleasure; whether they had ever, at different times, pleaded for and against the same cause, and cited precedents to prove contrary opinions; whether they were a rich or a poor corporation; whether they received any pecuniary reward for pleading, or delivering their opinions; and, particularly, whether they were ever admitted as members in the lower senate.*

He fell next upon the management of our treasury; and said he thought my memory had failed me, because I computed our taxes at about five or six millions a year, and when I came to mention the issues, he found they sometimes amounted to more than double; for the notes he had taken were very particular in this point, because he hoped, as he told me, that the knowledge of our conduct might be useful to him, and he could not be deceived in his calcula-

---

* Swift's hatred to lawyers, both as a class and to many individuals of the profession, is well known. He had, indeed, by his writings, placed himself on many occasions in the power of the law, and would not be likely to forego any opportunity to assail either the laws themselves or the administration of them. Swift gives us his own opinion of the "glorious uncertainty of the law" in his "Thoughts on Various Subjects:" "I never heard a finer piece of satire against lawyers than that of astrologers, when they pretend, by rules of art, to tell when a suit will end, and whether to the advantage of the plaintiff or defendant; thus making the matter entirely depend upon the influence of the stars, without the least regard to the merits of the cause."

tions. But if what I told him were true, he was still at a loss how a kingdom could run out of its estate, like a private person. He asked me who were our creditors, and where we found money to pay them. He wondered to hear me talk of such chargeable and expensive wars; that certainly we must be a quarrelsome people, or live among very bad neighbors, and that our generals must needs be richer than our kings. He asked what business we had out of our own islands, unless upon the score of trade, or treaty, or to defend the coast with our fleets. Above all, he was amazed to hear me talk of a mercenary standing army, in the midst of peace and among a free people. He said, if we were governed by our own consent, in the persons of our representatives, he could not imagine of whom we were afraid, or against whom we were to fight; and would hear my opinion, whether a private man's house might not be better defended by himself, his children, and family, than by half a dozen rascals, picked up at a venture in the streets for small wages, who might get a hundred times more by cutting their throats.

He laughed at my odd kind of arithmetic, as he was pleased to call it, in reckoning the numbers of our people by a computation drawn from the several sects among us in religion and politics. He said he knew no reason why those who entertain opinions prejudicial to the public should be obliged to change, or should not be obliged to conceal them. And as it was tyranny in any government to require the first, so it was weakness not to enforce the second; for a man may be allowed to keep poisons in his closet, but not to vend them for cordials.

He observed, that among the diversions of our nobility and gentry I had mentioned gaming; he desired to know at what age this entertainment was usually taken up, and when it was laid down; how much of their time it employed; whether it ever went so high as to affect their fortunes; whether mean, vicious people, by their dexterity in that art, might not arrive at great riches, and sometimes keep our very nobles in dependence, as well as habituate them to vile companions: wholly take them from the improvement of their mind, and force them, by the losses they received, to learn and practice that infamous dexterity upon others.

He was perfectly astonished with the historical account I gave him of our affairs during the last century; protesting it was only a heap of conspiracies, rebellions, murders, massacres, revolutions, banishments; the very worst effects that avarice, faction, hypocrisy, perfidiousness, cruelty, rage, madness, hatred, envy, lust, malice, and ambition could produce.

His majesty, in another audience, was at the pains to recapitulate the sum of all I had spoken; compared the questions he made with the answers I had given; then, taking me into his hands, and stroking me gently, delivering himself in these words, which I shall never forget, nor the manner he spoke them in: "My little friend Grildrig, you have made a most admirable panegyric upon your country; you have clearly proved that ignorance, idleness, and vice are the proper ingredients for qualifying a legislator; that laws are best explained, interpreted, and applied by those whose interest and abilities lie in perverting, confounding, and eluding them. I observe among you some lines of an institution which in its original might have been tolerable, but these half erased, and the rest wholly blurred and blotted by corruption. It does not appear, from all you have said, how any one perfection is required toward the procurement of any one station among you; much less that men are ennobled on account of their virtue; that priests are advanced for their piety or learning; soldiers for their conduct or valor; judges for their integrity; senators for the love of their country; or counselors for their wisdom.

"As for yourself," continued the king, "who have spent the greatest part of your life in traveling, I am well disposed to hope you may hitherto have escaped many vices of your country. But by what I have gathered from your own relation, and the answers I have with much pains wringed and extorted from you, I cannot but conclude the bulk of your natives to be the most pernicious race of little odious vermin that Nature ever suffered to crawl upon the surface of the earth."*

* This opinion, delivered in the person of the philosophic monarch of the Brobdingnaggians, as his sentence upon the whole case of the English people and their institutions, is the last and heaviest stroke of Swift's bitter and misanthropic satire.

CHAPTER VII

*The Author's Love of His Country—He Makes a Proposal
of Much Advantage to the King, which Is Rejected—
The King's Great Ignorance in Politics—The Learning of
that Country Very Imperfect and Confined—The Laws,
Military Affairs, and Parties in the State.*

NOTHING but an extreme love of truth could have hindered
me from concealing this part of my story. It was in vain
to discover my resentments, which were always turned into
ridicule; and I was forced to rest with patience, while my
noble and beloved country was so injuriously treated. I am
as heartily sorry as any of my readers can possibly be that
such an occasion was given; but this prince happened to be
so curious and inquisitive upon every particular, that it
could not consist either with gratitude or good manners to
refuse giving him what satisfaction I was able. Yet this
much I may be allowed to say in my own vindication, that
I artfully eluded many of his questions, and gave to every
point a more favorable turn, by many degrees, than the
strictness of truth would allow. For I have always borne
that laudable partiality to my own country which Dionysius
Halicarnassensis, with so much justice, recommends to an
historian: I would hide the frailties and deformities of my
political mother, and place her virtues and beauties in the
most advantageous light. This was my sincere endeavor in
those many discourses I had with that monarch, although it
unfortunately failed of success.

But great allowance should be given to a king who lives
wholly secluded from the rest of the world, and must therefore be altogether unacquainted with the manners and
customs that most prevail in other nations: the want of

which knowledge will ever produce many prejudices, and a certain narrowness of thinking, from which we and the politer countries of Europe are wholly exempted. And it would be hard indeed if so remote a prince's notions of virtue and vice were to be offered as a standard for all mankind.

To confirm what I have now said, and further to show the miserable effects of a confined education, I shall here insert a passage, which will hardly obtain belief. In hopes to ingratiate myself further into his majesty's favor, I told him of an invention discovered between three and four hundred years ago, to make a certain powder, into a heap of which the smallest spark of fire falling would kindle the whole in a moment, although it were as big as a mountain, and make it all fly up in the air together, with a noise and agitation greater than thunder. That a proper quantity of this powder rammed into a hollow tube of brass or iron, according to its bigness, would drive a ball of iron or lead with such violence and speed as nothing was able to sustain its force. That the largest balls thus discharged would not only destroy whole ranks of an army at once, but batter the strongest walls to the ground; sink down ships, with a thousand men in each, to the bottom of the sea; and when linked together by a chain, would cut through masts and rigging, divide hundreds of bodies in the middle, and lay all waste before them. That we often put this powder into large hollow balls of iron, and discharged them by an engine into some city we were besieging, which would rip up the pavements, tear the houses to pieces, burst and throw splinters on every side, dashing out the brains of all who came near. That I knew the ingredients very well, which were cheap and common: I understood the manner of compounding them, and could direct his workmen how to make those tubes of a size proportionable to all other things in his majesty's kingdom, and the largest need not be above a hundred feet long; twenty or thirty of which tubes, charged with the proper quantity of powder and balls, would batter down the walls of the strongest town in his dominions in a few hours, or destroy the whole metropolis, if ever it should pretend to dispute his absolute commands. This I humbly offered to his majesty, as a small tribute of acknowledgment, in turn for so many marks that I had received of his royal favor and protection.

The king was struck with horror at the description I had given of those terrible engines, and the proposal I had made. He was amazed how so impotent and groveling an insect as I (these were his expressions) could entertain such inhuman ideas, and in so familiar a manner, as to appear wholly unmoved at all the scenes of blood and desolation which I had painted, as the common effects of those destructive machines; "whereof," he said, "some evil genius, enemy to mankind, must have been the first contriver." As for himself, he protested that, although few things delighted him so much as new discoveries in art or nature, yet he would rather lose half his kingdom than be privy to such a secret, which he commanded me, as I valued my life, never to mention any more.*

A strange effect of narrow principles and views! that a prince possessed of every quality which procures veneration, love, and esteem; of strong parts, great wisdom, and profound learning, endowed with admirable talents, and almost adored by his subjects, should, from a nice, unnecessary scruple, whereof in Europe we can have no conception, let slip an opportunity put into his hands that would have made him absolute master of the lives, the liberties, and the fortunes of his people. Neither do I say this with the least intention to detract from the many virtues of that excellent king, whose character, I am sensible, will, on this account, be very much lessened in the opinion of an English reader; but I take this defect among them to have arisen from their

* The rejection of this proposition of Gulliver, to make the sovereign of the Brobdingnags absolute over his people by means of physical force, is intended to convey a censure upon the designs attributed to George I. by the Tories, of intending, by means of standing armies, to make himself independent of his people and subvert their liberties.

ignorance, by not having hitherto reduced politics into a
science, as the more acute wits of Europe have done. For
I remember very well, in a discourse one day with the king,
when I happened to say there were several thousand books
among us written upon the art of government, it gave him
(directly contrary to my intention) a very mean opinion of
our understandings. He professed both to abominate and
despise all mystery, refinement, and intrigue, either in a
prince or a minister. He could not tell what I meant by
secrets of state, where an enemy, or some rival nation, were
not in the case. He confined the knowledge of governing
within very narrow bounds—to common-sense and reason,
to justice and lenity, to the speedy determination of civil
and criminal causes; with some other obvious topics, which
are not worth considering. And he gave it for his opinion,
that whoever could make two ears of corn or two blades of
grass to grow upon a spot of ground where only one grew
before, would deserve better of mankind, and do more es-
sential service to his country, than the whole race of politicians put together.*

The learning of this people is very defective—consisting
only of morality, history, poetry, and mathematics, wherein
they must be allowed to excel. But the last of these is
wholly applied to what may be useful in life, to the improvement of agriculture and all mechanical arts; so that
among us it would be little esteemed. And as to ideas,
entities, abstractions, and transcendentals, I could never
drive the least conception into their heads.

No law of that country must exceed in words the number
of letters in their alphabet, which consists only of two-and-
twenty. But, indeed, few of them extend even to that
length. They are expressed in the most plain and simple
terms, wherein those people are not mercurial enough to
discover above one interpretation; and to write a comment
upon any law is a capital crime. As to the decision of civil

* This aphorism has become celebrated, and is often quoted
by statesmen and political economists. It is as wise as it is
epigrammatic.

causes, or proceedings against criminals, their precedents are so few that they have little reason to boast of any extraordinary skill in either.

They have had the art of printing, as well as the Chinese, time out of mind; but their libraries are not very large, for that of the king, which is reckoned the largest, does not amount to above a thousand volumes, placed in a gallery of twelve hundred feet long, whence I had liberty to borrow what books I pleased. The queen's joiner had contrived in one of Glumdalclitch's rooms a kind of wooden machine, five-and-twenty feet high, formed like a standing ladder; the steps were each fifty feet long: it was, indeed, a movable pair of stairs, the lowest end placed at ten feet distance from the wall of the chamber. The book I had a mind to read was put up leaning against the wall; I first mounted to the upper step of the ladder, and, turning my face toward the book, began at the top of the page, and so walking to the right and left about eight or ten paces, according to the length of the lines, till I had gotten a little below the level of mine eyes, and then descending gradually till I came to the bottom; after which I mounted again, and began the other page in the same manner, and so turned over the leaf, which I could easily do with both my hands, for it was as thick and stiff as pasteboard, and in the largest folios not above eighteen or twenty feet long.

Their style is clear, masculine, and smooth, but not florid; for they avoid nothing more than multiplying unnecessary words, or using various expressions. I have perused many of their books, especially those on history and morality. Among the rest, I was much diverted with a little old treatise, which always lay in Glumdalclitch's bedchamber, and belonged to her governess, a grave elderly gentlewoman, who dealt in morality and devotion. The book treats of the weakness of human kind, and is in little esteem, except among the women and the vulgar. However, I was curious to see what an author of that country could say upon such a subject. This writer went through all the usual topics of European moralists, showing how diminutive, contemptible and helpless an animal was man in his own nature; how unable to defend himself from the inclemencies of the air, or the fury of wild beasts; how much he was excelled by one creature in strength, by another in speed, by a third in foresight, by a fourth in industry. He added, that nature was degenerated in these latter declining ages of the world, and could now produce only small abortive births, in comparison of those in ancient times. He said it was very reasonable to think, not only that the species of men were originally much larger, but also that there must have been giants in former ages;* which, as it is asserted by history and tradition, so it has been confirmed by huge bones and skulls, casually dug up in several parts of the kingdom, far exceeding the common dwindled race of men in our days. He argued that the very laws of nature absolutely required we should have been made, in the beginning, of a size more large and robust; not so liable to destruction from every little accident, of a tile falling from a house, or a stone cast from the hand of a boy, or being drowned in a little brook. From this way of reasoning, the author drew several moral applications, useful in the conduct of life, but needless here to repeat. For my own part, I could not avoid reflecting how universally this talent was spread of drawing lectures in morality, or indeed rather matter of discontent and repining, from the quarrels we raise with nature. And I believe, upon a strict inquiry, those quarrels might be shown as ill-grounded among us as they are among that people.

As to their military affairs, they boast that the king's army consists of a hundred and seventy-six thousand foot and thirty-two thousand horse; if that may be called an army which is made up of tradesmen in the several cities,

* We have already referred to the theories entertained by different nations in regard to the earlier races of man being of a stature much greater than their descendants. The argument used by Swift, drawn from the bones and skulls which have from time to time been dug up, has been proved to be fallacious, as these bones were ascertained not to be the bones of men.

and farmers in the country, whose commanders are only the
nobility or gentry, without pay or reward. They are indeed
perfect enough in their exercises, and under very good
discipline, wherein I saw no great merit; for how should it
be otherwise where every farmer is under the command of
his own landlord, and every citizen under that of the principal men in his own city, chosen, after the manner of
Venice, by ballot?

I have often seen the militia of Lorbrulgrud drawn out
to exercise, in a great field near the city, of twenty miles
square. They were in all not above twenty-five thousand
foot and six thousand horse; but it was impossible for me
to compute their number, considering the space of ground
they took up. A cavalier, mounted on a large steed, might
be about ninety feet high. I have seen this whole body of
horse, upon the word of command, draw their swords at
once and brandish them in the air. Imagination can picture nothing so grand, so surprising, and so astonishing; it
looked as if ten thousand flashes of lightning were darting
at the same time from every quarter of the sky.

I was curious to know how this prince, to whose dominions there is no access from any other country, came to
think of armies, or to teach his people the practice of military discipline. But I was soon informed, both by conversation and reading their histories; for in the course of many
ages they have been troubled with the same disease to
which the whole race of mankind is subject; the nobility
often contending for power, the people for liberty, and the
king for absolute dominion:* all which, however, happily

* Swift here again exhibits his dislike and jealousy of the
maintenance of a standing army, than which, it must be owned,
nothing could be more repugnant to the national prejudices of
the times. Mr. Hallam, in his "Constitutional History of England," makes the following very just observation on this subject:
"Nothing could be more idle, at any time since the Revolution,
than to suppose that the regular army would pull the speaker
out of his chair, or in any manner be employed to confirm a
despotic power in the Crown. Such power, I think, could never
have been the waking dream of either king or minister. But as

tempered by the laws of that kingdom, have been sometimes violated by each of the three parties, and have more than once occasioned civil wars; the last whereof was happily put an end to by this prince's grandfather, in a general composition; and the militia, then settled with common consent, has been ever since kept in the strictest duty.

---

the slightest inroads upon private rights and liberties are to be guarded against in any nation that deserves to be called free, we should always keep in mind not only that the military power should be subordinate to the civil, but, as this subordination must cease where the former is frequently employed, that it should never be called upon in aid of the peace without sufficient cause."

CHAPTER VIII

*The King and Queen Make a Progress to the Frontiers—
The Author Attends Them—The Manner in which He
Leaves the Country Very Particularly Related—He Re-
turns to England.*

I HAD always a strong impulse that I should some time recover my liberty, though it was impossible to conjecture by
what means, or to form any project with the least hope of
succeeding.   The ship in which I sailed was the first ever
known to be driven within sight of that coast, and the king
had given strict orders that if at any time another appeared, it should be taken ashore, and with all its crew and
passengers brought in a tumbril to Lorbrulgrud.   I was
indeed treated with much kindness: I was the favorite of a
great king and queen, and the delight of the whole court;
but it was upon such a footing as ill became the dignity of
human kind.   I could never forget those domestic pledges
I had left behind me.   I wanted to be among people with
whom I could converse upon even terms, and walk about
the streets and fields without being afraid of being trod to
death like a frog or a young puppy.   But my deliverance
came sooner than I expected, and in a manner not very
common; the whole story and circumstances of which I
shall faithfully relate.

I had now been two years in this country; and about the
beginning of the third, Glumdalclitch and I attended the
king and queen, in a progress to the south coast of the kingdom.   I was carried, as usual, in my traveling-box, which,
as I have already described, was a very convenient closet,
of twelve feet wide; and I had ordered a hammock to be
fixed, by silken ropes, from the four corners at the top, to

139

break the jolts, when a servant carried me before him on horseback, as I sometimes desired; and would often sleep in my hammock, while we were upon the road. On the roof of my closet, not directly over the middle of the hammock, I ordered the joiner to cut out a hole of a foot square, to give me air in hot weather, as I slept; which hole I shut at pleasure with a board that drew backward and forward through a groove.

When we came to our journey's end, the king thought proper to pass a few days at a palace he has near Flanflasnic, a city within eighteen English miles of the sea-side. Glumdalclitch and I were much fatigued. I had gotten a small cold, but the poor girl was so ill as to be confined to her chamber. I longed to see the ocean, which must be the only scene of my escape, if ever it should happen. I pretended to be worse than I really was, and desired leave to take the fresh air of the sea, with a page whom I was very fond of, and who had sometimes been trusted with me. I shall never forget with what unwillingness Glumdalclitch consented, nor the strict charge she gave the page to be careful of me, bursting at the same time into a flood of tears, as if she had some foreboding of what was to happen. The boy took me out in my box, about half an hour's walk from the palace, toward the rocks on the sea-shore. I ordered him to set me down, and lifting up one of my sashes, cast many a wistful, melancholy look toward the sea. I found myself not very well, and told the page that I had a mind to take a nap in my hammock, which I hoped would do me good. I got in, and the boy shut the window close down, to keep out the cold. I soon fell asleep, and all I conjecture is, while I slept, the page, thinking no danger could happen, went among the rocks to look for birds'-eggs, having before observed him from my window searching about, and picking up one or two in the clefts. Be that as it will, I found myself suddenly awaked with a violent pull upon the ring which was fastened at the top of my box, for the convenience of carriage. I felt my box raised very high in the air, and then borne forward with prodigious speed.

The first jolt had like to have shaken me out of my hammock, but afterward the motion was easy enough. I called out several times as loud as I could raise my voice, but all to no purpose. I looked toward my windows, and could see nothing but the clouds and sky. I heard a noise just over my head, like the clapping of wings, and then began to perceive the woful condition I was in; that some eagle had got the ring of my box in his beak, with an intent to let it fall on a rock, like a tortoise in a shell, and then pick out my body, and devour it; for the sagacity and smell of this bird enabled him to discover his quarry at a great distance, though better concealed than I could be within a two-inch board.

In a little time I observed the noise and flutter of wings to increase very fast, and my box was tossed up and down like a sign on a windy day. I heard several bangs or buffets, as I thought, given to the eagle (for such I am certain it must have been that held the ring of my box in his beak), and then, all on a sudden, felt myself falling perpendicularly down, for above a minute, but with such incredible swiftness that I almost lost my breath. My fall was stopped by a terrible squash, that sounded louder to my ears than the cataract of Niagara; after which I was quite in the dark for another minute, and then my box began to rise so high that I could see light from the tops of the windows. I now perceived I was fallen into the sea. My box, by the weight of my body, the goods that were in, and the broad plate of iron fixed for strength at the four corners of the top and bottom, floated about five feet deep in water. I did then and do now suppose that the eagle which flew away with my box was pursued by two or three others, and forced to let me drop, while he defended himself against the rest, who hoped to share in the prey. The plates of iron fastened at the bottom of the box (for those were the strongest) preserved the balance while it fell, and hindered it from being broken on the surface of the water. Every joint of it was well grooved; and the door did not move on hinges, but up and down like a sash, which kept my closet so tight that very little water came in. I got with much difficulty out of my hammock, having first ventured to draw back the slip-board on the roof already mentioned, contrived on purpose to let in air. for want of which I found myself almost stifled.

How often did I then wish myself with my dear Glumdalclitch, from whom one single hour had so far divided me! And I may say with truth, that in the midst of my own misfortunes I could not forbear lamenting my poor nurse, the grief she would suffer for my loss, the displeasure of the queen, and the ruin of her fortune. Perhaps many travelers have not been under greater difficulties and distress than I was at this juncture, expecting every moment to see my box dashed to pieces, or at least overset by the first violent blast or rising wave. A breach in one pane of glass would have been immediate death; nor could anything have preserved the windows, but the strong lattice wires on the outside, against accidents in traveling. I saw the water ooze in at several crannies, although the leaks were not considerable, and I endeavored to stop them as well as I could. I was not able to lift up the roof of my closet, which otherwise I certainly should have done, and sat on the top of it, where I might at least preserve myself some hours longer than by being shut up (as I may call it) in the hold. Or if I escaped these dangers for a day or two, what could I expect but a miserable death of cold and hunger? I was four hours under these circumstances, expecting, and indeed wishing, every moment to be my last.

I have already told the reader that there were two strong staples fixed upon that side of my box which had no window, and into which the servant who used to carry me on horseback would put a leathern belt, and buckle it about his waist. Being in this disconsolate state, I heard, or at least thought I heard, some kind of grating noise on that side of my box where the staples were fixed; and soon after I began to fancy that the box was pulled or towed along the sea; for I now and then felt a sort of tugging, which made the waves rise near the tops of my windows, leaving me almost in the dark. This gave me some faint hopes of relief, although I was not able to imagine how it could be brought about. I ventured to unscrew one of my chairs, which were always fastened to the floor; and having made a hard shift to screw it down again, directly under the slipping-board that I had lately opened, I mounted on the chair, and putting my mouth as near as I could to the hole, I called for help in a loud voice, and in all the languages I understood. I then fastened my handkerchief to a stick I usually carried, and thrusting it up the hole, waved it several times in the air, that if any boat or ship were near, the seamen might conjecture some unhappy mortal to be shut up in the box.

I found no effect for all I could do, but plainly perceived my closet to be moved along; and in the space of an hour, or better, that side of the box where the staples were, and had no windows, struck against something that was hard. I apprehended it to be a rock, and found myself tossed more than ever. I plainly heard a noise upon the cover of my closet, like that of a cable, and the grating of it as it passed through the ring. I then found myself hoisted up, by degrees, at least three feet higher than I was before. Whereupon I again thrust up my stick and handkerchief, calling for help till I was almost hoarse. In return to which I heard a great shout repeated three times, giving me such transports of joy as are not to be conceived but by those who feel them. I now heard a trampling over my head, and somebody calling through the hole with a loud voice, in the English tongue, "If there be anybody below, let them speak." I answered I was an Englishman drawn by ill fortune into the greatest calamity that ever any creature underwent, and begged, by all that was moving, to be delivered out of the dungeon I was in. The voice replied I was safe, for my box was fastened to their ship; and the carpenter should immediately come and saw a hole in the cover, large enough to pull me out. I answered that was needless, and would take up too much time; for there was no more to be done but to let one of the crew put his finger into the ring, and take the box out of the sea into the ship, and so into the captain's cabin.* Some of them, upon hearing me talk so wildly, thought I was mad; others laughed; for indeed it never came into my head that I was now got among people of my own stature and strength. The carpenter came, and in a few minutes sawed a passage of about four feet square, then let down a small ladder, upon which I mounted, and thence was taken into the ship in a very weak condition.

The sailors were all in amazement, and asked me a thousand questions which I had no inclination to answer. I was equally confounded at the sight of so many pigmies, for such I took them to be, after having so long accustomed mine eyes to the monstrous objects I had left. But the captain, Mr. Thomas Wilcocks, an honest worthy Shropshire man, observing I was ready to faint, took me into his cabin, gave me a cordial to comfort me, and made me turn in upon his own bed, advising me to take a little rest, of which I had great need. Before I went to sleep I gave him to understand that I had some valuable furniture in my box, too good to be lost: a fine hammock, a handsome fieldbed, two chairs, a table, and a cabinet; that my closet was hung on all sides, or rather quilted, with silk and cotton;

---

* The art displayed by Swift in this incident is very remarkable. Gulliver's long habit of associating with beings so much larger than himself makes him refer everything to their enormous standard, and so he forgets himself when he comes among men of his own stature. None but a master of fiction would have made his hero commit a mistake so absurd and yet so natural. "The figure," says Thackeray, commenting on the humor of Swift, "suggests itself naturally to him, and comes out of his subject, as in that wonderful passage when, Gulliver's box having been dropped by the eagle into the sea, and Gulliver having been received into the ship's cabin, he calls upon the crew to bring the box into the cabin and put it on the table, the cabin being only a quarter the size of the box. It is the *veracity* of the blunder that is so admirable. Had a man come from such a country as Brobdingnag he would have blundered so." Indeed, the delusion continues for some time, and he again repeats his desire to have the box brought into the cabin, in his eagerness to have his furniture preserved.

that if he would let one of the crew bring my closet into his cabin, I would open it there before him, and show him my goods. The captain, hearing me utter these absurdities, concluded I was raving; however (I suppose to pacify me) he promised to give orders as I desired, and, going upon deck, sent some of his men down into my closet, whence (as I afterward found) they drew up all my goods and stripped off the quilting; but the chairs, cabinet, and bedstead, being screwed to the floor, were much damaged by the ignorance of the seamen, who tore them up by force. Then they knocked off some of the boards for the use of the ship, and when they had got all they had a mind for, let the hull drop into the sea, which, by reason of many breaches made in the bottom and sides, sunk outright. And, indeed, I was glad not to have been a spectator of the havoc they made; because I am confident it would have sensibly touched me, by bringing former passages into my mind which I would rather have forgot.

I slept some hours, but perpetually disturbed with dreams of the place I had left, and the dangers I had escaped. However, upon waking I found myself much recovered. It was now about eight o'clock at night, and the captain ordered supper immediately, thinking I had already fasted too long. He entertained me with great kindness, observing me not to look wildly, or talk inconsistently, and, when we were left alone, desired I would give him a relation of my travels, and by what accident I came to be set adrift in that monstrous wooden chest. He said that about twelve o'clock at noon, as he was looking through his glass, he espied it at a distance, and thought it was a sail, which he had a mind to make, being not much out of his course, in hopes of buying some biscuits, his own beginning to fall short. That upon coming nearer, and finding his error, he sent out his long boat, to discover what it was; that his men came back in a fright, saying they had seen a swimming house. That he laughed at their folly, and went himself in the boat, ordering his men to take a strong cable along with them. That the weather being calm, he rowed round me several times, observing my windows and wire lattices that defended them. That he discovered two staples upon one side, which was all of boards, without any passage for light. He then commanded his men to row up to that side, and, fastening a cable to one of the staples, ordered them to tow my chest, as they called it, toward the ship. When it was there, he gave directions to fasten another cable to the ring fixed in the cover, and to raise up my chest with pulleys, which all the sailors were not able to do above two or three feet. He said they saw my stick and handkerchief thrust out of the hole, and concluded that some unhappy man must be shut up in the cavity. I asked whether he or the crew had seen any prodigious birds in the air, about the time he first discovered me. To which he answered, that, discoursing this matter with the sailors while I was asleep, one of them said he had observed three eagles flying toward the north, but remarked nothing of their being larger than the usual size; which I suppose must be imputed to the great height they were at; and he could not guess the reason of my question. I then asked the captain how far he reckoned we might be from land. He said, by the best computation he could make, we were at least a hundred leagues. I assured him he must be mistaken by almost half, for I had not left the country whence I came above two hours before I dropped into the sea. Whereupon he began to think that my brain was disturbed, of which he gave me a hint, and advised me to go to bed in a cabin he had provided. I assured him I was well refreshed with his good entertainment and company, and as much in my senses as ever I was in my life. He then grew serious, and desired to ask me freely whether I were not troubled in my mind by the consciousness of some enormous crime, for which I was punished, at the command of some prince, by exposing me in that chest; as great criminals, in other countries, have been forced to sea in a leaky vessel, without provisions; for although he should be sorry to have taken so ill a man into his ship, yet he would engage his word to set me safe ashore, in the first port where we ar•

rived. He added, that his suspicions were much increased by some very absurd speeches I had delivered at first to his sailors, and afterward to himself, in relation to my closet or chest, as well as by my odd looks and behavior while I was at supper.

I begged his patience to hear me tell my story, which I faithfully did, from the last time I left England to the moment he first discovered me. And as truth always forces its way into rational minds, so this honest, worthy gentleman, who had some tincture of learning, and very good sense, was immediately convinced of my candor and veracity. But, further to confirm all I had said, I entreated him to give order that my cabinet should be brought, of which I had the key in my pocket; for he had already informed me how the seamen disposed of my closet. I opened it in his own presence, and showed him the small collection of rarities I made in the country from which I had been so strangely delivered. There was the comb I had contrived out of the stumps of the king's beard, and another of the same materials, but fixed into a paring of her majesty's thumb-nail, which served for the back. There was a collection of needles and pins, from a foot to half a yard long; four wasp-stings, like joiner's tacks; some combings of the queen's hair; a gold ring which one day she made me a present of in the most obliging manner, taking it from her little finger, and throwing it over my head like a collar. I desired the captain would please to accept this ring in return for his civilities; which he absolutely refused. I showed him a corn that I had cut off with my own hand from a maid of honor's toe; it was about the bigness of a Kentish pippin, and grown so hard that, when I returned to England, I got it hollowed into a cup, and set in silver. Lastly, I desired him to see the breeches I had then on, which were made of a mouse's skin.

I could force nothing on him but a footman's tooth, which I observed him to examine with great curiosity, and found he had a fancy for it. He received it with abundance of thanks, more than such a trifle could deserve. It was drawn by an unskillful surgeon, in a mistake, from one of Glumdalclitch's men, who was afflicted with the toothache, but it was as sound as any in his head. I got it cleaned, and put it into my cabinet. It was about a foot long and four inches in diameter.

The captain was very well satisfied with this plain relation I had given him, and said he hoped, when we returned to England, I would oblige the world by putting it on paper, and making it public. My answer was, that I thought we were overstocked with books of travels; that nothing could now pass which was not extraordinary; wherein I doubted some authors less consulted truth than their own vanity, or interest, or the diversion of ignorant readers; that my story could contain little beside common events, without those ornamental descriptions of strange plants, trees, birds, and other animals; or of the barbarous customs and idolatry of savage people, with which most writers abound. However, I thanked him for his good opinion, and promised to take the matter into my thoughts.

He said he wondered at one thing very much, which was to hear me speak so loud; asking me whether the king or queen of that country were thick of hearing. I told him it was what I had been used to for above two years past, and that I admired as much at the voices of him and his men, who seemed to me only to whisper, and yet I could hear them well enough. But when I spoke in that country, it was like a man talking in the streets to another looking out from the top of a steeple, unless when I was placed on a table, or held in any person's hand. I told him I had likewise observed another thing—that when I first got into the ship, and the sailors stood all about me, I thought they were the most contemptible little creatures I had ever beheld. For, indeed, while I was in that prince's country, I could never endure to look in a glass, after mine eyes had been accustomed to such prodigious objects, because the comparisons gave me so despicable a conceit of myself. The captain said that while we were at supper he observed me to look at everything with a sort of wonder, and that I often seemed hardly able to contain my laughter, which he knew not well how to take, but imputed it to some disorder in my brain. I answered, it was very true, and I wondered how I could forbear, when I saw his dishes of the size of a silver threepence, a leg of pork hardly a mouthful, a cup not so big as a nutshell; and so I went on, describing the rest of his household stuff and provisions after the same manner. For, although the queen had ordered a little equipage of all things necessary for me, while I was in her service, yet my ideas were wholly taken up with what I saw on every side of me, and I winked at my own littleness, as people do at their own faults.

The captain understood my raillery very well, and merrily replied with an old English proverb, that he doubted mine eyes were bigger than my belly, for he did not observe my stomach so good, although I had fasted all day; and continuing in his mirth, protested he would have gladly given a hundred pounds to have seen my chest in the eagle's bill, and afterward in its fall from so great a height into the sea; which would certainly have been a most astonishing object, worthy to have the description of it transmitted to future ages; and the comparison of Phaëton was so obvious, that he could not forbear applying it, although I did not much admire the conceit.

The captain having been at Tonquin, was, in his return to England, driven north-eastward to the latitude of 44 degrees and longitude of 143. But meeting a trade-wind two days after I came on board him, we sailed southward a long time, and coasting New Holland, kept our course west-south-west, and then south-south-west, till we doubled the Cape of Good Hope. Our voyage was very prosperous, but I shall not trouble the reader with a journal of it. The captain called in at one or two ports, and sent in his long-boat for provisions and fresh water; but I never went out of the ship till we came into the Downs, which was on the 3d day of June, 1706, about nine months after my escape. I offered to leave my goods in security for the payment of my freight, but the captain protested he would not receive one farthing. We took a kind leave of each other, and I made him promise he would come and see me at my house in Redriff. I hired a horse and guide for five shillings, which I borrowed of the captain.

As I was on the road, observing the littleness of the houses, the trees, the cattle, and the people, I began to think myself in Lilliput. I was afraid of trampling on every traveler I met, and often called aloud to have them stand out of the way, so that I had like to have gotten one or two broken heads for my impertinence.

When I came to my own house, for which I was forced to inquire, one of the servants opening the door, I bent down to go in (like a goose under a gate), for fear of striking my head. My wife ran out to embrace me, but I stooped lower than her knees, thinking she could otherwise never be able to reach my mouth. My daughter kneeled to ask my blessing, but I could not see her till she arose, having been so long used to stand with my head and eyes erect to above sixty feet; and then I went to take her up with one hand by the waist. I looked down upon the servants, and one or two friends who were in the house, as if they had been pigmies, and I a giant. I told my wife she had been too thrifty, for I found she had starved herself and her daughter to nothing. In short, I behaved myself so unaccountably, that they were all of the captain's opinion when he first saw me, and concluded I had lost my wits. This I mention as an instance of the great power of habit and prejudice.*

In a little time, I and my family and friends came to a

* The conduct of Gulliver upon his return to his native land is thoroughly consistent, and gives wonderful spirit and liveliness to the narrative. His fear of trampling on those whom he met, his bending down to go in at the door like a goose under a gate, his stooping to embrace his wife, and looking over his daughter, are all admirably humorous. "The sort of reaction," observes Scott, "which is produced upon the traveler's mind when restored to persons of his own size (particularly after his return from the land of giants), greatly reconciles us to a deception maintained with such accuracy and truth of description."

right understanding; but my wife protested I should never go to sea any more; although my evil destiny so ordered, that she had not power to hinder me, as the reader may know hereafter. In the meantime, I here conclude the second part of my unfortunate voyages.

*Among the complimentary poems which appeared after the pub-
lication of the first edition of the "Travels" was the
following by Arbuthnot:*

THE LAMENTATION OF GLUMDALCLITCH FOR THE LOSS OF GRILDRIG.

A PASTORAL.

Soon as Glumdalclitch miss'd her pleasing care,
She wept, she blubber'd, and she tore her hair:
No British miss sincerer grief has known,
Her squirrel missing, or her sparrow flown.
She furl'd her sampler, and haul'd in her thread,
And stuck her needle into Grildrig's bed;
Then spread her hands, and with a bounce let fall
Her baby, like the giant in Guildhall.
In peals of thunder now she roars—and now
She gently whimpers like a lowing cow;
Yet lovely in her sorrow still appears;
Her locks dishevelled, and her floods of tears
Seem like the lofty barn of some rich swain,
When from the thatch drips fast a shower of rain.
 In vain she searched each cranny of the house
Each gaping chink impervious to a mouse.
"Was it for this," she cried, "with daily care,
Within thy reach I set the vinegar?
And fill'd the cruet with the acid tide,
While pepper-water-worms thy bait supplied,
Where twined the silver eel around thy hook,
And all the little monsters of the brook;
Sure in that lake he dropp'd:—my Grilly's drown'd!"
She dragg'd the cruet and no Grildrigs found.
"Vain is thy courage, Grilly, vain thy boast;
But little creatures enterprise the most.
Trembling, I've seen thee dare the kitten's paw;
Nay, mix with children as they play'd at taw,
Nor fear the marbles as they bounding flew;
Marbles to them, but rolling rocks to you.
 "Why did I thrust thee with that giddy youth!
Who from a page can ever learn the truth?

Versed in court-tricks, that money-loving boy,
To some lord's daughter sold the living toy;
Or rent him limb from limb in cruel play,
As children tear the wings of flies away:
From place to place o'er Brobdingnag I'll roam,
And never will return; or bring thee home.
But who hath eyes to trace the passing wind?—
How, then, thy fairy footsteps can I find?
Dost thou, bewilder'd, wander all alone,
In the green thicket of a mossy stone?
Or tumbled from the toadstool's slippery round,
Perhaps all maim'd die grov'lling on the ground?
Dost thou, embosom'd in the lovely rose,
Or sunk within the peach's down, repose?
Within the king-cup, if thy limbs are spread,
Or in the golden cowslip's velvet head,
Oh, show me, Flora, 'midst those sweets, the flower
Where sleeps my Grildrig in the fragrant bower!
    "But, ah! I fear thy little fancy roves
On little females and on little loves,
Thy pigmy children and thy tiny spouse;
The baby playthings that adorn thy house—
Doors, windows, chimneys, and the spacious rooms,
Equal in size to cells of honeycombs.
Hast thou for these now ventured from the shore,
Thy bark a bean-shell, and a straw thine oar?
Or, in thy box, now bounding on the main,
Shall I ne'er bear thyself and house again?
And shall I set thee on my hand no more,
To see thee leap the lines, and traverse o'er
My spacious palm? Of stature scarce a span,
Mimic the actions of a real man?
No more behold thee turn my watch's key,
As seamen at a capstan anchor weigh?
    "How wert thou wont to walk with cautious tread,
A dish of tea, like milk-pail, on thy head!
How chase the mite that bore thy cheese away,
And keep the rolling maggot at a bay!"
    She spoke, but broken accents stopp'd her voice,
Soft as the speaking-trumpet's mellow noise;
She sobb'd a storm, and wiped her flowing eyes,
Which seem'd like two broad suns in misty skies:
Oh, squander not thy grief—those tears command
To weep upon our cod in Newfoundland;
The plenteous pickle shall preserve the fish,
And Europe taste thy sorrows in her dish.

A VOYAGE TO
LAPUTA, BALNIBARBI,
LUGGNAGG, GLUBBDUBDRIB,
AND JAPAN

A Voyage to Laputa*

CHAPTER I

The Author Sets Out on His Third Voyage—Is Taken by Pirates—The Malice of a Dutchman—His Arrival at an Island—He Is Received in Laputa.

I HAD not been at home above ten days when Captain William Robinson, a Cornishman, commander of the Hopewell, a stout ship of three hundred tons, came to my house. I had formerly been surgeon of another ship, where he was master, and a fourth part owner, in a voyage to the Levant. He had always treated me more like a brother than an inferior officer; and hearing of my arrival, made me a visit, as I apprehended only out of friendship, for nothing passed more than what is usual after long absences. But repeating his visits often, expressing his joy to find me in good health, asking whether I were now settled for life, adding that he intended a voyage to the East Indies in two months; at last he plainly invited me, though with some apologies, to be surgeon of the ship; that I should have

* The first two voyages of Gulliver were intended, as we have seen, to satirize the Whig Administration, and the members composing it, especially Sir Robert Walpole, and to comment on the defects in the political institutions of England. The object of the third voyage, that to Laputa, is to ridicule the mathematicians and philosophers of Swift's day, and in particular the members of the Royal Society, against some of whom he entertained a grudge. "He ridicules," says Lord Orrery, somewhat affectedly, "the vain attempts and irregular productions of those rash men who, like Ixion embracing a cloud instead of a goddess, plagued the world with centaurs, while Jupiter, from the embraces of a Juno and an Alcmena, blessed the earth with an Hebe and an Hercules."

another surgeon under me, besides our two mates; that my salary should be double to the usual pay; and that having experienced my knowledge in sea affairs to be at least equal to his, he would enter into any engagement to follow my advice, as much as if I had shared in the command.

He said so many other obliging things, and I knew him to be so honest a man, that I could not reject his proposal; the thirst I had for seeing the world, notwithstanding my past misfortunes, continuing as violent as ever. The only difficulty that remained was to persuade my wife, whose consent, however, I at last obtained, by the prospect of advantage she proposed to her children.

We set out the 5th day of August, 1706, and arrived at Fort St. George the 11th of April, 1707. We stayed there three weeks to refresh our crew, many of whom were sick. From thence we went to Tonquin, where the captain resolved to continue some time, because many of the goods he intended to buy were not ready, nor could he expect to be dispatched in several months. Therefore, in hopes to defray some of the charges he must be at, he bought a sloop, loaded it with several sorts of goods, wherewith the Tonquinese usually trade to the neighboring islands, and putting fourteen men on board, whereof three were of the country, he appointed me master of the sloop, and gave me power to traffic, while he transacted his affairs at Tonquin.

We had not sailed above three days when, a great storm arising, we were driven five days to the north-north-east, and then to the east; after which we had fair weather, but still with a pretty strong gale from the west. Upon the tenth day we were chased by two pirates, who soon overtook us; for my sloop was so deeply laden that she sailed very slow, neither were we in a condition to defend ourselves.

We were boarded about the same time by both the pirates, who entered furiously at the head of their men; but finding us all prostrate upon our faces (for so I gave

order), they pinioned us with strong ropes, and, setting
a guard upon us, went to search the sloop.

I observed among them a Dutchman, who seemed to be
of some authority, though he was not commander of
either ship. He knew us by our countenances to be
Englishmen, and, jabbering to us in our own language,
swore we should be tied back to back and thrown into the
sea. I spoke Dutch tolerably well; I told him who we
were, and begged him, in consideration of our being Chris-
tians and Protestants, of neighboring countries in strict
alliance, that he would move the captains to take some
pity on us. This inflamed his rage; he repeated the
threatenings, and, turning to his companions, spoke with
great vehemence in the Japanese language, as I suppose,
often using the word *Christianos.*

The largest of the two pirate ships was commanded by
a Japanese captain, who spoke a little Dutch, but very
imperfectly. He came up to me, and after several questions, which I answered in great humility, he said we
should not die. I made the captain a very low bow, and
then, turning to the Dutchman, said I was sorry to find
more mercy in a heathen than in a brother Christian.
But I had soon reason to repent those foolish words, for
that malicious reprobate, having often endeavored in vain
to persuade both the captains that I might be thrown
into the sea (which they would not yield to after the
promise made me that I should not die), however prevailed so far as to have a punishment inflicted on me
worse in all human appearance than death itself. My
men were sent by an equal division into both the pirate
ships, and my sloop new manned. As to myself it was
determined that I should be set adrift in a small canoe
with paddles and a sail and four days' provisions; which
last the Japanese captain was so kind as to double out
of his own stores, and would permit no man to search me.
I got down into the canoe, while the Dutchman, standing
upon the deck, loaded me with all the curses and injurious
terms his language could afford.

About an hour before we saw the pirates I had taken an observation, and found we were in the latitude of 46 N. and longitude of 183. When I was at some distance from the pirates I discovered by my pocket-glass several islands to the south-east. I set up my sail, the wind being fair, with a design to reach the nearest of those islands, which I made a shift to do in about three hours. It was all rocky; however, I got many birds' eggs, and striking fire, I kindled some heath and dry sea-weed, by which I roasted my eggs. I ate no other supper, being resolved to spare my provisions as much as I could. I passed the night under the shelter of a rock, strewing some heath under me, and slept pretty well.

The next day I sailed to another island, and thence to a third and fourth, sometimes using my sail, sometimes my paddles. But, not to trouble the reader with a particular account of my distresses, let it suffice that on the fifth day I arrived at the last island in my sight which lay south-south-east to the former.

This island was at a greater distance than I expected, and I did not reach it in less than five hours. I encompassed it almost round before I could find a convenient place to land in; which was a small creek, about three times the wideness of my canoe. I found the island to be all rocky, only a little intermingled with tufts of grass and sweet-smelling herbs. I took out my small provisions, and after having refreshed myself, I secured the remainder in a cave, whereof there were great numbers; I gathered plenty of eggs upon the rocks, and got a quantity of dry sea-weed and parched grass, which I designed to kindle the next day, and roast my eggs as well as I could, for I had about me my flint, steel, watch, and burning-glass. I lay all night in the cave where I had lodged my provisions. My bed was the same dry grass and sea-weed which I intended for fuel. I slept very little, for the disquiet of my mind prevailed over my weariness and kept me awake. I considered how impossible it was to preserve my life in so desolate a place, and how miserable my end must be; yet found myself so listless and desponding that I had not the heart to rise; and before I could get spirits enough to creep out of my cave, the day was far advanced. I walked awhile among the rocks: the sky was perfectly clear, and the sun so hot that I was forced to turn my face from it: when all on a sudden it became obscure, as I thought, in a manner very different from what happens by the interposition of a cloud. I turned back, and perceived a vast opaque body between me and the sun, moving forward toward the island; it seemed to be about two miles high, and hid the sun six or seven minutes; but I did not observe the air to be much colder, or the sky more darkened, than if I had stood under the shade of a mountain. As it approached nearer over the place where I was, it appeared to be a firm substance, the bottom flat, smooth, and shining very bright from the reflection of the sea below. I stood upon a height of about two hundred yards from the shore, and saw this vast body descending almost to a parallel with me, at less than an English mile distance. I took out my pocket perspective, and could plainly discover numbers of people moving up and down the sides of it, which appeared to be sloping; but what those people were doing I was not able to distinguish.

The natural love of life gave me some inward motion of joy, and I was ready to entertain a hope that this adventure might, some way or other, help to deliver me from the desolate place and condition I was in. But at the same time the reader can hardly conceive my astonishment to behold an island in the air, inhabited by men, who were able (as it should seem) to raise or sink, or put it into progressive motion, as they pleased. But not being at that time in a disposition to philosophize upon this phenomenon, I rather chose to observe what course the island would take, because it seemed for a while to stand still. Yet soon after it advanced nearer, and I could see the sides of it encompassed with several gradations of galleries and stairs, at certain intervals, to descend from one to the other. In the lowest gallery I beheld some people fishing with long angling-rods, and others looking on. I waved my cap (for my hat was long since worn out) and my handkerchief toward the island; and upon its nearer approach I called and shouted with the utmost strength of my voice; and then looking circumspectly, I beheld a crowd gathered to that side which was most in my view. I found, by their pointing toward me and to each other, that they plainly discovered me, although they made no return to my shouting. But I could see four or five men running in great haste up the stairs, to the top of the island, who then disappeared. I happened rightly to conjecture that these were sent for orders, to some person in authority, upon this occasion.

The number of people increased, and in less than half an hour the island was moved and raised in such a manner that the lowest gallery appeared in a parallel of less than a hundred yards' distance from the height where I stood. I then put myself in the most supplicating posture, and spoke in the humblest accent, but received no answer. Those who stood nearest over against me seemed to be persons of distinction, as I supposed by their habits. They conferred earnestly with each other, looking often upon me. At length one of them called out in a clear, polite, smooth dialect, not unlike in sound to the Italian; and therefore I returned an answer in that language, hoping at least that the cadence might be more agreeable to his ears. Although neither of us understood the other, yet my meaning was easily known, for the people saw the distress I was in.

They made signs for me to come down from the rock and go toward the shore, which I accordingly did; and the flying island being raised to a convenient height, the verge directly over me, a chain was let down from the lowest gallery, with a seat fastened to the bottom, to which I fixed myself, and was drawn up by pulleys.

CHAPTER II

*The Humors and Disposition of the Laputians Described—
An Account of Their Learning—Of the King and His
Court—The Author's Reception There—The Inhabitants
Subject to Fear and Disquietudes—An Account of the
Women.*

AT MY alighting I was surrounded by a crowd of people,
but those who stood nearest seemed to be of better quality.
They beheld me with all the marks and circumstances
of wonder: neither, indeed, was I much in their debt,
having never till then seen a race of mortals so singular
in their shapes, habits, and countenances. Their heads
were all reclined, either to the right or the left; one of
their eyes turned inward, and the other directly up to the
zenith.* Their outward garments were adorned with the
figures of suns, moons, and stars, interwoven with those
of fiddles, flutes, harps, trumpets, guitars, harpsichords,

* In this description of the people of Laputa, Swift intends to
satirize, if not philosophers in general, at all events those pre-
tenders to philosophy and persons who, in his time, as, indeed,
in every period of the world, have been found to devote themselves to vain and profitless speculations in science. The description of those people is very ingenious. By making their heads
always awry, turned either to the right or left, he indicates
pretty plainly that such people never took the right direction
or the straight course in their views. The eye turned inward
seems evidently to denote the abstraction and absence of mind
commonly attributed to those who are occupied with their own
cogitations; while the eye that was turned upward betokens
that the owner was engaged in the contemplation of visionary
and transcendental schemes, above the ken of ordinary humanity.
In neither case was the vision or the intellect directed to the
objects that lay before or around the man—the things, as it
were, at his feet—the common and necessary concerns of every-
day life.

and many other instruments of music, unknown to us in
Europe. I observed, here and there, many in the habit of
servants, with blown bladders, fastened like a flail to the
end of a stick, which they carried in their hands. In
each bladder was a small quantity of dried peas, or little
pebbles, as I was afterward informed. With these bladders they now and then flapped the mouth and ears of
those who stood near them, of which practice I could not
then conceive the meaning. It seems the minds of these
people are so taken up with intense speculations that they
can neither speak nor attend to the discourses of others
without being roused by some external action upon the
organs of speech and hearing; for which reason, those
persons who are able to afford it always keep a flapper
(the original is *climenole*) in their family, as one of their
domestics; nor ever walk abroad or make visits without
him. And the business of this officer is, when two, three,
or more persons are in company, gently to strike with his
bladder the mouth of him who is to speak, and the right
ear of him or them to whom the speaker addresses himself.
This flapper is likewise employed diligently to attend his
master in his walks, and upon occasion to give him a soft
flap on his eyes; because he is always so wrapped up in
cogitation that he is in manifest danger of falling down
every precipice, and bouncing his head against every post;
and in the streets, of jostling others, or being jostled himself into the kennel.*

* This idea of a flapper is as original as it is happy and
humorous; and his office of recalling the mind of his absorbed
master to the affairs of common life, and saving him from
knocking his head against everything and everybody, is aimed
as a satirical assault against the absence of mind with which
philosophers were popularly charged, and especially the great
Sir Isaac Newton, whom Swift desired, for his own reasons, to
turn into ridicule. The Dean on one occasion assured a relative
that Sir Isaac was the worst companion in the world, and that
if you asked him a question "he would revolve it in a circle in
his brain, round, and round, and round" (here Swift described
a circle on his own forehead), "before he could produce an
answer."

It is necessary to give the reader this information, without which he would be at the same loss with me to understand the proceedings of these people, as they conducted me up the stairs, to the top of the island, and from thence to the royal palace. While we were ascending, they forgot several times what they were about, and left me to myself, till their memories were again roused by their flappers; for they appeared altogether unmoved by the sight of my foreign habit and countenance, and by the shouts of the vulgar, whose thoughts and minds were more disengaged.

At last we entered the palace, and proceeded to the chamber of presence, where I saw the king seated on his throne, attended on each side by persons of prime quality. Before the throne was a large table filled with globes and spheres, and mathematical instruments of all kinds. His majesty took not the least notice of us, although our entrance was not without sufficient noise, by the concourse of all persons belonging to the court. But he was then deep in a problem; and we attended at least an hour before he could solve it. There stood by him, on each side, a young page with flaps in their hands, and when they saw he was at leisure, one of them gently struck his mouth, and the other his right ear; at which he startled like one awakened on a sudden, and looking toward me and the company I was in, recollected the occasion of our coming, whereof he had been informed before. He spoke some words; whereupon, immediately a young man with a flap came up to my side and flapped me gently on the right ear; but I made signs, as well as I could, that I had no occasion for such an instrument; which, as I afterward found, gave his majesty and the whole court a very mean opinion of my understanding. The king, as far as I could conjecture, asked me several questions, and I addressed myself to him in all the languages I had. When it was found I could neither understand nor be understood, I was conducted by his order to an apartment in his palace (this prince being distinguished above all his predecessors for his hospitality to strangers), where two servants were appointed to attend me. My dinner was brought, and four persons of quality, whom I remembered to have seen very near the king's person, did me the honor to dine with me. We had two courses, of three dishes each. In the first course there was a shoulder of mutton cut into an equilateral triangle, a piece of beef into a rhomboid, and a pudding into a cycloid. The second course was two ducks trussed up in the form of fiddles, sausages and puddings resembling flutes and hautboys, and a breast of veal in the shape of a harp. The servants cut our bread into cones, cylinders, parallelograms, and other mathematical figures.

While we were at dinner I made bold to ask the names of several things in their language, and those noble persons, by the assistance of their flappers, delighted to give me answers, hoping to raise my admiration of their great abilities, if I could be brought to converse with them. I was soon able to call for bread and drink, or whatever else I wanted.

After dinner my company withdrew, and a person was sent by the king's order, attended by a flapper. He brought with him pens, ink, and paper, and three or four books, giving me to understand, by signs, that he was sent to teach me the language. We sat together four hours, in which time I wrote down a great number of words in columns, with the translations over against them: I likewise made a shift to learn several short sentences; for my tutor would order some of my servants to fetch something, to turn about, to make a bow, to sit, or to stand or walk, and the like. Then I took down the sentence in writing. He showed me also, in one of the books, the figures of the sun, moon, and stars, the zodiac, the tropics, and polar circles, together with the denominations of many planes and solids. He gave me the names and descriptions of all their musical instruments, and the general terms of art in playing on each of them. After he had left me, I placed all my words, with their interpretations, in alphabetical order. And thus, in a few days, by the help of a very faithful memory, I got some insight into their language.

The word, which I interpret the flying or floating island, is in the original *Laputa*, whereof I could never learn the true etymology. *Lap*, in the old obsolete language, signifies high; and *untuh*, a governor; from which they say, by corruption, was derived *Laputa*, from *Lapuntuh*. But I do not approve of this derivation, which seems to be a little strained. I ventured to offer to the learned men among them a conjecture of my own, that Laputa was *quasi lap outed*: *lap*, signifying properly the dancing of the sunbeams in the sea; and *outed*, a wing; which, however, I shall not obtrude, but submit to the judicious reader.*

Those to whom the king had intrusted me, observing how ill I was clad, ordered a tailor to come next morning and take my measure for a suit of clothes. This operator did his office after a different manner from those of his trade in Europe. He first took my altitude by a quadrant, and then, with rule and compasses, described the dimensions and outlines of my whole body, all which he entered upon paper; and in six days brought my clothes very ill made, and quite out of shape, by happening to make a mistake of a figure in the calculation. But my comfort was, that I observed such accidents very frequent, and little regarded.

During my confinement for want of clothes, and by an indisposition that held me some days longer, I much enlarged my dictionary; and when I next went to court was able to understand many things the king spoke, and to return him some kind of answers. His majesty had given orders that the island should move north-east and by east, to the vertical point over Lagado, the metropolis of

* Gulliver's philological disquisition upon the etymology of the word Laputa—both the received derivation among the learned men of the island, and that which he suggests to them himself— is a piece of solemn ridicule of the many fanciful conjectures which philologists often hazard as to the derivation of words.

the whole kingdom below, upon the firm earth. It was about ninety leagues distant, and our voyage lasted four days and a half. I was not in the least sensible of the progressive motion made in the air by the island. On the second morning, about eleven o'clock, the king himself in person, attended by his nobility, courtiers, and officers, having prepared all their musical instruments, played on them for three hours, without intermission, so that I was quite stunned with the noise; neither could I possibly guess the meaning, till my tutor informed me. He said that the people of their island had their ears adapted to hear the music of the spheres, which always played at certain periods, and the court was now prepared to bear their part, in whatever instruments they most excelled.

In our journey toward Lagado, the capital city, his majesty ordered that the island should stop over certain towns and villages, from whence he might receive the petitions of his subjects. And to this purpose several pack-threads were let down, with small weights at the bottom. On these pack-threads the people strung their petitions, which mounted up directly, like the scraps of paper fastened by school-boys at the end of the string that holds the kite. Sometimes we received wine and victuals from below, which were drawn up by pulleys.

The knowledge I had in mathematics gave me great assistance in acquiring their phraseology, which depended much upon that science, and music; and in the latter I was not unskilled. Their ideas are perpetually conversant in lines and figures. If they would, for example, praise the beauty of a woman, or any other animal, they describe it by rhombs, circles, parallelograms, ellipses, and other geometrical terms, or by words of art drawn from music, needless here to repeat. I observed in the king's kitchen all sorts of mathematical and musical instruments, after the figures of which they cut up the joints that were served at his majesty's table.

Their houses are very ill built, the walls bevel, without one right angle in any apartment; and this defect arises from the contempt they bear to practical geometry, which they despise as vulgar and mechanical: those instructions they give being too refined for the intellects of their workmen, which occasion perpetual mistakes. And although they are dexterous enough upon a piece of paper, in the management of the rule, the pencil, and the divider, yet in the common actions and behavior of life I have not seen a more clumsy, awkward, and unhandy people, nor so slow and perplexed in their conceptions upon all other subjects except those of mathematics and music. They are very bad reasoners, and vehemently given to opposition, unless when they happen to be of the right opinion, which is seldom their case. Imagination, fancy, and invention they are wholly strangers to, nor have any words in their language by which those ideas can be expressed; the whole compass of their thoughts and mind being shut up within the two fore-mentioned sciences.

Most of them, and especially those who deal in the astronomical part, have great faith in judicial astrology, although they are ashamed to own it publicly. But what I chiefly admired, and thought altogether unaccountable, was the strong disposition I observed in them toward news and politics, perpetually inquiring into public affairs, giving their judgments in matters of state, and passionately disputing every inch of a party opinion. I have, indeed, observed the same disposition among most of the mathematicians I have known in Europe, although I could never discover the least analogy between the two sciences; unless those people suppose that because the smallest circle has as many degrees as the largest, therefore the regulation and management of the world require no more abilities than the handling and turning of a globe: but I rather take this quality to spring from a very common infirmity of human nature, inclining us to be most curious and conceited in matters where we have least concern, and for which we are least adapted by study or nature.

These people are under continual disquietudes, never enjoying a minute's peace of mind: and their disturbances proceed from causes which very little affect the rest of mortals. Their apprehensions arise from several changes they dread in the celestial bodies: for instance, that the earth, by the continual approaches of the sun toward it, must, in course of time, be absorbed, or swallowed up; that the face of the sun will, by degrees, be incrusted with its own effluvia, and give no more light to the world; that the earth very narrowly escaped a brush from the tail of the last comet, which would have infallibly reduced it to ashes; and that the next, which they have calculated for one-and-thirty years hence, will probably destroy us. For if, in its perihelion, it should approach within a certain degree of the sun (as by their calculations they have reason to dread), it will receive a degree of heat ten thousand times more intense than that of red-hot, glowing iron; and, in its absence from the sun, carrying a blazing tail ten hundred thousand and fourteen miles long; through which, if the earth should pass at the distance of one hundred thousand miles from the nucleus, or main body of the comet, it must in its passage be set on fire and reduced to ashes: that the sun, daily spending its rays without any nutriment to supply them, will at last be wholly consumed and annihilated; which must be attended with the destruction of this earth, and of all the planets that receive their light from it.

They are so perpetually alarmed with the apprehension of these and the like impending dangers that they can neither sleep quietly in their beds nor have any relish for the common pleasures and amusements of life. When they meet an acquaintance in the morning, the first question is about the sun's health, how he looked at his setting and rising, and what hopes they have to avoid the stroke of the approaching comet. This conversation they are apt to run into with the same temper that boys discover in delighting to hear terrible stories of spirits and hobgoblins, which they greedily listen to, and dare not go to bed for fear.

The women of the island have abundance of vivacity:

they contemn their husbands, and are exceedingly fond of strangers, whereof there is always a considerable number from the continent below, attending at court, either upon affairs of the several towns and corporations, or their own particular occasions, but are much despised, because they want the same endowments. Among these the ladies choose their gallants; for the husband is always so rapt in speculation that the mistress and lover may proceed to the greatest familiarities before his face, if he be but provided with paper and implements, and without his flapper at his side.

The wives and daughters lament their confinement to the island, although I think it the most delicious spot of ground in the world: and although they live here in the greatest plenty and magnificence, and are allowed to do whatever they please, they long to see the world, and take the diversions of the metropolis; which they are not allowed to do without a particular license from the king; and this is not easy to be obtained, because the people of quality have found, by frequent experience, how hard it is to persuade their women to return from below. I was told that a great court lady, who had several children—is married to the prime minister, the richest subject in the kingdom, a very graceful person, extremely fond of her, and lives in the finest palace of the island—went down to Lagado on the pretence of health, there hid herself for several months, till the king sent a warrant to search for her; and she was found in an obscure eating-house all in rags, having pawned her clothes to maintain an old deformed footman, who beat her every day, and in whose company she was taken, much against her will. And although her husband received her with all possible kindness, and without the least reproach, she soon after contrived to steal down again, with all her jewels, to the same gallant, and has not been heard of since.

This may, perhaps, pass with the reader rather for a European or English story than for one of a country so remote. But he may please to consider that the caprices of womankind are not limited by any climate or nation, and that they are much more uniform than can be easily imagined.

In about a month's time I had made a tolerable proficiency in their language, and was able to answer most of the king's questions, when I had the honor to attend him. His majesty discovered not the least curiosity to inquire into the laws, government, history, religion, or manners of the countries where I had been; but confined his questions to the state of mathematics, and received the account I gave him with great contempt and indifference, though often roused by his flapper on each side.

CHAPTER III

A Phenomenon Solved by Modern Philosophy and Astronomy—The Laputians' Great Improvements in the Latter—The King's Method of Suppressing Insurrections.

I DESIRED leave of this prince to see the curiosities of the island, which he was graciously pleased to grant, and ordered my tutor to attend me. I chiefly wanted to know to what cause in art or in nature it owed its several motions, whereof I will now give a philosophical account to the reader.

The flying or floating island is exactly circular, its diameter 7837 yards, or about four miles and a half, and consequently contains ten thousand acres.* It is three hundred yards thick. The bottom, or under surface, which appears to those who view it below, is one even regular plate of adamant, shooting up to the height of about two hundred yards. Above it lie the several minerals in their usual order, and over all is a coat of rich mould, ten or twelve feet deep. The declivity of the upper surface, from the circumference to the centre, is the natural cause why all the dews and rains which fall upon the island are conveyed in small rivulets toward the middle, where they are emptied into four large basins, each of about half a mile in circuit, and two hundred yards' distance from the centre. From these basins the water is continually exhaled by the sun in the day-time, which effectually prevents their overflowing. Besides, as it is in the power of the monarch to raise the island above the region of clouds and vapors, he can prevent the falling of dews and rain whenever he

* Swift's arithmetical calculation as to the contents of the floating island is quite correct. The superficial contents of a circle whose diameter is 7837 yards will be 10,000 acres.

173

pleases. For the highest clouds cannot rise above two miles, as naturalists agree; at least, they were never known to do so in that country.

At the centre of the island there is a chasm about fifty yards in diameter, whence the astronomers descend into a large dome, which is therefore called *flandona gagnole*, or the astronomers' cave, situated at the depth of a hundred yards beneath the upper surface of the adamant. In this cave are twenty lamps continually burning, which, from the reflection of the adamant, cast a strong light into every part. The place is stored with a great variety of sextants, quadrants, telescopes, astrolabes, and other astronomical instruments. But the greatest curiosity, upon which the fate of the island depends, is a loadstone of prodigious size, in shape resembling a weaver's shuttle. It is in length six yards, and in the thickest part at least three yards over. This magnet is sustained by a very strong axle of adamant passing through its middle, upon which it plays, and is poised so exactly that the weakest hand can turn it. It is hooped round with a hollow cylinder of adamant, four feet deep, as many thick, and twelve yards in diameter, placed horizontally, and supported by eight adamantine feet, each six yards high. In the middle of the concave side there is a groove twelve inches deep, in which the extremities of the axle are lodged, and turned round as there is occasion.

The stone cannot be removed from its place by any force, because the hoop and its feet are one continued piece with that body of adamant which constitutes the bottom of the island.

By means of this loadstone the island is made to rise and fall and move from one place to another. For, with respect to that part of the earth over which the monarch presides, the stone is endued at one of its sides with an attractive power, and at the other with a repulsive. Upon placing the magnet erect, with its attractive end toward the earth, the island descends; but when the repelling extremity points downward. the island mounts directly upward.

When the position of the stone is oblique, the motion of the island is so too: for in this magnet the forces always act in lines parallel to its direction.

By this oblique motion the island is conveyed to different parts of the monarch's dominions. To explain the manner of its progress let A B represent a line drawn across the dominions of Balnibarbi; let the line *c d* represent the loadstone, of which let *d* be the repelling end and *c* the attracting end, the island being over C: let the stone be placed in position *c d*, with its repelling end downward; then the island will be driven upward obliquely toward D. When it is arrived at D, let the stone be turned upon its axle, till its attracting end points toward E, and then the island will be carried obliquely toward E; where, if the stone be again turned upon its axle till it stands in the position E F, with its repelling point downward, the island will rise obliquely toward F, where, by directing the attracting end toward G, the island may be carried to G, and from G to H, by turning the stone so as to make its repelling extremity point directly downward. And thus, by changing the situation of the stone as often as there is occasion, the island is made to rise and fall by turns in an oblique direction, and by those alternate risings and fallings (the obliquity being not considerable) is conveyed from one part of the dominions to the other.

But it must be observed that this island cannot move beyond the extent of the dominions below, nor can it rise above the height of four miles; for which the astronomers (who have written large systems concerning the stone) assign the following reason: that the magnetic virtue does not extend beyond the distance of four miles, and that the mineral, which acts upon the stone in the bowels of the earth, and in the sea about six leagues distant from the shore, is not diffused through the whole globe, but terminates with the limits of the king's dominions; and it was easy, from the great advantage of such a superior situation, for a prince to bring under his obedience whatever country lay within the attraction of that magnet.

When the stone is put parallel to the plane of the horizon, the island stands still; for in that case the extremities of it, being at equal distances from the earth, act with equal force, the one in drawing downward, and the other in pushing upward, and consequently no motion can ensue.

This loadstone is under the care of certain astronomers, who, from time to time, give it such positions as the monarch directs. They spend the greatest part of their lives in observing the celestial bodies, which they do by the assistance of glasses, far excelling ours in goodness. For, although their largest telescopes do not exceed three feet, they magnify much more than those of a hundred with us, and show the stars with greater clearness. This advantage has enabled them to extend their discoveries much farther than our astronomers in Europe; for they have made a catalogue of ten thousand fixed stars, whereas the largest of ours does not contain above one third part of that number. They have likewise discovered two lesser stars, or satellites, which revolve about Mars; whereof the innermost is distant from the centre of the primary planet exactly three of his diameters, and the outermost five: the former revolves in the space of ten hours, and the latter in twenty-one and a half: so that the squares of their periodical times are very nearly in the same proportion with the cubes of their distance from the centre of Mars; which evidently shows them to be governed by the same law of gravitation that influences the other heavenly bodies.*

They have observed ninety-three different comets, and settled their periods with great exactness. If this be true (and they affirm it with great confidence), it is much to be wished that their observations were made public, whereby the theory of comets, which at present is very lame and

* Professor de Morgan observes upon these astronomical statements, that Swift has correctly placed his satellites of Mars so as to have the squares of the times as the cubes of the distances —one of Kepler's well-known laws

defective, might be brought to the same perfection as other parts of astronomy.*

The king would be the most absolute prince in the universe if he could but prevail on his ministry to join with him; but these having their estates below on the continent, and considering that the office of a favorite has a very uncertain tenure, would never consent to the enslaving of their country.

If any town should engage in rebellion or mutiny, fall into violent factions, or refuse to pay the usual tribute, the king has two methods of reducing them to obedience. The first and the mildest course is by keeping the island hovering over such a town and the lands about it, whereby he can deprive them of the benefit of the sun and the rain, and consequently afflict the inhabitants with dearth and diseases: and if the crime deserve it, they are at the same time pelted from above with great stones, against which they have no defence but by creeping into cellars or caves, while the roofs of their houses are beaten to pieces. But if they still continue obstinate, or offer to raise insurrections, he proceeds to the last remedy, by letting the island drop directly upon their heads, which makes a universal destruction both of houses and men. However, this is an extremity to which the prince is seldom driven; neither, indeed, is he willing to put it into execution; nor dare his ministers advise him to an action which, as it would render them odious to the people, so it would be a great damage to their own estates, which lie all below; for the island is the king's demesne.

But there is still, indeed, a more weighty reason why the kings of this country have been always averse from executing so terrible an action, unless upon the utmost necessity. For, if the town intended to be destroyed should

* The subject of comets very much engaged the attention of the learned men of Swift's time, as will be seen by a reference to the transactions of the Royal Society, in which there are many papers upon them, and details of observations made by astronomers in various parts of Europe.

have in it any tall rocks, as it generally falls out in the
larger cities—a situation probably chosen at first with a
view to prevent such a catastrophe—or if it abound in high
spires or pillars of stone, a sudden fall might endanger the
bottom or under surface of the island, which, although it
consists, as I have said, of one entire adamant, two hundred yards thick, might happen to crack by too great a
shock, or burst by approaching too near the fires from
the houses below, as the backs, both of iron and stone, will
often do in our chimneys. Of all this the people are well
apprised, and understand how far to carry their obstinacy,
where their liberty or property is concerned. And the
king, when he is highest provoked, and most determined
to press a city to rubbish, orders the island to descend
with great gentleness, out of a pretence of tenderness to
his people, but, indeed, for fear of breaking the adamantine
bottom; in which case, it is the opinion of all their philosophers that the loadstone could no longer hold it up, and the
whole mass would fall to the ground.

By a fundamental law of this realm, neither the king
nor either of his two eldest sons are permitted to leave
the island; nor the queen, till she has attained a certain age.

CHAPTER IV

The Author Leaves Laputa—Is Conveyed to Balnibarbi—Arrives at the Metropolis—A Description of the Metropolis and the Country Adjoining—The Author Hospitably Received by a Great Lord—His Conversation with that Lord.

ALTHOUGH I cannot say that I was ill treated in this island, yet I must confess I thought myself too much neglected, not without some degree of contempt; for neither prince nor people appeared to be curious in any part of knowledge, except mathematics and music, wherein I was far their inferior, and upon that account very little regarded.

On the other side, after having seen all the curiosities of the island, I was very desirous to leave it, being heartily weary of those people. They were indeed excellent in two sciences for which I have great esteem, and wherein I am not unversed; but, at the same time, so abstracted and involved in speculation that I never met with such disagreeable companions. I conversed only with women, tradesmen, flappers, and court pages, during two months of my abode there, by which, at last, I rendered myself extremely contemptible; yet these were the only people from whom I could ever receive a reasonable answer.

I had obtained, by hard study, a good degree of knowledge in their language: I was weary of being confined to an island, where I received so little countenance, and resolved to leave it with the first opportunity.

There was a great lord at court, nearly related to the king, and for that reason alone treated with respect. He was universally reckoned the most ignorant and stupid person among them. He had performed many eminent

services for the crown, had great natural and acquired
parts, adorned with integrity and honor, but so ill an ear for
music that his detractors reported "he had been often known
to beat time in the wrong place;" neither could his tutors,
without extreme difficulty, teach him to demonstrate the
most easy proposition in the mathematics. He was pleased
to show me many marks of favor; often did me the honor
of a visit; desired to be informed in the affairs of Europe,
the laws and customs, the manner and learning of the
several countries where I had travelled. He listened to me
with great attention, and made very wise observations on
all I spoke. He had two flappers attending him for state,
but never made use of them, except at court and in visits
of ceremony, and would always command them to withdraw
when we were alone together.

I entreated with this illustrious person to intercede in
my behalf with his majesty for leave to depart; which he
accordingly did, as he was pleased to tell me, with regret:
for, indeed, he had made me several offers, very advantageous, which, however, I refused with expressions of the
highest acknowledgement.

On the 16th of February I took leave of his majesty and
the court. The king made me a present, to the value of
about two hundred pounds English; and my protector, his
kinsman, as much more, together with a letter of recommendation to a friend of his in Lagado, the metropolis.
The island being then hovering over a mountain about two
miles from it, I was let down from the lowest gallery, in
the same manner as I had been taken up.

The continent, as far as it is subject to the monarch
of the flying island, passes under the general name of
Balnibarbi; and the metropolis, as I said before, is called
Lagado. I felt some little satisfaction in finding myself on
firm ground. I walked to the city without any concern,
being clad like one of the natives, and sufficiently instructed
to converse with them. I soon found out the person's
house to whom I was recommended, presented my letter
from his friend. the grandee, in the island, and was re-

ceived with much kindness. This great lord, whose name was Munodi, ordered me an apartment in his own house, where I continued during my stay, and was entertained in a most hospitable manner.

The next morning after my arrival he took me in his chariot to see the town, which is about half the bigness of London; but the houses were strangely built, and most of them out of repair. The people in the streets walked fast, looked wild, their eyes fixed, and were generally in rags. We passed through one of the town gates, and went about three miles into the country, where I saw many laborers working with several sorts of tools in the ground, but was not able to conjecture what they were about; neither did I observe any expectation either of corn or grass, although the soil appeared to be excellent. I could not forbear admiring at these odd appearances, both in town and country; and I made bold to desire my conductor that he would be pleased to explain to me what could be meant by so many busy heads, hands, and faces, both in the streets and in the fields, because I did not discover any good effect they produced; but, on the contrary, I never knew a soil so unhappily cultivated, houses so ill-contrived and so ruinous, or a people whose countenances and habits expressed so much misery and want.*

This Lord Munodi was a person of the first rank, and had been some years governor of Lagado, but, by a cabal of ministers, was discharged for inefficiency. However, the king treated him with tenderness, as a well-meaning man, but of low, contemptible understanding.†

* In this character Swift has been supposed to have portrayed his friend Lord Bolingbroke, and there are certainly points of resemblance. The dismission by the intrigues of a cabal of ministers, and the tenderness of treatment by the king, would seem to point at the impeachment of Bolingbroke by Walpole and his committee, and the partial removal of the attainder and restoration to favor by George I.

† By Balnibarbi, Swift intends England, and Lagado is designed to represent its capital, London. The condition of the people in the streets, with their wild looks and hurried manner

When I gave that free censure of the country and its inhabitants, he made no further answer than by telling me that I had not been long enough among them to form a judgment, and that the different nations of the world had different customs, with other common topics to the same purpose. But, when we returned to his palace, he asked me how I liked the building, what absurdities I observed, and what quarrel I had with the dress or looks of his domestics. This he might safely do; because everything about him was magnificent, regular, and polite. I answered that his excellency's prudence, quality, and fortune had exempted him from those defects which folly and beggary had produced in others. He said, if I would go with him to his country house, about twenty miles distant, where his estate lay, there would be more leisure for this kind of conversation. I told his excellency that I was entirely at his disposal, and accordingly we set out next morning.

During our journey he made me observe the several methods used by farmers in managing their lands, which to me were wholly unaccountable; for, except in some very few places, I could not discover one ear of corn or blade of grass. But in three hours' travelling the scene was wholly

---

of walking, is an allusion to the state of the public mind under the excitement of the many schemes and speculations which came out during the years 1719, 1720, and 1721, under the name of "bubbles," and were pursued by the people with almost a frenzy. The first, as it was the chief of these, for its enormity, was that gigantic national delusion which, under the name of "The South Sea Scheme," for a time actually absorbed the attention of every one, high and low, to the neglect of the legitimate pursuits of commerce and agriculture (symbolized by Swift in the state of neglect of the houses, and the absence of corn and grass). Other schemes and chimerical adventures in trade sprang up almost daily. There were companies not only for fisheries, for insurances, for working mines, and for almost every possible sort of commercial adventures, but even for making wigs and shoes, for making of oil from sunflowers, for importing jackasses from Spain, for trading in human hair, for fatting hogs, and for a wheel for a perpetual motion.

altered: we came into a most beautiful country—farmers' houses, at small distances, neatly built; the fields inclosed, containing vineyards, corn-grounds, and meadows. Neither do I remember to have seen a more delightful prospect. His excellency observed my countenance to clear up; he told me, with a sigh, that there his estate began, and would continue the same till we should come to his house; that his countrymen ridiculed and despised him for managing his affairs no better, and for setting so ill an example to the kingdom; which, however, was followed by very few, such as were old, and willful, and weak, like himself.

We came, at length, to the house, which was indeed a noble structure, built according to the best rules of architecture. The fountains, gardens, walks, avenues, and groves were all disposed with exact judgment and taste. I gave due praises to everything I saw, whereof his excellency took not the least notice till after supper, when, there being no third companion, he told me, with a very melancholy air, that he doubted he must throw down his houses in town and country, to rebuild them after the present mode; destroy all his plantations, and cast others into such a form as modern usage required, and give the same directions to all his tenants, unless he would submit to incur the censure of pride, singularity, affectation, ignorance, caprice, and perhaps increase his majesty's displeasure; that the admiration I appeared to be under would cease or diminish when he had informed me of some particulars which, probably, I never heard of at court; the people there being too much taken up in their own speculations to have regard to what passed here below.

The sum of his discourse was to this effect: that about forty years ago certain persons went up to Laputa, either upon business or diversion, and, after five months' continuance, came back with a very little smattering in mathematics, but full of volatile spirits, acquired in that airy region; that these persons, upon their return, began to dislike the management of everything below, and fell into schemes of putting all arts, sciences, languages, and mechanics upon a new footing. To this end they procured a royal patent for erecting an academy of projectors in Lagado; and the humor prevailed so strongly among the people that there is not a town of any consequence in the kingdom without such an academy. In these colleges the professors contrive new rules and methods of agriculture and building, and new instruments and tools for all trades and manufactures; whereby, as they undertake one man shall do the work of ten, a palace may be built in a week, of materials so durable as to last forever without repair. All the fruits of the earth shall come to maturity at whatever season they think fit to choose, and increase a hundredfold more than they do at present, with innumerable other happy proposals. The only inconvenience is that none of these projects are yet brought to perfection, and in the mean time the whole country lies miserablv waste, the houses in ruins, and the people without food or clothes. By all which, instead of being discouraged, they are fifty times more violently bent upon prosecuting their schemes, driven equally on by hope and despair; that, as for himself, being not of an enterprising spirit, he was content to go on in the old forms, to live in the house his ancestors had built, and act as they did, in every part of life, without innovation; that some few other persons of quality and gentry had done the same, but were looked on with an eye of contempt and ill-will, as enemies to art, ignorant, and ill commonwealth's men, preferring their own ease and sloth before the general improvement of their country.

His lordship added that he would not, by any further particulars, prevent the pleasure I should certainly take in viewing the grand academy, whither he was resolved I should go. He only desired me to observe a ruined building, upon the side of a mountain about three miles distant, of which he gave me this account: that he had a very convenient mill within half a mile of his house, turned by a current from a large river, and sufficient for his own family, as well as a great number of his tenants; that, about seven years ago, a club of those projectors came to him with proposals to destroy this mill, and build another on the side of that mountain, on the long ridge whereof a long canal must be cut, for a repository of water, to be conveyed up by pipes and engines to supply the mill; because the wind and air upon a height agitated the water, and thereby made it fitter for motion; and because the water, descending down a declivity, would turn the mill with half the current of a river, whose course is more upon a level. He said that, being then not very well with the court, and pressed by many of his friends, he complied with the proposal, and, after employing a hundred men for two years, the work miscarried, the projectors went off, laying the blame entirely upon him, railing at him ever since, and putting others upon the same experiment, with equal assurance of success, as well as equal disappointment.

In a few days we came back to town; and his excellency, considering the bad character he had in the academy, would not go with me himself, but recommended me to a friend of his to bear me company thither. My lord was pleased to represent me as a great admirer of projects, and a person of much curiosity and easy belief—which, indeed, was not without truth, for I had myself been a sort of projector in my younger days.

CHAPTER V *

The Author Permitted to See the Grand Academy of Lagado—The Academy Largely Described—The Arts Wherein the Professors Employ Themselves.

THIS academy is not an entire single building, but a continuation of several houses on both sides of a street, which, growing waste, was purchased and applied to that use.

I was received very kindly by the warden, and went for many days in the academy. Every room has in it one or more projectors; and I believe I could not be in fewer than five hundred rooms.

The first man I saw was of a very meagre aspect, with sooty hands and face, his hair and beard long, ragged, and singed in several places. His clothes, shirt, and skin were all of the same color. He had been eight years upon a project for extracting sunbeams out of cucumbers, which were to be put in vials hermetically sealed, and let out to warm the air in raw, inclement summers. He told me he did not doubt that in eight years more he should be able to supply the governor's gardens with sunshine at a reasonable rate; † but he complained that his stock was

* In this and the following chapter Swift indulges himself in the most unrestrained sallies of ridicule against the professors of speculative learning, representing every sort of absurdity as the concoction of their fantasies.

† There is an amusing paper of Swift's, entitled "The Humble Petition of the Colliers, Cooks, Cookmaids, Blacksmiths, Jackmakers, Braziers, and others," to the Mayor and Aldermen of the City of London, against "certain *virtuosi*, taking upon them the name and title of the Catoptrical Victualers;" complaining of their "gathering, breaking, folding, and bundling up the sunbeams, by the help of certain glasses, to make, produce, and kindle up several new focuses or fires within these His Majesty's dominion; and there to boil, bake, stew, fr and dress all sorts

low, and entreated me to give him something as an encouragement to ingenuity, especially since this had been a very dear year for cucumbers. I made him a small present, for my lord had furnished me with money on purpose, because he knew their practice of begging from all who go to see them.

I saw another at work to calcine ice into gunpowder, who likewise showed me a treatise he had written concerning the malleability of fire, which he intended to publish.

There was a most ingenious architect, who had contrived a new method for building houses, by beginning at the roof and working downward to the foundation, which he justified to me by the like practice of those two prudent insects, the bee and the spider.

There was a man born blind, who had several apprentices in his own condition. Their employment was to mix colors for painters, which their master taught them to distinguish by feeling and smelling. It was indeed my misfortune to find them at that time not very perfect in their lessons, and the professor himself happened to be generally mistaken. This artist is much encouraged and esteemed by the whole fraternity.*

In another apartment I was highly pleased with a projector who had found a device of ploughing the ground with hogs, to save the charges of ploughs, cattle, and labor.

---

* Swift ridicules the opinions of some learned men, who maintained that it was not impossible for the blind to be taught to distinguish colors by the touch.

---

of victuals and provisions; to brew, distill spirits, smelt ore, and in general to perform all the offices of culinary fires;" and also stating that "the said Catoptrical Victualers have undertaken, by burning-glasses made of ice, to roast an ox on the Thames next winter;" and then setting forth very humorously the evils to result from the operations of the company. This *jeu d'esprit* is of a piece with the satire in the text, and may be supposed with reason to have been directed against similar philosophical absurdities. It was not real science that Swift attacked, but those chimerical and spurious studies with which the name has been too often injuriously associated.

The method is this: in an acre of ground you bury, at six inches' distance and eight deep, a quantity of acorns, dates, chestnuts, and other mast or vegetables whereof these animals are fondest; then you drive six hundred of them into the field, where, in a few days, they will root up the whole ground in search of their feed, and make it fit for sowing, at the same time manuring it with their dung. It is true, upon experiment, they found the charge and trouble very great, and they had little or no crop. However, it is not doubted that his invention may be capable of great improvement.

I went into another room, where the walls and ceiling were all hung round with cobwebs, except a narrow passage for the artist to go in and out. At my entrance he called aloud to me not to disturb his webs. He lamented the fatal mistake the world had been so long in of using silkworms while we had such plenty of domestic insects who infinitely excelled the former, because they understood how to weave as well as spin. And he proposed further that, by employing spiders, the charge of dyeing silks should be wholly saved, whereof I was fully convinced when he showed me a vast number of flies most beautifully colored, wherewith he fed his spiders, assuring us that the webs would take a tincture from them; and as he had them of all hues, he hopes to fit everybody's fancy, as soon as he could find proper food for the flies, of certain gums, oils, and other glutinous matter, to give a strength and consistence to the threads.*

* It may reasonably be presumed that Swift was aware that a few years previously an ingenious Frenchman, of the name of Bon, had actually succeeded in manufacturing the web of the spider, and had made stockings and gloves of it; and, as a pair of each of these were presented to the Royal Society, our author probably had seen them. In "Rees' Cyclopædia," article "Silk Spider," a full account of the whole process, as well as of the species of spiders which produce the silk, will be found, extracted from the "Memoir of M. Bon," presented to the Société Royale de France in 1710, and the report of M. Reaumur thereon. M. Bon states that the silk spider makes a silk every way as beautiful, glossy, and strong as the silkworm; that it

There was an astronomer who had undertaken to place a sun-dial upon the great weathercock on the town-house, by adjusting the annual and diurnal motions of the earth and sun so as to answer and coincide with all accidental turnings of the wind.

I visited many other apartments, but shall not trouble my reader with all the curiosities I observed, being studious of brevity.

I had hitherto seen only one side of the academy, the other being appropriated to the advancers of speculative learning, of whom I shall say something, when I have mentioned one illustrious person more, who is called among them the "Universal Artist." He told us he had been thirty years employing his thoughts for the improvement of human life. He had two large rooms full of wonderful curiosities, and fifty men at work. Some were condensing air into a dry, tangible substance, by extracting the nitre and letting the aqueous or fluid particles percolate; others softening marble for pillows and pin-cushions; others petrifying the hoofs of a living horse, to preserve them from foundering. The artist himself was at that time busy upon two great designs: the first, to sow land with chaff, wherein he affirmed the true seminal virtue to be contained, as he demonstrated by several experiments, which I was not skillful enough to comprehend. The other was, by a certain composition of gums, minerals, and vegetables, outwardly applied, to prevent the growth of wool upon two young lambs; and he hoped, in a reasonable time, to propagate the breed of naked sheep all over the kingdom.

We crossed a walk to the other part of the academy, where, as I have already said, the projectors in speculative learning resided.

---

takes all kinds of dyes, and may be worked into all kinds of stuffs. The report, however, of M. Reaumur was not favorable to the process as of commercial value. The spiders, too, were so ferocious that the larger ones killed all the smaller. M. Bon also asserted that the silk spider contained volatile salt, which might be procured by distillation.

The first professor I saw was in a very large room, with forty pupils about him. After salutation, observing me to look earnestly upon a frame, which took up the greatest part of both the length and breadth of the room, he said perhaps I might wonder to see him employed in a project for improving speculative knowledge, by practical and mechanical operations. But the world would soon be sensible of its usefulness; and he flattered himself that a more noble, exalted thought never sprang in any other man's head. Every one knew how laborious the usual method is of attaining to arts and sciences; whereas, by his contrivance, the most ignorant person, at a reasonable charge, and with a little bodily labor, might write books in philosophy, poetry, politics, laws, mathematics, and theology, without the least assistance from genius or study. He then led me to the frame, about the sides whereof all his pupils stood in ranks. It was twenty feet square, placed in the middle of the room. The superficies were composed of several bits of wood, about the bigness of a die, but some larger than others. They were all linked together by slender wires. These bits of wood were covered, on every square, with paper pasted on them; and on these papers were written all the words of their language, in their several moods, tenses, and declensions, but without any order. The professor then desired me to observe, for he was going to set his engine at work. The pupils, at his command, took each of them hold of an iron handle, whereof there were forty fixed round the edges of the frame; and giving them a sudden turn, the whole disposition of the words was entirely changed. He then commanded six-and-thirty of the lads to read the several lines softly, as they appeared upon the frame; and where they found three or four words together that might make part of a sentence, they dictated to the four remaining boys, who were scribes. This work was repeated three or four times; and at every turn the engine was so contrived that the words shifted into new places, as the square bits of wood moved upside down.

Six hours a day the young students were employed in
this labor; and the professor showed me several volumes
in large folio already collected of broken sentences, which
he intended to piece together, and out of those rich materials to give the world a complete body of all arts and
sciences; which, however, might be still improved and much
expedited if the public would raise a fund for making and
employing five hundred such frames in Lagado, and oblige
the managers to contribute in common their several col-
lections.

He assured me that the invention had employed all his
thoughts from his youth; that he had emptied the whole
vocabulary into his frame, and made the strictest computation of the general proportion there is in books between
the number of particles, nouns, and verbs, and other parts
of speech.

I made my humblest acknowledgment to this illustrious
person for his great communicativeness; and promised, if
ever I had the good-fortune to return to my native country,
that I would do him justice, as the sole inventor of this
wonderful machine; the form and contrivance of which I
desired leave to delineate on paper. I told him, although
it was the custom of our learned in Europe to steal inventions from each other, who had thereby at least this advantage, that it became a controversy which was the right
owner, yet I would take such caution that he should have
the honor entire, without a rival.

We next went to the school of languages, where three
professors sat in consultation upon improving that of their
own country.

The first project was to shorten discourse, by cutting
polysyllables into one, and leaving out verbs and parti-
ciples; because in reality all things imaginable are but
nouns.

The other project was a scheme for entirely abolishing
all words whatsoever; and this was urged as a great advantage in point of health as well as brevity. For it is plain
that every word we speak is, in some degree, a diminution

of our lungs by corrosion, and consequently contributes to the shortening of our lives. An expedient was therefore offered, that since words are only names for things, it would be more convenient for all men to carry about them such things as were necessary to express a particular business they are to discourse on. And this invention would certainly have taken place, to the great ease as well as health of the subject, if the women, in conjunction with the vulgar and illiterate, had not threatened to raise a rebellion unless they might be allowed the liberty to speak with their tongues, after the manner of their forefathers; such constant, irreconcilable enemies to science are the common people. However, many of the most learned and wise adhere to the new scheme of expressing themselves by things, which has only this inconvenience attending it, that if a man's business be very great, and of various kinds, he must be obliged, in proportion, to carry a greater bundle of things upon his back, unless he can afford one or two strong servants to attend him. I have often beheld two of these sages almost sinking under the weight of their packs, like peddlers among us; who, when they met in the street, would lay down their loads, open their packs, hold conversation for an hour, and then put up their implements, help each other to resume their burdens, and take their leave.

But for short conversations a man may carry implements in his pockets, and under his arms, enough to supply him; and in his house he cannot be at a loss. Therefore the room where company meet who practice this art is full of all things, ready at hand, requisite to furnish matter for this kind of artificial converse.

Another great advantage proposed by this invention was that it would serve as a universal language, to be understood in all civilized nations, whose goods and utensils are generally of the same kind, or nearly resembling, so that their uses might easily be comprehended. And thus ambassadors would be qualified to treat with foreign princes or ministers of state, to whose tongues they were utter strangers.

I was at the mathematical school, where the master taught his pupils after a method scarcely imaginable to us in Europe. The proposition and demonstration were fairly written on a thin wafer, with ink composed of a cephalic tincture. This the student was to swallow upon a fasting stomach, and for three days following eat nothing but bread and water. As the wafer digested the tincture mounted to his brain, bearing the proposition along with it. But the success has not hitherto been answerable, partly by some error in the quantum or composition, and partly by the perverseness of the lads, to whom this bolus is so nauseous that they generally steal aside and discharge it upward before it can operate; neither have they been yet persuaded to use so long an abstinence as the prescription requires.

CHAPTER VI

A Further Account of the Academy—The Author Proposes
Some Improvements, Which Are Honorably Received.

IN THE school of political projectors I was but ill entertained, the professors appearing, in my judgment, wholly out of their senses, which is a scene that never fails to make me melancholy. These unhappy people were proposing schemes for persuading monarchs to choose favorites upon the score of their wisdom, capacity, and virtue; of teaching ministers to consult the public good; of rewarding merit, great abilities, and eminent services; of instructing princes to know their true interest, by placing it on the same foundation with that of their people; of choosing for employments persons qualified to exercise them; with many other wild, impossible chimeras, that never entered before into the heart of a man to conceive; and confirmed in me the old observation, that "there is nothing so extravagant and irrational which some philosophers have not affirmed for truth."

But, however, I shall so far do justice to this part of the academy as to acknowledge that all of them were not so visionary. There was a most ingenious doctor, who seemed to be perfectly versed in the whole nature and system of government. This illustrious person had very usefully employed his studies in finding out effectual remedies for all diseases and corruptions to which the several kinds of public administration are subject, by the vices and infirmities of those who govern as well as by the licentiousness of those who are to obey. For instance: Whereas all writers and reasoners have agreed that there is a strict universal resemblance between the natural and political body, can there be anything more evident than that the health of

194

both must be preserved, and the diseases cured, by the same prescriptions? It is allowed that senates and great councils are often troubled with redundant, ebullient, and other peccant humors; with many diseases of the head, and more of the heart; with strong convulsions, with grievous contractions of the nerves and sinews in both hands, but especially the right; with spleen, flatus, vertigoes, and deliriums; with scrofulous tumors, full of fœtid purulent matter; with canine appetites and crudeness of digestion, beside many others, needless to mention. This doctor therefore proposed that, upon the meeting of the senate, certain physicians should attend at the three first days of their sitting, and at the close of each day's debate feel the pulses of every senator; after which, having maturely considered and consulted upon the nature of the several maladies, and the methods of cure, they should, on the fourth day, return to the senate-house, attended by their apothecaries stored with proper medicines, and before the members sat administer to each of them lenitives, aperients, abstersives, corrosives, restringents, palliatives, laxatives, cephalalgics, icterics, aphphlegmatics, acoustics, as the several cases required; and, according as these medicines should operate, repeat, alter, or omit them at the next meeting.

This project could not be of any great expense to the public, and might, in my poor opinion, be of much use for the dispatch of business in those countries where senates have any share in the legislative power; beget unanimity, shorten debates, open a few mouths which are now closed, and close many more which are now open; curb the petulancy of the young, and correct the positiveness of the old; rouse the stupid, and damp the pert.

Again: because it is a general complaint that the favorites of princes are troubled with short and weak memories, the same doctor proposed that whoever attended a first minister, after having told his business, with the utmost brevity and in the plainest words, should, at his departure, give the said minister a tweak by the nose, or tread on his

corns, or lug him thrice by both ears, or pinch his arm
black and blue to prevent forgetfulness; and at every
levee day repeat the same operation till the business were
done or absolutely refused.

He likewise directed that every senator in the great
council of a nation, after he had delivered his opinion and
argued in the defence of it, should be obliged to give his
vote directly contrary; because, if that were done, the
result would infallibly terminate in the good of the public.

When parties in a state are violent, he offered a wonderful contrivance to reconcile them. The method is this:
You take a hundred leaders of each party; you dispose
them into couples of such whose heads are nearest of a
size; then let two nice operators saw off the occiput of
each couple at the same time, in such a manner that the
brains may be equally divided. Let the occiputs thus cut
off be interchanged, applying each to the head of his
opposite party-man. It seems, indeed, to be a work that
requires some exactness, but the professor assured us that
if it were dexterously performed the cure would be infallible. For he argued thus: that the two half brains, being
left to debate the matter between themselves within the
space of one skull, would soon come to a good understanding, and produce that moderation as well as regularity of
thinking so much to be wished for in the heads of those
who imagine they come into the world only to watch and
govern its motions; and as to the difference of brains, in
quantity or quality, among those who are the directors in
faction, the doctor assured us, from his own knowledge,
that it was a perfect trifle.

I heard a very warm debate between two professors
about the most commodious and effectual ways and means
of raising money without grieving the subject. The first
affirmed the justest method would be to lay a certain tax
upon vice and folly; and the sum fixed upon every man
to be rated, after the fairest manner, by a jury of his
neighbors. The second was of an opinion directly contrary
—to tax those qualities of body and mind for which men

chiefly value themselves; the rate to be more or less, according to the degrees of excelling; the decision whereof should be left entirely to their own breasts. Wit, valor, and politeness were likewise proposed to be largely taxed, and collected in the same manner, by every person's giving his own word for the quantum of what he possessed. But as to honor, justice, wisdom, and learning, they shall not be taxed at all, because they are qualifications of so singular a kind that no man will either allow them in his neighbor or value them in himself.

The women were proposed to be taxed according to their beauty and skill in dressing, wherein they had the same privilege with men, to be determined by their own judgment.

To keep senators in the interest of the crown it was proposed that the members shall raffle for employments, every man first taking an oath and giving security that he would vote for the court, whether he won or not; after which, the losers had, in their turn, the liberty of raffling upon the next vacancy. Thus, hope and expectation would be kept alive; none would complain of broken promises, but impute their disappointments wholly to fortune, whose shoulders are broader and stronger than those of a ministry.

Another professor showed me a large paper of instructions for discovering plots and conspiracies against the government. The whole discourse was written with great acuteness, containing many observations, both curious and useful for politicians, but, as I conceived, not altogether complete. This I ventured to tell the author, and offered, if he pleased, to supply him with some additions. He received my proposition with more compliance than is usual among writers, especially those of the projecting species, professing he would be glad to receive further information.

I told him that in the kingdom Tribnia, by the natives called Langden,* where I sojourned some time in my travels, "the bulk of the people consist in a manner wholly of

* Tribnia and Langden, neither of which names are mentioned in the original edition of 1726, are both anagrams, the former for Britain, the latter for England.

discoverers, witnesses, informers, accusers, prosecutors, evidences, swearers, together with their several subervient and subaltern instruments, all under the colors, the conduct, and the pay of ministers of state and their deputies. The plots in that kingdom are usually the workmanship of those persons who desire to raise their own characters of profound politicians; to restore new vigor to a crazy administration; to stifle or divert general discontents; to fill their coffers with forfeitures; and raise or sink the opinions of public credit, as either shall best answer their private advantage. It is first agreed and settled among them what suspected persons should be accused of a plot, then effectual care is taken to secure all their letters and papers, and put the owners in chains. These papers are delivered to a set of artists, very dexterous in finding out the mysterious meanings of words, syllables, and letters; for instance, they can discover a flock of geese to signify a senate; a lame dog,* an invader; the plague, a standing army; a buzzard, a prime minister; the gout, a high priest; a gibbet, a secretary of state; a sieve, a court lady; a broom, a revolution; a mouse-trap, an employment; a sink, a court; a cap and bells, a favorite; a broken reed, a court of justice; an empty tun, a general; a running sore, the administration.

"When this method fails they have two others more effectual, which the learned among them call acrostics and anagrams. First, they can decipher all initial letters into political meanings. Thus, N shall signify a plot; B, a regiment of horse; L, a fleet at sea; or secondly, by transposing the letters of the alphabet in any suspected paper, they can lay open the deepest designs of a discontented party. And this is the anagrammatic method."

The professor made me great acknowledgments for communicating these observations, and promised to make honorable mention of me in his treatise.

I saw nothing in this country to invite me to a longer continuance, and began to think of returning to England.

* The allusion here is to a piece of circumstantial evidence relied upon by the Commons' Committee against Atterbury.

CHAPTER VII

The Author Leaves Lagado—Arrives at Maldonada—No Ship Ready—He Takes a Short Voyage to Glubbdubdrib —His Reception by the Governor.

THE continent, of which this kingdom is a part, extends itself, as I have reason to believe, eastward to that unknown tract of America westward of California; and north to the Pacific Ocean, which is not above a hundred and fifty miles from Lagado, where there is a good port, and much commerce from the great island of Luggnagg, situated to the northwest about 29 degrees north latitude and 140 longitude. This island of Luggnagg stands south-estward of Japan, about a hundred leagues distant. There is a strict alliance between the Japanese emperor and the king of Luggnagg, which affords frequent opportunities of sailing from one island to the other. I determined therefore to direct my course this way, in order to my return to Europe. I hired two mules, with a guide to show me the way and carry my small baggage. I took leave of my noble protector who had shown me so much favor, and made me a generous present at my departure.

My journey was without any accident or adventure worth relating. When I arrived at the port of Maldonada (for so it is called), there was no ship in the harbor bound for Luggnagg, nor likely to be for some time. The town is about as large as Portsmouth. I soon fell into some acquaintance, and was very hospitably received. A gentleman of distinction said to me that since the ships bound for Luggnagg could not be ready in less than a month, it might be no disagreeable amusement for me to take a trip to the little island of Glubbdubdrib, about five leagues off to the south-west. He offered himself and a friend to accompany me, and that I should be provided with a small convenient bark for the voyage.

Glubbdubdrib, as near as I can interpret the word, signifies the island of sorcerers or magicians. It is about one third as large as the Isle of Wight, and extremely fruitful: it is governed by the head of a certain tribe, who are all magicians. This tribe marries only among each other, and the eldest in succession is prince or governor. He has a noble palace, and a park of three thousand acres, surrounded by a wall of hewn stone twenty feet high. In this park are several small inclosures for cattle, corn, and gardening.

The governor and his family are served and attended by domestics of a kind somewhat unusual. By his skill in necromancy he has a power of calling whom he pleases from the dead, and commanding their service for twenty-four hours, but no longer; nor can he call the same persons up again in less than three months, except upon very extraordinary occasions.

When we arrived at this island, which was about eleven in the morning, one of the gentlemen who accompanied me went to the governor, and desired admittance for a stranger, who came on purpose to have the honor of attending on his highness. This was immediately granted, and we all three entered the gate of the palace between two rows of guards, armed and dressed after a very antique manner, and something in their countenances that made my flesh creep with a horror I cannot express. We passed through several apartments, between servants of the same sort, ranked on each side as before, till we came to the chamber of presence; where, after three profound obeisances and a few general questions, we were permitted to sit on three stools, near the lowest step of his highness's throne. He understood the language of Balnibarbi, although it was different from that of this island. He desired me to give him some account of my travels; and to let me see that I should be treated without ceremony, he dismissed all his attendants with a turn of his finger; at which, to my great astonishment, they vanished in an instant, like visions in a dream when we awake on a sudden. I could not recover myself in some time, till the governor assured me that I should receive no hurt; and observing my two companions to be under no concern, who had been often entertained in the same manner, I began to take courage, and related to his highness a short history of my several adventures, yet not without some hesitation, and frequently looking behind me to the place where I had seen those domestic spectres. I had the honor to dine with the governor, where a new set of ghosts served up the meat and waited at table. I now observed myself to be less terrified than I had been in the morning. I stayed till sunset, but humbly desired his highness to excuse me for not accepting his invitation of lodging in the palace. My two friends and I lay at a private house in the town adjoining, which is the capital of this little island; and the next morning we returned to pay our duty to the governor, as he was pleased to command us.

After this manner we continued in the island for ten days, most part of every day with the governor, and at night in our lodging. I soon grew so familiarized to the sight of spirits that after the third or fourth time they gave me no emotion at all; or if I had any apprehensions left, my curiosity prevailed over them. For his highness the governor ordered me to call up whatever persons I might choose to name, and in whatever numbers, among all the dead from the beginning of the world to the present time, and command them to answer any questions I should think fit to ask; with this condition, that my question be confined within the compass of the times they lived in. And one thing I might depend upon, that they would certainly tell me the truth, for lying was a talent of no use in the lower world.*

I made my humble acknowledgments to his highness for so great a favor. We were in a chamber from whence

* The idea of introducing his readers into the company of the departed was probably suggested to Swift by Lucian's "Dialogues of the Dead."

there was a fair prospect into the park. And because my first inclination was to be entertained with scenes of pomp and magnificence, I desired to see Alexander the Great at the head of his army, just after the battle of Arbela, which, upon a motion of the governor's finger, immediately appeared in a large field, under the window where we stood. Alexander was called up into the room; it was with great difficulty I understood his Greek, and had but little of my own. He assured me upon his honor that he was not poisoned, but died of a bad fever by excessive drinking.*

Next I saw Hannibal passing the Alps, who told me he had not a drop of vinegar in his camp.†

I saw Cæsar and Pompey at the head of their troops

* Lord Orrery's criticism on this passage is neither acute nor just. "After a hint from Gulliver that we have lost the true Greek idiom, the conqueror of the universe is made to declare that he died of excessive drinking, not by poison," which he calls a trifling and improper observation, when he should have spoken of some of the great events of his life. Dr. Hawkesworth has better appreciated the point of Swift's satire. "The appearance of Alexander with a victorious army after the battle of Arbela produces only a declaration that he died by drunkenness: thus inadequate and ridiculous in the eye of reason is the ultimate purpose for which Alexander with his army marched into a remote country, subverted a mighty empire, and deluged a nation with blood; he gained no more than an epithet to his name, which, after a few repetitions, was no longer regarded even by himself. Thus the purpose of his resurrection appears to be at least equally important with that of his life, upon which it is a satire not more bitter than just." We think there is a higher moral here which even Dr. Hawkesworth has overlooked—namely, that while the deeds that filled the world have perished and are not worth a thought, the truth is eternal and all-important; and so the highest mission for the dead hero was to proclaim the truth, and thus clear the character of Antipater, even at the expense of his own.

† There is here a plain intimation of the author's disbelief in the story told by Livy, of Hannibal having burst a rock which opposed his passage through the Alps, by burning wood upon it till it was heated, and then pouring vinegar upon it. Polybius makes no mention of this, and modern writers, while admitting that vinegar might produce the effect, doubt the possibility of Hannibal having a sufficient quantity to accomplish such a feat.

just ready to engage. I saw the former in the last great triumph. I desired that the senate of Rome might appear before me, in one large chamber, and a modern representative in counterview, in another. The first seemed to be an assembly of heroes and demigods; the other, a knot of peddlers, pickpockets, highwaymen, and bullies.*

The governor, at my request, gave the sign for Cæsar and Brutus to advance toward us. I was struck with a profound veneration at the sight of Brutus, and could easily discover the most consummate virtue, the greatest intrepidity and firmness of mind, the truest love of his country, and general benevolence of mankind, in every lineament of his countenance. I observed, with much pleasure, that these two persons were in good intelligence with each other; and Cæsar freely confessed to me that the greatest actions of his own life were not equal, by many degrees, to the glory of taking it away. I had the honor to have much conversation with Brutus, and was told that his ancestors, Junius, Socrates, Epaminondas, Cato the younger, Sir Thomas More, and himself were perpetually together—a sextumvirate to which all the ages in the world cannot add a seventh.

It would be tedious to trouble the reader with relating what vast numbers of illustrious persons were called up, to gratify that insatiable desire I had to see the world in every period of antiquity placed before me. I chiefly fed mine eyes with beholding the destroyers of tyrants and usurpers, and the restorers of liberty to oppressed and injured nations. But it is impossible to express the satisfaction I received in my own mind, after such a manner as to make it a suitable entertainment to the reader.

* Pompey and Cæsar only appear to grace the entry of Brutus.

CHAPTER VIII

A Further Account of Glubbdubdrib—Ancient and Modern History Corrected.

HAVING a desire to see those ancients who were most renowned for wit and learning, I set apart one day on purpose. I proposed that Homer and Aristotle might appear at the head of all their commentators; but these were so numerous that some hundreds were forced to attend in the court and outward rooms of the palace. I knew and could distinguish those two heroes, at first sight, and not only from the crowd but from each other. Homer was the comelier person of the two, walked very erect for one of his age, and his eyes were the most quick and piercing I ever beheld. Aristotle stooped much, and made use of a staff. His visage was meager, his hair lank and thin, and his voice hollow.* I soon discovered that both of them were perfect strangers to the rest of the company, and had never seen or heard of them before; and I had a whisper from a ghost who shall be nameless, that these commentators al-

* Swift, like Lord Orrery, seems to have failed to appreciate the character or mind of Aristotle. By representing him as stooping much, and making use of a staff, our author indicates that the reputation of the great philosopher has not stood the test of time. Perhaps Swift and Orrery are both fair exponents of the opinions of their own day. But the philosophers of the age that succeeded, and of the present—Kant, Hegel, Brandis, Cousin, and Sir William Hamilton—have vindicated the greatness of Aristotle, and restored to the high place which he so long occupied one of the most profound and subtle thinkers that the world has ever seen, whose mind has left its impress on all systems of philosophy and all modes of thought since his own time, and of whose "Organon" Kant and Hegel have asserted that no man has added to the logic of Aristotle, or taken anything from it.

ways kept in the most distant quarters from their princi-
pals in the lower world, through a consciousness of shame
and guilt, because they had so horribly misrepresented the
meaning of those authors to posterity. I introduced Didy-
mus and Eustathius to Homer, and prevailed on him to
treat them better than perhaps they deserved, for he soon
found they wanted a genius to enter into the spirit of a
poet. But Aristotle was out of all patience with the account I gave him of Scotus and Ramus, as I presented them
to him; and he asked them whether the rest of the tribe
were as great dunces as themselves.

I then desired the governor to call up Descartes and
Gassendi, with whom I prevailed to explain their systems
to Aristotle. This great philosopher freely acknowledged
his own mistakes in natural philosophy, because he proceeded in many things upon conjecture, as all men must do;
and he found that Gassendi who had made the doctrine of
Epicurus as palatable as he could, and the vortices of Descartes, were equally to be exploded.* He predicted the

* By the introduction of Descartes and Gassendi, and the
judgment passed upon them by Aristotle, Swift wishes to express
his own unfavorable estimate of both. But the Dean's opinion
of philosophers or philosophy is not greatly to be relied on.
Descartes, with all his speculations, must be looked on as one
of the great pioneers of modern psychology, leading the way for
Locke in England, Leibnitz in Germany, and Condillac in France.
His doctrine of the vortices, to which Swift alludes, was that
the heavens were one vast fluid, revolving like a vortex round
the sun. Scherk, one of his best German commentators, says
that on these questions of physics his head swam round in one
of his own vortices; and that, had not his natural genius and
powerful understanding hindered it, he would hardly have left
behind him, as physical theories went, a single idea that has
retained any kind of credit to the present day. Gassendi, the
contemporary and opponent of Descartes, on the subject of the
origin of our knowledge, was a man of great genius and varied
learning, of whom it was said that he was "le meilleur littéra-
teur des philosophes, et le meilleur philosophe des littérateurs."
He published two great works, "De Vitâ et Moribus Epicuri,"
and "Syntagma Philosophiæ Epicuri," in which he endeavored
to reconstruct the theory of Epicurus, one which, overpraised
by the ancients and overcensured by the moderns, can never be

same fate to attraction, whereof the present learned are such zealous assertors. He said that new systems of nature were but new fashions, which would vary in every age; and even those who pretend to demonstrate them from mathematical principles would flourish but a short period of time, and be out of vogue when that was determined.

I spent five days in conversing with many others of the ancient learned. I saw most of the Roman emperors. I prevailed on the governor to call up Heliogabalus's cooks to dress us a dinner, but they could not show us much of their skill, for want of materials. A helot of Agesilaus made us a dish of Spartan broth, but I was not able to get down a second spoonful.

The two gentlemen who conducted me to the island were pressed by their private affairs to return in three days, which I employed in seeing some of the modern dead, who had made the greatest figure for two or three hundred years past, in our own and other countries of Europe; and having been always a great admirer of old illustrious families, I desired the governor would call up a dozen or two of kings, with their ancestors, in order, for eight or nine generations. But my disappointment was grievous and unexpected. For, instead of a long train with royal diadems, I saw in one family two fiddlers, three spruce courtiers, and an Italian prelate; in another, a barber, an abbot, and two cardinals. I have too great a veneration for crowned heads to dwell any longer on so nice a subject. But as to counts, marquises, dukes, earls, and the like, I was not so scrupulous. And I confess it was not without some pleasure that I found myself able to trace the particular features by which certain families are distinguished up to their originals. I could plainly discover whence one family derives

---

defended. Lord Orrery says, with some truth: "His natural philosophy is absurd; his moral philosophy wants its proper basis, the fear of God." Bayle, though an advocate of that philosopher, admits, "On ne scauroit pas dire assez de bien de l'honnêteté de se mœurs, ni assez de mal de ses opinions sur la religion."

a long chin; why a second has abounded with knaves for
two generations, and fools for two more; why a third happened to be crack-brained, and a fourth to be sharpers:
whence it came, what Polydore Virgil says of a certain great
house, *Nec vir fortis, nec fœmina casta;* how cruelty, falsehood, and cowardice grew to be characteristics by which
certain families are distinguished as much as by their coats
of arms. Neither could I wonder at all this, when I saw
such an interruption of lineages, by pages, lackeys, valets,
coachmen, gamesters, fiddlers, players, captains, and pickpockets.

I was chiefly disgusted with modern history. For having
strictly examined all the persons of greatest name in the
courts of princes, for a hundred years past, I found how
the world had been misled by writers, to ascribe the greatest exploits in war to cowards; the wisest counsel to fools;
sincerity to flatterers; Roman virtue to betrayers of their
country; piety to atheists; truth to informers; how many
innocent and excellent persons had been condemned to
death or banishment by the practising of great ministers
upon the corruption of judges and the malice of factions;
how many villains had been exalted to the highest places
of trust, power, dignity, and profit; how great a share in
the motions and events of courts, councils, and senates
might be challenged by parasites and buffoons. How low an
opinion I had of human wisdom and integrity, when I was
truly informed of the springs and motives of great enterprises and revolutions in the world, and of the contemptible accidents to which they owed their success!

Here I discovered the roguery and ignorance of those who
pretend to write anecdotes or secret history; who send so
many kings to their graves with a cup of poison; will repeat the discourse between a prince and chief minister,
where no witness was by; unlock the thoughts and cabinets of ambassadors and secretaries of state; and have the
perpetual misfortune to be mistaken. Here I discovered
the true causes of many great events that have surprised
the world. A general confessed, in my presence, that he

got a vistory purely by the force of cowardice and ill-con-
duct; and an admiral, that for want of proper intelligence
he beat the enemy to whom he intended to betray the fleet.*
Three kings protested to me that in their whole reigns they
never did once prefer any person of merit, unless by mistake, or treachery of some minister in whom they confided;
neither would they do it if they were to live again; and
they showed, with great strength of reason, that the royal
throne could not be supported without corruption, because
that positive, confident, restive temper which virtue infused
into a man was a perpetual clog to public business.†

I had the curiosity to inquire in a particular manner by
what methods great members had procured to themselves
high titles of honor and prodigious estates; and I confined
my inquiry to a very modern period: however, without
grating upon present times, because I would be sure to
give no offence even to foreigners; for I hope the reader
need not be told that I do not in the least intend my own
country in what I say upon this occasion. A great number
of persons concerned were called up; and, upon a very

* It is very probable that Swift here alludes, according to the
conjecture of Sir Walter Scott, to the conduct of Admiral Russell, previous to the battle off La Hogue, in 1692. Russell, at
the time, was in command of the English and Dutch fleets, and
though he had received many rewards and honors from William
III., whom he had invited to come over to England, his ambition
and greed were still unsatisfied, and he carried on at the very
time a treasonable correspondence with James II. for the purpose of restoring him to the throne, and even proposed to get
out of the way with the fleet, so as to give the invaders an
opportunity of landing. And yet, with all his readiness to play
the traitor, he had enough of English feeling, and perhaps
professional spirit, to intimate to the enemy "that if he met
the French fleet he would fight it, even though the king himself
were on board." In this he was as good as his word. On the
19th of May he engaged the French fleet off La Hogue, and
gained a signal victory, which demolished the hopes of the
prince whom he was plotting to restore to his kingdom.

† Scott conjectures, what is very likely, that the three monarchs alluded to here are Charles II., James II., and William
III., none of whom stood high in Swift's good graces.

slight examination, discovered such a scene of infamy that I cannot reflect upon it without some seriousness. Perjury, oppression, subornation, fraud, panderism, and the like infirmities were among the most excusable arts they had to mention; and for these I made, as it was reasonable, great allowance. But when some confessed they owed their greatness and wealth to debauchery; other to the betraying of their country or their prince; some to poisoning; more to the perverting of justice, in order to destroy the innocent; I hope I may be pardoned if these discoveries inclined me a little to abate of that profound veneration which I am naturally apt to pay to persons of high rank, who ought to be treated with the utmost respect due to their sublime dignity, by us their inferiors.

I had often read of some great services done to princes and states, and desired to see the persons by whom those services were performed. Upon inquiry I was told that their names were to be found on no record, except a few of them, whom history has represented as the vilest of rogues and traitors. As to the rest, I had never once heard of them. They all appeared with dejected looks, and in the meanest habits, most of them telling me they died in poverty and disgrace, and the rest on a scaffold or on a gibbet.

Among others, there was one person whose case appeared a little singular. He had a youth about eighteen years old standing by his side. He told me he had for many years been commander of a ship, and in the sea-fight at Actium had the good-fortune to break through the enemy's great line of battle, sink three of their capital ships, and take a fourth, which was the sole cause of Antony's flight, and of the victory that ensued; that the youth standing by him, his only son, was killed in the action. He added that, upon the confidence of some merit, the war being at an end, he went to Rome, and solicited at the court of Augustus to be preferred to a greater ship, whose commander had been killed; but, without any regard to his pretensions, it was given to a boy who had never seen the sea, the son of Libertina, who waited on one of the emperor's mistresses.

Returning back to his own vessel, he was charged with neglect of duty, and the ship given to a favorite page of Publicola, the vice-admiral; whereupon he retired to a poor farm at a great distance from Rome, and there ended his life. I was so curious to know the truth of this story that I desired Agrippa might be called, who was admiral in that fight. He appeared, and confirmed the whole account; but with much more advantage to the captain, whose modesty had extenuated or concealed a great part of his merit.

I was surprised to find corruption grown so high and so quick in that empire, by the force of luxury so lately introduced, which made me less wonder at many parallel cases in other countries, where vices of all kinds have reigned so much longer, and where the whole praise, as well as pillage, has been engrossed by the chief commander, who, perhaps, had the least title to either.

As every person called up made exactly the same appearance he had done in the world, it gave me melancholy reflections to observe how much the race of human kind was degenerated among us within these hundred years past; how disease, under all its consequences and denominations, had altered every lineament of an English countenance, shortened the size of bodies, unbraced the nerves, relaxed the sinews and muscles, introduced a sallow complexion, and rendered the flesh loose and rancid.

I descended so low as to desire some English yeomen of an old stamp might be summoned to appear; once so famous for the simplicity of their manners, diet, and dress; for justice in their dealings; for their true spirit of liberty; for their valor, and love of their country. Neither could I be wholly unmoved, after comparing the living with the dead, when I considered how all these pure native virtues were prostituted for a piece of money by their grandchildren, who in selling their votes and managing at elections, have acquired every vice and corruption that can possibly be learned in a court.

CHAPTER IX

The Author Returns to Maldonada—Sails to the Kingdom of Luggnagg—The Author Confined—He Is Sent for to Court—The Manner of His Admittance—The King's Great Lenity to His Subjects.

THE day of our departure being come, I took leave of his highness, the governor of Glubbdubdrib, and returned with my two companions to Maldonada, where, after a fortnight's waiting, a ship was ready to sail for Luggnagg. The two gentlemen, and some others, were so generous and kind as to furnish me with provisions and see me on board. I was a month on this voyage. We had one violent storm, and were under a necessity of steering westward to get into the trade-wind, which holds for about sixty leagues. On the 21st of April, 1708, we sailed into the river of Clumegnig, which is a seaport town, at the south-east point of Luggnagg. We cast anchor within a league of the town, and made a signal for a pilot. Two of them came on board in less than half an hour, by whom we were guided between certain shoals and rocks which are very dangerous in the passage, to a large basin, where a fleet may ride in safety within a cable's length of the town wall.

Some of our sailors, either out of treachery or inadvertance, had informed the pilots that I was a stranger, and a great traveler; whereof these gave notice to a custom-house officer, by whom I was examined very strictly upon my landing. This officer spoke to me in the language of Balnibarbi, which, by the force of much commerce, is generally understood in that town, especially by seamen and those employed in the customs. I gave him a short account of some particulars, and made my story as plausible and consistent as I could; but I thought it necessary to

disguise my country and call myself a Hollander; because
my intentions were for Japan, and I knew the Dutch were
the only Europeans permitted to enter into that kingdom.
I therefore told the officer, that having been shipwrecked on
the coast of Balnibarbi, and cast on a rock, I was received
up into Laputa, or the flying island (of which he had often
heard), and was now endeavoring to get to Japan, whence
I might find a convenience of returning to my own country. The officer said I must be confined till he could receive orders from court, for which he would write immediately, and hoped to receive an answer in a fortnight. I
was carried to a convenient lodging, with a sentry placed
at the door; however, I had the liberty of a large garden,
and was treated with humanity enough, being maintained
all the time at the king's charge. I was visited by several
persons, chiefly out of curiosity, because it was reported
that I came from countries very remote, of which they had
never heard.

I hired a young man, who came in the same ship, to be
an interpreter; he was a native of Luggnagg, but had lived
some years at Maldonada, and was a perfect master of both
languages. By his assistance I was able to hold a conversation with those who came to visit me, but this consisted
only of their questions and my answers.

The dispatch came from court about the time we expected. It contained a warrant for conducting me and my
retinue to *Traldragdubh*, or *Trildrogdrib* (for it is pronounced both ways as near as I can remember), by a party
of ten horse. All my retinue was that poor lad for an interpreter, whom I persuaded into my service, and, at my
humble request, we had each of us a mule to ride on. A
messenger was dispatched half a day's journey before us,
to give the king notice of my approach, and to desire that
his majesty would please to appoint a day and hour when
it would be his gracious pleasure that I might have the
honor to lick the dust before his footstool. This was the
court style, and I found it to be more than matter of form;
for, upon my admittance two days after my arrival, I was

commanded to crawl upon my belly and lick the floor as I advanced; but, on account of my being a stranger, care was taken to have it made so clean that the dust was not offensive.* However, this was a peculiar grace, not allowed to any but persons of the highest rank, when they desire an admittance. Nay, sometimes the floor is strewed with dust on purpose, when the person to be admitted happens to have powerful enemies at court; and I have seen a great lord with his mouth so crammed that when he had crept to the proper distance from the throne he was not able to speak a word. Neither is there any remedy; because it is capital for those who receive an audience to spit or wipe their mouth in his majesty's presence. There is indeed another custom, which I cannot altogether approve of: when the king has a mind to put any of his nobles to death in a gentle, indulgent manner, he commands the floor to be strewed with a certain brown powder of a deadly composition, which, being licked up, infallibly kills him in twenty-four hours. But in justice to this prince's great clemency, and the care he has of his subjects' lives (wherein it were much to be wished that the monarchs of Europe would imitate him), it must be mentioned for his honor that strict orders are given to have the infected parts of the floor well washed after every such execution, which, if his domestics neglect, they are in danger of incurring his royal displeasure. I myself heard him give directions that one of his pages should be whipped, whose turn it was to give notice about washing the floor after an execution, but maliciously had omitted it; by which neglect a young lord of great hopes, coming to an audience, was unfortunately poisoned, although the king at that time had no design against his

---

* There is here an obvious allusion to the humiliation to which men must submit who seek to rise in courts. Few men knew better than Swift what arts were practiced at court, and there are few courts in which patronage was more venal than in that of George I. The surest road to favor was to pay homage, and something more substantial than homage, to the favorites of the king, both male and female, whose rapacity was such that they made sale of everything.

life. But this good prince was so gracious as to forgive the poor page his whipping upon promise that he would do so no more, without special orders.

To return from this digression: when I had crept to within four yards of the throne I raised myself gently upon my knees, and then, striking my forehead seven times against the ground, I pronounced the following words, as they had been taught me the night before: *Inckpling gloff-throbb squw tserumm blhiop mlashnalt zwin tnodbalkuff hsthiophad kurdlubhasht*. This is the compliment, established by the laws of the land, for all persons admitted to the king's presence. It may be rendered into English thus: "May your celestial majesty outlive the sun, eleven moons and a half!" * To this the king returned some answer, which, although I could not understand, yet I replied, as I had been directed: *Flute drin yalerick dwuldom prtasrad mirpush*, which properly signifies, "My tongue is in the mouth of my friend;" and by this expression was meant that I desired leave to bring my interpreter; whereupon the young man already mentioned was accordingly introduced, by whose intervention I answered as many questions as his majesty could put in about an hour. I spoke in the Balnibarbian tongue, and my interpreter delivered my meaning in that of Luggnagg. The king was much delighted with my company, and ordered his *bliffmarklub*, or high chamberlain, to appoint a lodging in the court for me and my interpreter, with a daily allowance for my table, and a large piece of gold for my common expenses.

I stayed three months in this country out of perfect obedience to his majesty, who was pleased highly to favor me, and made me very honorable offers. But I thought it more consistent with prudence and justice to pass the remainder of my days with my wife and family.

* The description of the ceremonial of the introduction to the King of Luggnagg and the hyperbolical language addressed to him are intended, we may infer, to ridicule and reprove the extravagant and adulatory terms in which the Houses of Parliament were in the habit of addressing the English sovereign.

CHAPTER X*

The Luggnaggians Commended—A Particular Description of the Struldbrugs, with Many Conversations Between the Author and Some Eminent Persons Upon that Subject.

THE Luggnaggians are a polite and generous people, and although they are not without some share of that pride which is peculiar to all Eastern countries, yet they show themselves courteous to strangers, especially such as are countenanced by the court. I had many acquaintances, and among persons of the best fashion; and being always attended by my interpreter the conversation we had was not disagreeable.

One day, in much good company, I was asked by a person of quality whether I had seen any of their *struldbrugs*, or immortals. I said I had not, and desired he would explain to me what he meant by such an appellation, applied to a mortal creature. He told me that sometimes, though very rarely, a child happened to be born in a family, with a red circular spot on the forehead, directly over the left eyebrow, which was an infallible mark that it would never die. The spot, as he described it, was about the compass of a silver threepence, but in the course of time grew larger and

---

* "The description of the struldbrugs," says Lord Orrery, "is an instructive piece of morality; for, if we consider it in a serious light, it tends to reconcile us to our final dissolution. Death, when set in contrast to the immortality of the struldbrugs, is no longer the king of terrors; he loses his sting; he appears to us as a friend, and we cheerfully obey his summons, because it brings certain relief to the greatest miseries. It is in this description that Swift shines in a particular manner. He probably felt in himself the effects of approaching age, and tacitly dreaded the period of life in which he might become a representative of those miserable immortals."

changed its color; for at twelve years old it became green, so continued till five-and-twenty, then turned to a deep blue; at five-and-forty it grew coal black, and as large as an English shilling, but never admitted any further alteration. He said these births were so rare that he did not believe there could be above eleven hundred *struldbrugs,* of both sexes, in the whole kingdom; of which he computed about fifty in the metropolis, and among the rest a young girl born about three years ago: that these productions were not peculiar to any family, but a mere effect of chance; and the children of the *struldbrugs* themselves were equally mortal with the rest of the people.

I freely own myself to have been struck with inexpressible delight upon hearing this account; and the person who gave it me happening to understand the Balnibarbian language, which I spoke very well, I could not forbear breaking out into expressions perhaps a little too extravagant. I cried out, as in a rapture, "Happy nation, where every child has at least a chance of being immortal! Happy people, who enjoy so many living examples of ancient virtue, and have masters ready to instruct them in the wisdom of all former ages! but happiest, beyond all comparison, are those excellent *struldbrugs,* who, being born exempt from that universal calamity of human nature, have their minds free and disengaged, without the weight and depression of spirits caused by the continual apprehension of death." I discovered my admiration that I had not observed any of these illustrious persons at court, the black spot on the forehead being so remarkable a distinction that I could not have easily overlooked it; and it was impossible that his majesty, a most judicious prince, should not provide himself with a good number of such wise and able counselors. Yet perhaps the virtue of those reverend sages was too strict for the corrupt and libertine manners of a court; and we often find, by experience, that young men are too opinionated and volatile to be guided by the sober dictates of their seniors. However, since the king was pleased to allow me access to his royal person, I was resolved, upon the very first occasion, to deliver my opinion to him on this matter freely and at large, by the help of my interpreter; and whether he would please to take my advice or not, yet in one thing I was determined: that his majesty, having frequently offered me an establishment in this country, I would, with great thankfulness, accept the favor, and pass my life here in the conversation of those superior beings, the *struldbrugs*, if they would be pleased to admit me.

The gentleman to whom I addressed my discourse, because (as I have already observed) he spoke the language of Balnibarbi, said to me, with a sort of a smile, which usually arises from them to the ignorant, that he was glad of any occasion to keep me among them, and desired my permission to explain to the company what I had said. He did so, and they talked together for a long time in their own language, whereof I understood not a syllable, neither could I observe by their countenances what impression my discourse had made on them. After a short silence the same person told me that his friends and mine (so he thought fit to express himself) were very much pleased with the judicious remarks I had made on the great happiness and advantages of immortal life, and they were desirous to know, in a particular manner, what scheme of living I should have formed to myself, if it had fallen to my lot to have been born a *struldbrug*.

I answered it was easy to be eloquent on so copious and delightful a subject, especially to me, who had been often apt to amuse myself with visions of what I should do if I were a king, a general, or a great lord; and upon this very case, I had frequently run over the whole system how I should employ myself, and pass the time, if I were sure to live forever.

"If it had been my good-fortune to come into the world a *struldbrug*, as soon as I could discover my own happiness, by understanding the difference between life and death, I would first resolve, by all arts and methods whatsoever, to procure myself riches: in pursuit of which, by thrift and management, I might reasonably expect, in about two hundred years, to be the wealthiest man in the kingdom. In the second place, I would, from my earliest youth, apply myself to the study of arts and sciences, by which I should arrive in time to excel all others in learning. Lastly, I would carefully record every action and event of consequence that happened in the public, impartially draw the characters of the several successions of princes and great ministers of state, with my own observations on every point. I would exactly set down the several changes and customs, language, fashions of dress, diet, and diversions; by all which acquirements I should be a good treasure of knowledge and wisdom, and certainly become the oracle of the nation.

"I would never marry after threescore, but live in an hospitable manner, yet still on the saving scale. I would entertain myself in forming and directing the minds of hopeful young men, by convincing them, from my own remembrance, experience, and observation, fortified by numerous examples, of the usefulness of virtue in public and private life. But my choice and constant companions should be a set of my own immortal brotherhood, among whom I would elect a dozen, from the most ancient down to my own contemporaries. Where any of these wanted fortunes, I would provide them with convenient lodges round my own estate, and have some of them always at my table; only mingling a few of the most valuable among you mortals, whom length of time would harden me to lose with little or no reluctance, and treat your posterity after the same manner; just as a man diverts himself with the annual succession of pinks and tulips in his garden without regretting the loss of those which withered the preceding year.

"These *struldbrugs* and I would mutually communicate our observations and memorials, through the course of time; remark the several gradations by which corruption steals into the world, and oppose it in every step, by giving perpetual warning and instruction to mankind; which, added to the strong influence of our own example, would

probably prevent that continual degeneracy of human na‑
ture, so justly complained of in all ages.

"Add to this the pleasure of seeing the various revolu‑
tions of states and empires; the changes in the lower and
upper world; ancient cities in ruins, and obscure villages
become the seats of kings; famous rivers lessening into
shallow brooks; the ocean leaving one coast dry, and over‑
whelming another; the discovery of many countries yet un‑
known; barbarity overrunning the politest nations, and the
most barbarous becoming civilized. I should then see the
discovery of the longitude, the perpetual motion, the uni‑
versal medicine, and many other great inventions, brought
to the utmost perfection.

"What wonderful discoveries should we make in astron‑
omy, by outliving and confirming our own predictions; by
observing the progress and returns of comets, with the
changes of motion in the sun, moon, and stars!"

I enlarged upon many other topics, which the natural
desire of endless life and sublunary happiness could easily
furnish me with. When I had ended, and the sum of my
discourse had been interpreted, as before, to the rest of
the company, there was a good deal of talk among them
in the language of the country, not without some laughter
at my expense. At last the same gentleman who had been
my interpreter said, "He was desired by the rest to set
me right in a few mistakes, which I had fallen into through
the common imbecility of human nature, and upon that
allowance was less answerable for them. That this breed of
struldbrugs was peculiar to their country, for there were
no such people either in Balnibarbi or Japan, where he
had the honor to be ambassador from his majesty, and
found the natives in both these kingdoms very hard to be‑
lieve that the fact was possible; and it appeared from my
astonishment when he first mentioned the matter to me,
that I received it as a thing wholly new, and scarcely to
be credited. That in the two kingdoms above mentioned,
where during his residence he had conversed very much, he
observed long life to be the universal desire and wish of

mankind. That whoever had one foot in the grave was sure to hold back the other as strongly as he could. That the oldest had still hopes of living one day longer, and looked on death as the greatest evil, from which nature always prompted him to retreat. Only in this island of Luggnagg the appetite for living was not so eager, from the continual example of the *struldbrugs* before their eyes.

"That the system of living contrived by me was unreasonable and unjust; because it supposed a perpetuity of youth, health, and vigor, which no man could be so foolish to hope, however extravagant he may be in his wishes.* That the question therefore was not whether a man would choose to be always in the prime of youth, attended with prosperity and health, but how he would pass a perpetual life, under all the usual disadvantages which old age brings along with it; for although few men will avow their desires of being immortal, upon such hard conditions, yet in the two kingdoms before mentioned, of Balnibarbi and Japan, he observed that every man desired to put off death some time longer, let it approach ever so late; and he rarely heard of any man who died willingly, except he were incited by the extremity of grief or torture. And he appealed to me, whether in those countries I had traveled, as well as my own, I had not observed the same general disposition."

After this preface, he gave me a particular account of the *struldbrugs* among them. He said they commonly acted like mortals till about thirty years old; after which, by degrees, they grew melancholy and dejected, increasing in both till they came to fourscore. This he learned from their own confession; for otherwise, there not being above two

* "To this it may possibly be objected that the perpetuity of youth, health, and vigor would be less a prodigy than the perpetuity of life in a body subject to gradual decay, and might therefore be hoped without greater extravagance of folly; but the sentiment here expressed is that of a being to whom immortality, though not perpetual youth, was familiar, and in whom the wish of a perpetual youth only would have been extravagant, because that only appeared from the facts to be impossible."—*Hawkesworth.*

or three of that species born in an age, they were too few to form a general observation by. When they came to fourscore years, which is reckoned the extremity of living in this country, they had not only all the follies and infirmities of other old men, but many more which arose from the dreadful prospect of never dying. They were not only opinionated, peevish, covetous, morose, vain, talkative, but incapable of friendship, and dead to all natural affection, which never descended below their grandchildren. "Envy and impotent desires are their prevailing passions. But those objects against which their envy seems principally directed are the vices of the younger sort, and the deaths of the old. By reflecting on the former they find themselves cut off from all possibility of pleasure, and whenever they see a funeral they lament and repine that others are gone to a harbor of rest, to which they themselves never can hope to arrive. They have no remembrance of anything but what they learned and observed in their youth and middle age, and even that is very imperfect; and for the truth or particulars of any fact it is safer to depend on common tradition than upon their best recollections. The least miserable among them appear to be those who turn to dotage and entirely lose their memories; these meet with more pity and assistance, because they want many bad qualities which abound in others.

"If a *struldbrug* happen to marry one of his own kind, the marriage is dissolved, of course, by the courtesy of the kingdom, as soon as the younger of the two comes to the fourscore; for the law thinks it a reasonable indulgence that those who are condemned, without any fault of their own, to perpetual continuance in the world should not have their miseries doubled by the load of a wife.

"As soon as they have completed the term of eighty years they are looked on as dead in law; their heirs immediately succeed to their estates; only a small pittance is reserved for their support; and the poor ones are maintained at the public charge. After that period they are held incapable of any employment of trust or profit; they cannot purchase

lands or take leases; neither are they allowed to be wit‑
nesses in any cause, either civil or criminal, not even for the
decision of meers and bounds.

"At ninety they lose their teeth and hair; they have at
that age no distinction of taste, but eat and drink whatever
they can get, without relish or appetite. The diseases they
were subject to still continue, without increasing or dimin‑
ishing. In talking, they forget the common appellation of
things, and the names of persons, even of those who are
their nearest friends and relations. For the same reason,
they never can amuse themselves with reading, because
their memory will not serve to carry them from the begin‑
ning of a sentence to the end; and by this defect they are
deprived of the only entertainment whereof they might
otherwise be capable.

"The language of this country being always upon the
flux, the *struldbrugs* of one age do not understand those of
another; neither are they able after two hundred years to
hold any conversation (further than by a few general
words) with their neighbors the mortals; and thus they lie
under the disadvantage of living like foreigners in their own
country."

This was the account give me of the *struldbrugs*, as near
as I can remember. I afterward saw five or six of different
ages, the youngest not above two hundred years old, who
were brought to me at several times by some of my friends;
but although they were told that I was a great traveler, and
had seen all the world, they had not the least curiosity to
ask me a question; only desired I would give them *slums-
kudash*, or a token of remembrance, which is a modest way
of begging, to avoid the law, that strictly forbids it, because
they are provided for by the public, although indeed with a
very scanty allowance.

They are despised and hated by all sorts of people. When
one of them is born, it is reckoned ominous, and their birth
is recorded very particularly; so that you may know their
age by consulting the register, which, however, has not been
kept above a thousand years past, or at least has been de

stroyed by time or public disturbances. But the usual way of computing how old they are is by asking them what kings or great persons they can remember, and then consulting history; for infallibly the last prince in their mind did not begin his reign after they were fourscore years old.

They were the most mortifying sight I ever beheld; and the women were more horrible than the men. Besides the usual deformities in extreme old age, they acquired additional ghastliness, in proportion to their number of years, which is not to be described; and among half a dozen I soon distinguished which was the eldest, although there was not above a century or two between them.

The reader will easily believe that, from what I had heard and seen, my keen appetite for perpetuity of life was much abated. I grew heartily ashamed of the pleasing visions I had formed, and thought no tyrant could invent a death into which I would not run with pleasure from such a life. The king heard of all that had passed between me and my friends upon this occasion, and rallied me very pleasantly, wishing I could send a couple of *struldbrugs* to my own country to arm our people against the fear of death; but this, it seems, is forbidden by the fundamental laws of the kingdom, or else I should have been well content with the trouble and expense of transporting them.

I could not but agree that the laws of this kingdom relative to the *struldbrugs* were founded upon the strongest reasons, and such as any other country would be under the necessity of enacting, in the like circumstances. Otherwise, as avarice is the necessary consequent of old age, those immortals would in time become proprietors of the whole nation, and engross the civil power, which, for want of abilities to manage, must end in the ruin of the public.

CHAPTER XI

The Author Leaves Luggnagg, and Sails to Japan—From Thence He Returns in a Dutch Ship to Amsterdam, and from Amsterdam to England.

I THOUGHT this account of the *struldbrugs* might be some entertainment to the reader, because it seems to be a little out of the common way; at least I do not remember to have met the like in any book of travels that has come to my hands; and if I am deceived, my excuse must be that it is necessary for travelers who describe the same country, very often to agree in dwelling on the same particulars, without deserving the censure of having borrowed or transcribed from those who wrote before them.

There is indeed a perpetual commerce between this kingdom and the great empire of Japan; and it is very probable that the Japanese authors may have given some account of the *struldbrugs;* but my stay in Japan was so short, and I was so entirely a stranger to the language, that I was not qualified to make any inquiries. But I hope the Dutch, upon this notice, will be curious and able enough to supply my defects.

His majesty, having often pressed me to accept some employment in his court, and finding me absolutely determined to return to my native country, was pleased to give me his license to depart, and honored me with a letter of recommendation, under his own hand, to the Emperor of Japan. He likewise presented me with four hundred and forty-six large pieces of gold (this nation delighted in even numbers), and a red diamond, which I sold in England for eleven hundred pounds.

On the 6th of May, 1709, I took a solemn leave of his majesty and all my friends. This prince was so gracious as

to order a guard to conduct me to Glanguenstald, which
is a royal port to the south-west part of the island. In six
days I found a vessel ready to carry me to Japan, and
spent fifteen days in the voyage. We landed at a small
port town, called Xamoschi, situated on the south-east part
of Japan; the town lies on the western point, where there
is a narrow strait leading northward into a long arm of
the sea, upon the north-west part of which Yedo, the metropolis, stands. At landing I showed the custom-house
officer my letter from the King of Luggnagg to his imperial majesty. They knew the seal perfectly well; it was
as broad as the palm of my hand. The impression was,
"A king lifting up a lame beggar from the earth." The
magistrates of the town, hearing of my letter, received me
as a public minister; they provided me with carriages and
servants, and bore my charges to Yedo, where I was admitted to an audience, and delivered my letter, which was
opened with great ceremony, and explained to the emperor
by an interpreter; who then gave me notice, by his majesty's order, that I should signify my request, and, whatever it were, it should be granted, for the sake of his royal
brother of Luggnagg. This interpreter was a person employed to transact affairs with the Hollanders: he soon conjectured, by my countenance, that I was a European, and
therefore repeated his majesty's commands in Low Dutch,
which he spoke perfectly well. I answered, as I had before
determined, that I was a Dutch merchant, shipwrecked in
a very remote country, whence I had traveled by sea and
land to Luggnagg, and then took shipping for Japan, where
I knew my countrymen often traded, and with some of
these I hoped to get an opportunity of returning into
Europe. I therefore most humbly entreated his royal favor,
to give order that I should be conducted in safety to Nangasac. To this I added another petition, that, for the sake
of my patron, the King of Luggnagg, his majesty would condescend to excuse my performing the ceremony imposed on
my countrymen, of trampling upon the crucifix; because I
had been thrown into this kingdom by my misfortunes,

without any intention of trading. When this latter petition was interpreted to the emperor, he seemed a little surprised, and said he believed I was the first of my countrymen who ever made any scruple on this point, and that he began to doubt whether I was a real Hollander or not, but rather suspected I must be a Christian. However, for the reasons I had offered, but chiefly to gratify the King of Luggnagg by an uncommon mark of his favor, he would comply with the singularity of my humor; but the affair must be managed with dexterity and his officers should be commanded to let me pass, as it were by forgetfulness; for he assured me that if the secret should be discovered by my countrymen, the Dutch, they would cut my throat in the voyage. I returned my thanks, by the interpreter, for so unusual a favor; and some troops being at that time on the march to Nangasac, the commanding officer had orders to convey me safe thither, with particular instructions about the business of the crucifix.*

On the 9th of June, 1709, I arrived at Nangasac, after a very long and troublesome journey. I soon fell into the company of some Dutch sailors belonging to the Amboyna of Amsterdam, a stout ship of 450 tons. I had lived long in Holland, pursuing my studies in Leyden, and I spoke Dutch well. The seamen soon knew whence I came last; they were curious to inquire into my voyages and course of life. I made up a story as short and probable as I could, but concealed the greatest part. I knew many persons in Holland; I was able to invent names for my parents, whom I pretended to be obscure people in the province of Guelderland. I would have given the captain (one Theodorus Vangrult) what he pleased to ask for my voyage to Holland; but understanding I was a surgeon, he was contented to take half the usual rate, on condition that I would serve him in the way of my calling. Before we took shipping I was often asked by some of the crew whether I had per-

---

* In this account of Gulliver's reception at Japan, Swift refers to the popular but erroneous belief that the Dutch merchants were compelled, when entering Japan, to trample on the crucifix.

formed the ceremony above mentioned. I evaded the question by general answers—that I had satisfied the emperor and court in all particulars. However, a malicious rogue of a skipper went to an officer, and, pointing to me, told him I had not yet trampled on the crucifix; but the other, who had received instructions to let me pass, gave the rascal twenty strokes on the shoulders with a bamboo; after which I was no more troubled with such questions.

Nothing happened worth mentioning in this voyage. We sailed with a fair wind to the Cape of Good Hope, where we stayed only to take in fresh water. On the 10th of April, 1710, we arrived safe at Amsterdam, having lost only three men by sickness in the voyage, and a fourth, who fell from the foremast into the sea, not far from the coast of Guinea. From Amsterdam I soon after set sail for England, in a small vessel belonging to that city.

On the 16th of April we put in at the Downs. I landed next morning, and saw once more my native country, after an absence of five years and six months complete. I went straight to Redriff, where I arrived the same day, at two in the afternoon, and found my wife and family in good health.

A VOYAGE TO THE COUNTRY
OF THE HOUYHNHNMS

A Voyage to the
Houyhnhnms[*]

CHAPTER I

The Author Sets Out as Captain of a Ship—His Men Conspire Against Him, Confine Him a Long Time to His Cabin, and Set Him on Shore in an Unknown Land—He Travels Up Into the Country—The Yahoos, a Strange Sort of Animal, Described—The Author Meets Two Houyhnhnms.

I CONTINUED at home with my wife and children about five months in a very happy condition, if I could have learned the lesson of knowing when I was well. I left my poor wife once more, and accepted an advantageous offer made me to be captain of the Adventure, a stout merchantman of 350 tons; for I understood navigation well, and being grown weary of a surgeon's employment at sea, which, however, I could exercise upon occasion. I took a skillful young man of that calling, one Robert Purefoy, into my ship. We set sail from Portsmouth upon the 7th day of September, 1710; on the 14th we met with Captain Pocock, of Bristol, at

---

[*] From satires against individuals, institutions, and philosophers—against kings and courts, ministers and politicians—which have occupied us during the three preceding voyages of Gulliver, we now turn to an attack more comprehensive in its range, for it assails humanity on every point that is vulnerable.

Teneriffe, who was going to the Bay of Campechy to cut logwood. On the 16th he was parted from us by a storm; I heard since my return that his ship foundered, and none escaped but one cabin boy. He was an honest man and a good sailor, but a little too positive in his own opinions, which was the cause of his destruction, as it has been of several others; for if he had followed my advice he might have been safe at home with his family at this time as well as myself.

I had several men die in my ship of calentures, so that I was forced to get recruits out of Barbadoes and the Leeward Islands, where I touched, by the direction of the merchants who employed me; which I had soon too much cause to repent; for I found afterward that most of them had been buccaneers.* I had fifty hands on board; and my orders were that I should trade with the Indians in the South Sea, and make what discoveries I could. These rogues, whom I had picked up, debauched my other men, and they all formed a conspiracy to seize the ship and secure me; which they did one morning, rushing into my cabin, and binding me hand and foot, threatening to throw me overboard if I offered to stir. I told them I was their prisoner, and would submit. This they made me swear to do, and then they unbound me, only fastening one of my

* This society of freebooters, one of the most extraordinary that ever existed, had been completely broken up in the early part of the eighteenth century, and its remaining members dispersed through the world, so that Swift very naturally supplies Gulliver's crew with them. Originally the name was applied to the first French settlers in St. Domingo, who hunted animals for their skins, supporting themselves on fish and flesh, which they used to dry and smoke (boucaner). The term was subsequently assumed by those famous piratical adventurers, chiefly English and French, who joined together to commit depredations on the Spaniards of America. Their last great exploit was in 1697, when 1200 of them, in seven ships, under the command of Pointis, assaulted and took Carthagena, and gained a booty of £1,750,000. Without any regular system, without laws, without subordination, and even without any fixed revenue, they became the astonishment of the age in which they lived, as they will be of posterity.

fegs with a chain, near my bed, and placed a sentry at my door with his piece charged, who was commanded to shoot me dead if I attempted my liberty. They sent me down victuals and drink, and took the government of the ship to themselves. Their design was to turn pirates, and plunder the Spaniards, which they could not do till they got more men. But first they resolved to sell the goods in the ship, and then go to Madagascar* for recruits, several among them having died since my confinement. They sailed many weeks, and traded with the Indians; but I knew not what course they took, being kept a close prisoner in my cabin, and expecting nothing less than to be murdered, as they often threatened me.

Upon the 9th day of May, 1711, one James Welch came down to my cabin and said he had orders from the captain to set me ashore. I expostulated with him, but in vain; neither would he so much as tell me who their new captain was. They forced me into the long-boat, letting me put on my best suit of clothes, which were as good as new, and take a small bundle of linen, but no arms, except my hanger; and they were so civil as not to search my pockets, into which I conveyed what money I had, with some other little necessaries. They rowed about a league, and then set me down on a strand. I desired them to tell me what country it was. They all swore they knew no more than myself; but said that the captain (as they called him) was resolved, after they had sold the lading, to get rid of me in the first place where they could discover land. They pushed off immediately, advising me to make haste, for fear of being overtaken by the tide, and so bade me farewell.

In this desolate condition I advanced forward, and soon got upon firm ground, where I sat down on a bank to rest myself, and consider what I had best do. When I was a little refreshed I went up into the country, resolving to deliver myself to the first savages I should meet, and purchase

* The Island of Madagascar was a principal rendezvous of the buccaneers. Every one of their chiefs had, at one period, a sort of settlement upon the island.

my life from them by some bracelets, glass rings, and other toys, with which sailors usually provide themselves in those voyages, and whereof I had some. The land was divided by long rows of trees, not regularly planted, but naturally growing; there was plenty of grass, and several fields of oats. I walked very circumspectly, for fear of being sur• prised, or suddenly shot with an arrow from behind or on either side. I fell into a beaten road, where I saw many tracks of human feet, and some of cows, but most of horses. At last I beheld several animals in a field, and one or two of the same kind sitting on trees. Their shape was very singular and deformed, which a little discomposed me, so that I lay down behind a thicket to observe them better. Some of them coming forward near the place where I lay, gave me an opportunity of distinctly marking their form. They climbed high trees as nimbly as a squirrel, for they had strong extended claws before and behind, terminating in sharp points, and hooked. They would often spring, and bound, and leap with prodigious agility. The females were not so large as the males; they had long lank hair on their heads, but none on their faces. Upon the whole, I never beheld, in all my travels, so disagreeable an animal, or one against which I naturally conceived so strong an antipathy; so that thinking I had seen enough, full of contempt and aversion, I got up, and pursued the beaten road, hoping it might direct me to the cabin of some Indian. I had not gone far when I met one of these creatures full in my way, and coming up directly to me. The ugly monster, when he saw me, distorted several ways every feature of his visage, and stared, as at an object he had never seen before; then approaching nearer, lifted up his fore-paw, whether out of curiosity or mischief I could not tell; but I drew my hanger, and gave him a good blow with the flat side of it, for I durst not strike with the edge, fearing the inhabitants might be provoked against me if they should come to know that I had killed or maimed any of their cattle. When the beast felt the smart he drew back, and roared so loud that a herd of at least forty came flocking about me from the next field, howling and making hideous faces; but I ran to the body of a tree, and, leaning my back against it, kept them off by waving my hanger.

In the midst of this distress I observed them all to run away on a sudden as fast as they could; at which I ventured to leave the tree and pursue the road, wondering what it was that could put them into this fright. But looking on my left hand I saw a horse walking softly in the field, which my persecutors having sooner discovered was the cause of their flight. The horse started a little when he came near me, but soon recovering himself, looked full in my face with manifest tokens of wonder. He viewed my hands and feet, walking round me several times. I would have pursued my journey, but he placed himself directly in the way, yet looking with a very mild aspect, never offering the least violence. We stood gazing at each other for some time: at last I took the boldness to reach my hand toward his neck, with a design to stroke it, using the common style and whistle of jockeys, when they are going to handle a strange horse. But this animal seemed to receive my civilities with disdain, shook his head and bent his brows, softly raising up his right fore-foot to remove my hand. Then he neighed three or four times, but in so different a cadence that I almost began to think he was speaking to himself, in some language of his own.

When he and I were thus employed, another horse came up, who applying himself first in a very formal manner, they gently struck each other's right hoof before, neighing several times by turns, and varying the sound, which seemed to be almost articulate. They went some paces off, as if it were to confer together, walking side by side, backward and forward, like persons deliberating upon some affair of weight, but often turning their eyes toward me, as it were to watch that I might not escape. I was amazed to see such actions and behavior in brute beasts, and concluded with myself that if the inhabitants of this country were endued with a proportionable degree of reason they must needs be the wisest people upon earth. This thought gave me so

much comfort that I resolved to go forward until I could
discover some house or village, or meet with any of the
natives, leaving the two horses to discourse together as they
pleased. But the first, who was a dapple gray, observing
me to steal off, neighed after me in so expressive a tone
that I fancied myself to understand what he meant; whereupon I turned back and came near to him to expect his
further commands, but concealing my fear as much as I
could; for I began to be in some pain how this adventure
might terminate; and the reader will easily believe I did
not much like my present situation.

The two horses came up close to me, looking with great
earnestness upon my face and hands. The gray steed
rubbed my hat all round with his right fore-hoof, and discomposed it so much that I was forced to adjust it better
by taking it off and settling it again, whereat both he and
his companion (who was a brown bay) appeared to be
much surprised; the latter felt the lappet of my coat, and
finding it to hang loose about me, they both looked with
new signs of wonder. He stroked my right hand, seeming
to admire the softness and color; but he squeezed it so hard
between his hoof and his pastern that I was forced to roar;
after which they both touched me with all possible tenderness. They were under great perplexity about my shoes
and stockings, which they felt very often, neighing to each
other, and using various gestures, not unlike those of a
philosopher when he would attempt to solve some new and
difficult phenomenon.

Upon the whole the behavior of these animals was so
orderly and rational, so acute and judicious, that I at last
concluded they must needs be magicians, who had thus
metamorphosed themselves upon some design, and, seeing a
stranger in the way, resolved to divert themselves with him;
or perhaps were really amazed at the sight of a man so
very different in habit, feature, and complexion from those
who might probably live in so remote a climate. Upon the
strength of this reasoning I ventured to address them in the
following manner: "Gentlemen, if you be conjurers, as I

have good cause to believe, you can understand any language; therefore I make bold to let your worships know that I am a poor distressed Englishman, driven by my misfortunes upon your coast; and I entreat one of you to let me ride on his back, as if he were a real horse, to some house or village where I can be relieved. In return for which favor I will make you a present of this knife and bracelet;" taking them out of my pocket. The two creatures stood silent while I spoke, seeming to listen with great attention; and when I had ended they neighed frequently toward each other, as if they were engaged in serious conversation. I plainly observed that their language expressed the passions very well, and the words might with little pains be resolved into an alphabet more easily than the Chinese.

I could frequently distinguish the word *Yahoo*,* which was repeated by each of them several times; and although it was impossible for me to conjecture what it meant, yet while the two horses were busy in conversation I endeavored to practice this word upon my tongue; and as soon as they were silent I boldly pronounced *Yahoo* in a loud voice, imitating at the same time, as near as I could, the neighing of a horse; at which they were both visibly surprised; and the gray repeated the same word twice, as if he meant to teach the right accent; wherein I spoke after him as well as I could, and found myself perceivably to improve every time, though very far from any degree of perfection. Then the bay tried me with a second word, much harder to be pronounced; but reducing it to the English orthography may be spelt thus, *Houyhnhnm*. I did not succeed in this so well as in the former; but after two or three further trials I had better fortune, and they both appeared amazed at my capacity.

After some further discourse, which I then conjectured might relate to me, the two friends took their leaves, with

* Here, for the first time, occurs a name that, like "Lilliputian," has grown so universally into use that it has attained a permanent place in our literature.

the same compliment of striking each other's hoof; and the gray made me signs that I should walk before him; wherein I thought it prudent to comply till I could find a better director. When I offered to slacken my pace he would cry *hhuun, hhuun:* I guessed his meaning, and gave him to understand, as well as I could, that I was weary, and not able to walk faster; upon which he would stand awhile, to let me rest.

CHAPTER II

*The Author Conducted by a Houyhnhnm to His House—
The House Described—The Author's Reception—The
Food of the Houyhnhnms—The Author in Distress for
Want of Meat—Is at Last Relieved—His Manner of
Feeding in This Country.*

HAVING traveled about three miles we came to a long kind
of building, made of timber stuck in the ground, and wattled
across; the roof was low, and covered with straw. I now
began to be a little comforted, and took out some toys,
which travelers usually carry for presents to the savage
Indians of America and other parts, in hopes the people of
the house would be thereby encouraged to receive me
kindly. The horse made me a sign to go in first; it was a
large room, with a smooth clay floor, and a rack and
manger, extending the whole length on one side. There
were three nags and two mares, not eating, but some of
them sitting down upon their hams, which I very much
wondered at; but wondered more to see the rest employed
in domestic business: these seemed but ordinary cattle;
however, this confirmed my first opinion, that a people who
could so far civilize brute animals must needs excel in wisdom all the nations of the world. The gray came in just
after, and thereby prevented any ill treatment which the
others might have given me. He neighed to them several
times in a style of authority, and received answers.

Beyond this room there were three others, reaching the
length of the house, to which you passed through three
doors, opposite to each other, in the manner of a vista; we
went through the second room toward the third. Here the
gray walked in first, beckoning me to attend. I waited in
the second room, and got ready my presents for the master

and mistress of the house: they were two knives, three bracelets of false pearls, a small looking-glass, and a bead necklace. The horse neighed three or four times, and I waited to hear some answers in a human voice, but I heard no other returns than in the same dialect, only one or two a little shriller than his. I began to think that this house must belong to some person of great note among them, because there appeared so much ceremony before I could gain admittance. But that a man of quality should be served all by horses was beyond my comprehension; I feared my brain was disturbed by my sufferings and misfortunes. I roused myself, and looked about me in the room where I was left alone: this was furnished like the first, only after a more elegant manner. I rubbed my eyes often, but the same objects still occurred. I pinched my arms and sides to awake myself, hoping I might be in a dream. I then absolutely concluded that all these appearances could be nothing else but necromancy and magic. But I had no time to pursue these reflections; for the gray horse came to the door, and made me a sign to follow him into the third room, where I saw a very comely mare, together with a colt and foal, sitting on their haunches upon mats of straw, not unartfully made, and perfectly neat and clean.

The mare, soon after my entrance, rose from her mat, and coming up close, after having nicely observed my hands and face, gave me a most contemptuous look; and turning to the horse, I heard the word *Yahoo* often repeated betwixt them; the meaning of which word I could not then comprehend, although it was the first I had learned to pronounce; but I was soon better informed, to my everlasting mortification; for the horse, beckoning to me with his head, and repeating the *hhuun, hhuun,* as he did upon the road, which I understood was to attend him, led me out into a kind of court, where was another building at some distance from the house. Here we entered, and I saw three of those detestable creatures which I first met after my landing, feeding upon roots and the flesh of some animals, which I afterward found to be that of asses and dogs, and now and then

a cow, dead by accident or disease. They were all tied by
the neck with strong withes fastened to a beam; they held
their food between the claws of their fore-feet, and tore it
with their teeth.

The master horse ordered a sorrel nag, one of his servants, to untie the largest of these animals, and take him
into the yard. The beast and I were brought close together,
and our countenances diligently compared both by master
and servant, who thereupon repeated several times the word
Yahoo. My horror and astonishment are not to be described, when I observed, in this abominable animal, a perfect human figure: the face of it indeed was flat and broad,
the nose depressed, the lips large, and the mouth wide; but
the differences are common to all savage nations, where the
lineaments of the countenances are distorted, by the natives
suffering their infants to lie groveling on the earth, or by
carrying them on their backs, nuzzling with their face
against the mother's shoulders. The fore-feet of the *Yahoo*
differed from my hands in nothing else but the length of
the nails, the coarseness and brownness of the palms, and
the hairiness on the backs. There was the same resemblance
between our feet, with the same differences; which I knew
very well, though the horses did not, because of my shoes
and stockings: the same in every part of our bodies, except
as to hairiness and color, which I have already described.

The great difficulty that seemed to stick with the two
horses was to see the rest of my body so very different from
that of a *Yahoo*, for which I was obliged to my clothes,
whereof they had no conception.

About noon I saw coming toward the house a kind of
vehicle drawn like a sledge by four *Yahoos*. There was in
it an old steed, who seemed to be of quality; he alighted
with his hind feet forward, having by accident got a hurt
in his left fore-foot. He came to dine with our horse, who
received him with great civility. They dined in the best
room, and had oats boiled with milk for the second course,
which the old horse ate warm, but the rest cold. Their
mangers were placed circular in the middle of the room, and

divided into several partitions, round which they sat on their haunches, upon bosses of straw. In the middle was a large rack, with angles answering to every partition of the manger; so that each horse and mare ate their own hay, and their own mash of oats and milk, with much decency and regularity. The behavior of the young colt and foal appeared very modest, and that of the master and mistress extremely cheerful and complaisant to their guest. The gray ordered me to stand by him; and much discourse passed between him and his friend concerning me, as I found by the stranger often looking on me, and the frequent repetition of the word *Yahoo*.

I happened to wear my gloves, which the master gray observing, seemed perplexed, discovering signs of wonder what I had done to my fore-feet; he put his hoof three or four times to them, as if he would signify that I should reduce them to their former shape, which I presently did, pulling off both my gloves and putting them into my pocket.

This occasioned further talk, and I saw the company were pleased with my behavior, whereof I soon found the good effects. I was ordered to speak the few words I understood; and while they were at dinner the master taught me the names for oats, milk, fire, water, and some others, which I could readily pronounce after him, having from my youth a great facility in learning languages.

When dinner was done the master horse took me aside, and by signs and words made me understand the concern he was in that I had nothing to eat. Oats in their tongue are called *hlunnh*. This word I pronounced two or three times; for although I had refused them at first, yet upon second thoughts I considered that I could contrive to make of them a kind of bread, which might be sufficient, with milk, to keep me alive, till I could make my escape to some other country, and to creatures of my own species. The horse immediately ordered a white mare-servant of his family to bring me a good quantity of oats in a sort of wooden tray. These I heated before the fire as well as I

could, and rubbed them till the husks came off, which I
made a shift to winnow from the grain; I ground and beat
them between two stones, and then took water and made
them into a paste or cake, which I toasted at the fire, and
ate warm with milk. It was at first a very insipid diet,
though common enough in many parts of Europe, but grew
tolerable by time; and having been often reduced to hard
fare in my life, this was not the first experiment I had
made how easily nature is satisfied. And I cannot but observe that I never had one hour's sickness while I stayed in
this island. It is true I sometimes made a shift to catch a
rabbit, or bird, by springs made of *Yahoos'* hairs; and I
often gathered wholesome herbs, which I boiled, and ate as
salads with my bread; and now and then, for a rarity, I
made a little butter, and drank the whey. I was at first
at a great loss for salt, but custom soon reconciled me to
the want of it; and I am confident that the frequent use
of salt among us is an effect of luxury, and was first introduced only as a provocative to drink, except where it is
necessary for preserving flesh in long voyages, or in places
remote from great markets; for we observe no animal to
be fond of it but man; and as to myself, when I left this
country it was a great while before I could endure the taste
of it in anything that I ate.

This is enough to say upon this subject of my diet, wherewith other travelers fill their books, as if the readers were
personally concerned whether we fare well or ill. However,
it was necessary to mention this matter, lest the world
should think it impossible that I could find sustenance for
three years in such a country, and among such inhabitants.

When it grew toward evening, the master horse ordered
a place for me to lodge in; it was but six yards from the
house, and separated from the stable of the *Yahoos.* Here
I got some straw, and covering myself with my own clothes,
slept very sound. But I was in a short time better accom-
modated, as the reader shall know hereafter, when I come
to treat more particularly about my way of living.

CHAPTER III

*The Author Studies to Learn the Language—The Houy-
hnhnm, His Master, Assists in Teaching Him—The Language Described—Several Houyhnhnms of Quality Come
Out of Curiosity to See the Author—He Gives His Master a Short Account of His Voyage.*

MY principal endeavor was to learn the language, which my
master (for so I shall henceforth call him) and his children,
and every servant of his house, were desirous to teach me;
for they looked upon it as a prodigy that a brute animal
should discover such marks of a rational creature. I pointed
to everything, and inquired the name of it, which I wrote
down in my journal-book when I was alone, and corrected
my bad accent by desiring those of the family to pronounce
it often. In this employment a sorrel nag, one of the under-
servants, was very ready to assist me.

In speaking, they pronounce through the nose and throat,
and their language approaches nearest to the High Dutch,
or German, of any I know in Europe; but it is much more
graceful and significant. The Emperor Charles V. made
almost the same observation when he said that if he were
to speak to his horse it should be in High Dutch.* The
curiosity and impatience of my master were so great that
he spent many hours of his leisure to instruct me. He was
convinced (as he afterward told me) that I must be a
Yahoo; but my teachableness, civility, and cleanliness astonished him, which were qualities altogether opposite to

* This observation of Charles V. is well known; that he would
address his God in Spanish, his mistress in Italian, and his
horse in German. Swift may here have taken occasion to show
his distaste for the new order of things under the Hanoverian
dynasty and German influences.

those animals. He was most perplexed about my clothes, reasoning sometimes with himself whether they were a part of my body; for I never pulled them off till the family were asleep, and got them on before they woke in the morning. My master was eager to learn whence I came; how I acquired those appearances of reason which I discovered in all my actions; and to know my story from my own mouth, which he hoped he should soon do by the great proficiency I made in learning and pronouncing their words and sentences. To help my memory I formed all I learned into the English alphabet, and wrote the words down, with the translations. This last, after some time, I ventured to do in my master's presence. It cost me much trouble to explain to him what I was doing, for the inhabitants have not the least idea of books or literature.

In about ten weeks' time I was able to understand most of his questions, and in three months could give some tolerable answers. He was extremely curious to know from what part of the country I came, and how I was taught to imitate rational creatures; because the *Yahoos* (whom he saw I exactly resembled in my head, hands, and face, which were only visible), with some appearance of cunning and the strongest disposition to mischief, were observed to be the most unteachable of all brutes. I answered that I came over the sea from a far place, with many others of my own kind, in a great hollow vessel, made of the bodies of trees; that my companions forced me to land on this coast, and then left me to shift for myself. It was with some difficulty, and by the help of many signs, that I brought him to understand me. He replied that I must needs be mistaken, or that I said the thing which was not, for they have no word in their language to express lying or falsehood.* He knew it was impossible that there could be a country beyond the

* When Swift makes the Houyhnhnm incapable of conceiving the possibility of willfully stating what is false, and tells us there is no word in their language to express lying, he rebukes man for a sin which strikes at the root of all that is good and noble in his nature, and degrades him indeed below the brute.

sea, or that a parcel of brutes could move a wooden vessel whither they pleased upon water. He was sure no *Houyhnhnms* alive could make such a vessel, nor would trust *Yahoos* to manage it.

The word *Houyhnhnm*, in their tongue, signifies a horse, and, in its etymology, the perfection of nature. I told my master that I was at a loss for expression, but would improve as fast as I could; and hoped, in a short time, I should be able to tell him wonders. He was pleased to direct his own mare, his colt, and foal, and the servants of the family, to take all opportunities of instructing me; and every day, for two or three hours, he was at the same pains himself. Several horses and mares of quality in the neighborhood came often to our house, upon the report spread of "a wonderful *Yahoo*, that could speak like a *Houyhnhnm*, and seemed, in his words and actions, to discover some glimmerings of reason." These delighted to converse with me: they put many questions, and received such answers as I was able to return. By all these advantages I made so great a progress that in five months from my arrival I understood whatever was spoken, and could express myself tolerably well.

The *Houyhnhnms*, who came to visit my master out of a design of seeing and talking with me, could hardly believe me to be a right *Yahoo*, because my body had a different covering from others of my kind. They were astonished to observe me without the usual hair or skin, except on my head, face, and hands; but I discovered that secret to my master upon an accident which happened about a fortnight before.

I had hitherto concealed the secret of my dress, in order to distinguish myself, as much as possible, from that cursed race of *Yahoos;* but now I found it in vain to do so any longer. Besides, I considered that my clothes and shoes would soon wear out, which already were in a declining condition, and must be supplied by some contrivance from the hides of *Yahoos*, or other brutes; whereby the whole secret would be known. I therefore told my master that, in the country whence I came, those of my kind always covered their bodies with hairs of certain animals prepared by art, as well for decency as to avoid the inclemencies of the air, both hot and cold; of which, as to my own person, I would give him immediate conviction, if he pleased to command me; whereupon I first unbuttoned my coat, and pulled it off. I did the same with my waistcoat. I drew off my shoes, stockings, and breeches. I let my shirt down to my waist, and drew up the bottom, fastening it like a girdle about my middle.

My master observed the whole performance with great signs of curiosity and admiration. He took up all my clothes in his pastern, one piece after another, and examined them diligently; he then stroked my body very gently, and looked round me several times; after which he said it was plain I must be a perfect *Yahoo*, but that I differed very much from the rest of my species in the softness, whiteness, and smoothness of my skin, the shape and shortness of my claws behind and before, and my affectation of walking continually on my two hinder feet. He desired to see no more, and gave me leave to put on my clothes again, for I was shuddering with cold.

I expressed my uneasiness at his giving me so often the appellation of *Yahoo*, an odious animal, for which I had so utter a hatred and contempt. I begged he would forbear applying that word to me, and make the same order in his family, and among his friends whom he suffered to see me. I requested likewise that the secret of my having a false covering to my body might be known to none but himself, at least as long as my present clothing should last; for as to what the sorrel nag, his valet, had observed, his honor might command him to conceal it.

All this my master very graciously consented to, and thus the secret was kept till my clothes began to wear out, which I was forced to supply by several contrivances that shall hereafter be mentioned. In the mean time he desired I would go on with my utmost diligence to learn their language, because he was more astonished at my capacity for

speech and reason than at the figure of my body, whether
it were covered or not, adding that he waited with some
impatience to hear the wonders which I promised to tell
him.

Thenceforward he doubled the pains he had been at to
instruct me; he brought me into all company, and made
them treat me with civility, because, as he told them privately, this would put me into good humor and make me
more diverting.

Every day, when I waited on him, besides the trouble he
was at in teaching, he would ask me several questions concerning myself, which I answered as well as I could; and by
these means he had already received some general ideas,
though very imperfect. It would be tedious to relate the
several steps by which I advanced to a more regular conversation; but the first account I gave of myself in any
order and length was to this purpose:

That I came from a very far country, as I already had
attempted to tell him, with about fifty more of my own
species; that we traveled upon the seas in a great hollow
vessel, made of wood, and larger than his honor's house. I
described the ship to him in the best terms I could, and
explained, by the help of my handkerchief displayed, how
it was driven forward by the wind; that, upon a quarrel
among us, I was set on shore on this coast, where I walked
forward, without knowing whither, till he delivered me from
the persecutions of those execrable *Yahoos*. He asked me
who made the ship, and how it was possible that the
Houyhnhnms of my country would leave it to the management of brutes. My answer was that I durst proceed no
further in my relation, unless he would give me his word of
honor that he would not be offended. He agreed; and I
went on by assuring him that the ship was made by creatures like myself, who, in all the countries I had traveled as
well as in my own, were the only governing rational animals, and that upon my arrival hither I was as much astonished to see the *Houyhnhnms* act like rational creatures
as he or his friends could be in finding some marks of rea-

son in a creature he was pleased to call a *Yahoo*, to which I
owned my resemblance in every part, but could not account
for their degenerate and brutal nature. I said further, that
if good-fortune ever restored me to my native country to
relate my travels hither, as I resolved to do, everybody
would believe that I said the thing that was not, that I
invented the story out of my own head, and (with all possible respect to himself, his family, and friends, and under
his promise of not being offended) our countrymen would
hardly think it probable that a *Houyhnhnm* should be the
presiding creature of a nation, and a *Yahoo* the brute.*

* This discourse between Gulliver and the Houyhnhnm contains a summary of Swift's design—namely, to make man the
unreasoning and the brute the reasoning animal. In his poem
of "The Logicians Refuted," he deals with the idea of the superiority of the brute over the man, of instinct over reason, in his
usual vein of bitter and sarcastic humor.

CHAPTER IV

The Houyhnhnm's Notion of Truth and Falsehood—The Author's Discourse Disapproved by His Master—The Author Gives a More Particular Account of Himself and the Accidents of His Voyage.

DURING my relation my master's countenance indicated great appearance of uneasiness; because doubting or not believing are so little known in this country that the inhabitants cannot tell how to behave themselves under such circumstances; and I remember, in frequent discourses with my master concerning the nature of manhood in other parts of the world, having occasion to talk of lying and false representation, it was with much difficulty that he comprehended what I meant, although he had otherwise a most acute judgment. For he argued thus: that the use of speech was to make us understand one another and to receive information of facts; now, if any one said the thing which was not, these ends were defeated, because I cannot properly be said to understand him, and I am so far from receiving information that he leaves me worse than in ignorance, for I am led to believe a thing black when it is white, and short when it is long. And these were all the notions he had concerning that faculty of lying, so perfectly well understood and so universally practiced among human creatures.*

To return from this digression. When I asserted that the *Yahoos* were the only governing animals in my country, which my master said was altogether past his conception,

* The remark that speech was given to us to express our thoughts, while language is often used to conceal them, has been, in many epigrammatic forms, attributed to different wits and philosophers.

he desired to know whether we had *Houyhnhnms* among us, and what was their employment. I told him we had great numbers; that in summer they grazed in the fields, and in winter were kept in houses with hay and oats, where *Yahoo* servants were employed to rub their skins smooth, comb their manes, pick their feet, serve them with food, and make their beds. "I understand you well," said my master; "it is now very plain, from all you have spoken, what whatever share of reason the *Yahoos* pretend to, the *Houyhnhnms* are your masters; I heartily wish our *Yahoos* would be so tractable." I begged his honor would please to excuse me from proceeding any further, because I was very certain that the account he expected from me would be highly displeasing. But he insisted in commanding* me to let him know the best and the worst. I told him he should be obeyed. I owned that the *Houyhnhnms* among us, whom we called "horses," were the most generous and comely animals we had; that they excelled in strength and swiftness, and, when they belonged to persons of quality, were employed in traveling, racing, or drawing chariots; they were treated with much kindness and care, till they fell into diseases or became foundered in the feet; but then they were sold, and used to all kind of drudgery till they died, after which their skins were stripped and sold for what they were worth, and their bodies left to be devoured by dogs and birds of prey. But the common race of horses had not so good fortune, being kept by farmers, and carriers, and other mean people, who put them to greater labor and fed them worse.

I described, as well as I could, our way of riding, the shape and use of a bridle, a saddle, a spur, and a whip, of harness and wheels. I added that we fastened plates of a certain hard substance, called iron, at the bottoms of their

* Sheridan censures this form of expression, "insisted in commanding," as not being English. It is at all events unusual, but it may be a provincialism. One might suspect that *in* was a typographical error for *on*, but that it is found in all the editions.

feet, to preserve their hoofs from being broken by the stony ways, on which we often traveled.

My master, after some expressions of great indignation, wondered how we dared to venture upon a *Houyhnhnm's* back, for he was sure that the weakest servant in his house would be able to shake off the strongest *Yahoo;* or, by lying down and rolling on his back, squeeze the brute to death. I answered that our horses were trained up, from three or four years old, to the several uses we intended them for; that if any of them proved intolerably vicious, they were employed for carriages; that they were severely beaten, while they were young, for any mischievous tricks; that they were indeed sensible of rewards and punishments: but his honor would please to consider that they had not the least tincture of reason, any more than the *Yahoos* in this country.

It put me to the pains of many circumlocutions to give my master a right idea of what I spoke; for their language does not abound in variety of words, because their wants and passions are fewer than among us. But it is impossible to express his noble resentment at our savage treatment of the *Houyhnhnm* race. He said if it were possible there could be any country where *Yahoos* alone were endued with reason, they certainly must be the governing animal, because reason, in time, will always prevail against brutal strength. But, considering the frame of our bodies, and especially of mine, he thought no creature of equal bulk was so ill-contrived for employing that reason in the common offices of life; whereupon he desired to know whether those among whom I lived resembled me or the *Yahoos* of this country. I assured him that I was as well shaped as most of my age, but the younger and the females were much more soft and tender, and the skins of the latter generally as white as milk. He said I differed indeed from other *Yahoos,* being much more cleanly and not altogether so deformed; but, in point of real advantage, he thought I differed for the worse; that my nails were of no use either to my fore or hinder feet; as to my fore feet, he could not

properly call them by that name, for he never observed me
to walk upon them; that they were too soft to bear the
ground; that I generally went with them uncovered; neither
was the covering I sometimes wore on them of the same
shape or so strong as that on my feet behind; that I could
not walk with any security, for if either of my hinder feet
slipped, I must inevitably fall. He then began to find fault
with other parts of my body—the flatness of my face, the
prominence of my nose, my eyes placed directly in front,
so that I could not look on either side without turning my
head; that I was not able to feed myself without lifting one
of my fore-feet to my mouth, and therefore nature had
placed those joints to answer that necessity. He knew not
what could be the use of those several clefts and divisions
in my feet behind; that these were too soft to bear the
hardness and sharpness of stones without a covering made
from the skin of some other brute; that my whole body
wanted a fence against heat and cold, which I was forced
to put on and off every day, with tediousness and trouble;
and, lastly, that he observed every animal in this country
naturally to abhor the *Yahoos*, whom the weaker avoided,
and the stronger drove from them. So that, supposing us
to have the gift of reason, he could not see how it were
possible to cure that natural antipathy which every creature discovered against us, nor, consequently, how we could
tame and render them serviceable. However, he would, as
he said, debate the matter no farther, because he was more
desirous to know my own story, the country where I was
born, and the several actions and events of my life before
I came hither.

I assured him how extremely desirous I was that he
should be satisfied on every point; but I doubted much
whether it would be possible for me to explain myself on
several subjects, whereof his honor could have no conception, because I saw nothing in his country to which I could
resemble them; that, however, I would do my best, and
strive to express myself by similitudes, humbly desiring his

assistance when I wanted proper words, which he was
pleased to promise me.

I said, my birth was of honest parents, in an island called
England, which was remote from this country as many
days' journey as the strongest of his honor's servants could
travel in the annual course of the sun; that I was bred a
surgeon, whose trade it is to cure wounds and hurts in the
body, gotten by accident or violence; that my country was
governed by a female man, whom we called queen; that I
left it to get riches, whereby I might maintain myself and
family when I should return; that, in my last voyage, I was
commander of the ship, and had about fifty *Yahoos* under
me, many of which died at sea, and I was forced to supply
them by others, picked out from several nations; that our
ship was twice in danger of being sunk, the first time by a
great storm, and the second by striking against a rock.
Here my master interposed by asking me how I could persuade strangers, out of different countries, to venture with
me, after the losses I had sustained and the hazards I had
run. I said they were fellows of desperate fortunes, forced
to fly from the places of their birth on account of their
poverty or their crimes, and therefore they were under the
necessity of seeking a livelihood in other places.

During this discourse my master was pleased to interrupt me several times. I had made use of many circumlocutions in describing to him the nature of the several
crimes for which most of our crew had been forced to fly
their country. This labor took up several days' conversation before he was able to comprehend me. He was wholly
at a loss to know what could be the use or necessity of
practicing those vices. To clear up which I endeavored to
give some ideas of the desire of power and riches; of the
terrible effects of lust, intemperance, malice, and envy. All
this I was forced to define and describe by putting cases
and making suppositions; after which, like one whose imagination was struck with something never seen or heard before, he would lift up his eyes with amazement and indignation. Power, government, war, law, punishment, and a

thousand other things, had no term wherein that language could express them, which made the difficulty almost insuperable to give my master any conception of what I meant. But being of an excellent understanding, much improved by contemplation and converse, he at last arrived at a competent knowledge of what human nature, in our parts of the world, is capable to perform, and desired I would give him some particular account of that land which we call Europe, but especially of my own country.*

* The discourse between the Houyhnhnm and the human Yahoo is very happily conceived, as well as very amusing. The simplicity and purity of the former, his sense of honor and truth, his almost total incapacity to conceive vice, or the temptations which assail and so often overcome man with all his boasted power of reasoning, are well contrasted with the catalogue of crimes of mankind which Gulliver details, to the indignation and amazement of his auditor. The conviction of the horse that the physical construction of the man was the worst possible that could be contrived for discharging the common offices of life, and the reasoning upon which that opinion was founded, present a not uninstructive commentary upon ignorance and self-conceit.

CHAPTER V *

*The Author, at His Master's Command, Informs Him of
the State of England—The Causes of War Among the
Princes of Europe—The Author Begins to Explain the
English Constitution.*

THE reader may please to observe that the following extract
of many conversations I had with my master contains a
summary of the most material points which were discoursed,
at several times, for above two years. His honor often
desiring fuller satisfaction as I farther improved in the
Houyhnhnm tongue, I laid before him, as well as I could,
the whole state of Europe; I discoursed of trade and manufactures, of arts and sciences; and the answers I gave to all
the questions he made, as they arose upon several subjects,
were a fund of conversation not to be exhausted. But I
shall here only set down the substance of what passed between us concerning my own country, reducing it in order
as well as I can, without any regard to time or other circumstances, while I strictly adhere to truth. My only concern is that I shall hardly be able to do justice to my
master's arguments and expressions, which must needs suffer
by my want of capacity, as well as by a translation into
our barbarous English.

In obedience, therefore, to his honor's commands, I related to him the revolution under the Prince of Orange; the
long war with France, entered into by the said prince, and
renewed by his successor, the present queen, wherein the

* As in his former voyages Gulliver gave accounts of the
manners and customs of his own country, so in this chapter,
and those that follow, we have some notices, not only of the
history of Swift's own time and country, but of European
politics, of wars and their causes, and of laws and their administration.

greatest powers of Christendom were engaged, and which still continued; I computed, at his request, that about a million of *Yahoos* might have been killed in the whole progress of it, and perhaps a hundred or more cities taken, and five times as many ships burned or sunk.

He asked me what were the usual causes or motives that made one country go to war with another. I answered, they were innumerable, but I should only mention a few of the chief. Sometimes the ambition of princes, who never think they have land or people enough to govern; sometimes the corruption of ministers, who engage their master in a war in order to stifle or divert the clamor of the subjects against their evil administration. Difference in opinion has cost many millions of lives; for instance, whether flesh be bread, or bread be flesh; whether the juice of a certain berry be blood or wine; whether whistling be a vice or virtue; whether it be better to kiss a post or throw it into the fire; what is the best color for a coat, whether black, white, red, or gray, and whether it should be long or short, narrow or wide, dirty or clean, with many more. Neither are any wars so furious and bloody, or of so long continuance, as those occasioned by difference of opinion, especially if it be in things indifferent.

Sometimes the quarrel between two princes is to decide which of them shall dispossess a third of his dominions where neither of them pretend to any right; sometimes one prince quarrels with another, for fear the other should quarrel with him; sometimes a war is entered upon because the enemy is too strong, and sometimes because he is too weak; sometimes our neighbors want the things which we have, or have the things which we want, and we both fight till they take ours or give us theirs. It is a very justifiable cause of a war to invade a country after the people have been wasted by famine, destroyed by pestilence, or embroiled by factions among themselves. It is justifiable to enter into war against our nearest ally when one of his towns lies convenient for us, or a territory of land that would render our dominions round and compact. If a prince sends forces into a nation where the people are poor and ignorant, he may lawfully put half of them to death, and make slaves of the rest, in order to civilize and reduce them from their barbarous way of living. It is a very kingly, honorable, and frequent practice, when one king desires the assistance of another, to secure him against an invasion, that the assistant, when he has driven out the invader, should seize on the dominions himself, and kill, imprison, or banish the prince he came to relieve. Alliance by blood or marriage is a frequent cause of war between princes; and the nearer the kindred is, the greater their disposition to quarrel: poor nations are hungry, and rich nations are proud, and pride and hunger will ever be at variance. For these reasons the trade of a soldier is held the most honorable of all others, because a soldier is a *Yahoo* hired to kill, in cold blood, as many of his own species, who have never offended him, as he possibly can.*

There is likewise a kind of beggarly princes in Europe, not able to make war by themselves, who hire out their troops to richer nations for so much a day to each man, of which they keep three fourths to themselves, and it is the best part of their maintenance; such are those in many northern parts of Europe.†

"What you have told me," said my master, "upon the subject of war, does indeed discover most admirably the effects of that reason you pretend to; however, it is happy that the shame is greater than the danger, and that nature has left you utterly incapable of doing much mischief. For,

* The various causes here assigned by Swift for war will readily find their illustration in the mind of every person acquainted with history.

† The conduct of George I. in hiring German mercenaries from Hesse, at the expense of England, in order to provide for the defence of his Hanoverian dominions, created great dissatisfaction among the people, and is here assailed by Swift, to whom that policy was particularly distasteful. Immediately after the king's death a grant of £230,923 for 12,000 Hessians was moved for in Parliament, and met with a vigorous, though unsuccessful opposition.

your mouths lying flat with your faces, you can hardly bite each other to any purpose, unless by consent. Then as to the claws upon your feet, before and behind, they are so short and tender that one of our *Yahoos* would drive a dozen of yours before him. And, therefore, in recounting the numbers of those who had been killed in battle, I cannot but think you have said the thing which is not."

I could not forbear shaking my head, and smiling a little at his ignorance; and, being no stranger to the art of war, I gave him a description of cannons, culverins, muskets, carabines, pistols, bullets, powder, swords, bayonets, battles, sieges, retreats, attacks, undermines, countermines, bombardments, sea-fights, ships sunk with a thousand men, twenty thousand killed on each side, dying groans, limbs flying in the air, smoke, noise, confusion, trampling to death under horses' feet, flight, pursuit, victory; fields strewed with carcases left for food to dogs and wolves and birds of prey; plundering, stripping, burning, and destroying. And, to set forth the valor of my own dear countrymen, I assured him that I had seen them blow up a hundred enemies at once in a siege, and as many in a ship; and beheld the dead bodies drop down in pieces from the clouds, to the great diversion of the spectators.

I was going on to more particulars, when my master commanded me silence. He said, whoever understood the nature of the *Yahoos* might easily believe it possible for so vile an animal to be capable of every action I had named, if their strength and cunning equalled their malice. But as my discourse had increased his abhorrence of the whole species, so he found it gave him a disturbance in his mind, to which he was wholly a stranger before. He thought his ears, being used to such abominable words, might, by degrees, admit them with less detestation; that although he hated the *Yahoos* of this country, yet he no more blamed them for their odious qualities than he did a *gnnayh* (a bird of prey) for its cruelty, or a sharp stone for cutting his hoof. But when a creature pretending to reason could be capable of such enormities, he dreaded lest the corruption of that faculty might be worse than brutality itself. He seemed confident that, instead of reason, we were only possessed of some quality fitted to increase our natural vices; as the reflection from a troubled stream returns the image of an ill-shapen body, not only larger, but more distorted.*

He added that he had heard too much upon the subject of war, both in this and some further discourses. There was another point which a little perplexed him at present. I had informed him that some of our crew left their country on account of being ruined by law; that I had already explained the meaning of the word; but he was at a loss how it should come to pass that the law, which was intended for every man's preservation, should be any man's ruin. Therefore he desired to be further satisfied what I meant by law, and the dispensers thereof, according to the present practice in my own country; because he thought nature and reason were sufficient guides for a reasonable animal, as we pretended to be, in showing us what we ought to do, and what to avoid.

I assured his honor that law was a science, in which I had

* "It would perhaps be impossible, by the most labored argument or forcible eloquence, to show the absurd injustice and horrid cruelty of war so effectually as by this simple exhibition of them in a new light. With war, including every species of iniquity and every art of destruction, we become familiar, by degrees, under specious terms, which are seldom examined, because they are learned at an age in which the mind implicitly receives and retains whatever is impressed. Thus it happens that when one man murders another to gratify his lust, we shudder; but when one man murders a million to gratify his vanity, we approve and we admire, we envy and we applaud. If, when this and the preceding pages are read, we discover with astonishment that when the same events have occurred in history we felt no emotion, and acquiesced in wars which we could not but know to have commenced for such causes, and to have been carried on by such means, let him not be censured for too much debasing his species who has contributed to their felicity and preservation by stripping off the veil of custom and prejudice, and holding up in their native deformity the vices by which they become wretched, and the arts by which they are destroyed."—*Hawkesworth.*

not much conversed, further than by employing advocates in vain, upon some injustice that had been done me: however, I would give him all the satisfaction I was able.

I said there was a society of men among us, bred up from their youth in the art of proving, by words multiplied for the purpose, that white is black, and black is white, according as they are paid. To this society all the rest of the people are slaves. For example, if my neighbor has a mind to my cow, he has a lawyer to prove that he ought to have my cow from me. I must then hire another to defend my right, it being against all rules of law that any man should be allowed to speak for himself. "Now, in this case, I, who am the right owner, lie under two great disadvantages: first, my lawyer, being practiced almost from his cradle in defending falsehood, is quite out of his element when he would be an advocate for justice, which is an unnatural office he always attempts with great awkwardness, if not with ill-will. The second disadvantage is, that my lawyer must proceed with great caution, or else he will be reprimanded by the judges, and abhorred by his brethren, as one that would lessen the practice of the law. And therefore I have but two methods to preserve my cow. The first is, to gain over my adversary's lawyer with a double fee, who will then betray his client by insinuating that he has justice on his side. The second way is for my lawyer to make my cause appear as unjust as he can, by allowing the cow to belong to my adversary; and this, if it be skilfully done, will certainly bespeak the favor of the bench. Now your honor is to know that these judges are persons appointed to decide all controversies of property as well as for the trial of criminals, and picked out from the most dexterous lawyers, who have grown old or lazy; and having been biased all their lives against truth and equity, lie under such a fatal necessity of favoring fraud, perjury, and oppression, that I have known some of them refuse a large bribe from the side where justice lay, rather than injure the faculty by doing anything unbecoming their nature or their office.

"It is a maxim among these lawyers, that whatever has

been done before may legally be done again; and therefore they take special care to record all the decisions formerly made against common justice and the general reason of mankind. These, under the name of precedents, they produce as authorities to justify the most iniquitous opinions; and the judges never fail of directing accordingly.

"In pleading, they studiously avoid entering into the merits of the cause; but are loud, violent, and tedious in dwelling upon all circumstances which are not to the purpose. For instance, in the case already mentioned, they never desire to know what claim or title my adversary has to my cow, but whether the said cow were red or black, her horns long or short; whether the field I graze her in be round or square; whether she was milked at home or abroad; what diseases she is subject to, and the like; after which they consult precedents, adjourn the case from time to time, and in ten, twenty, or thirty years come to an issue.

"It is likewise to be observed that this society has a peculiar cant and jargon of their own that no other mortal can understand, and wherein all their laws are written, which they take special care to multiply; whereby they have wholly confounded the very essence of truth and falsehood, of right and wrong; so that it will take thirty years to decide whether the field left me by my ancestors for six generations belongs to me or to a stranger three hundred miles off.*

* While every one must admit that this picture of law and lawyers is grossly distorted and overcolored, it is impossible not to be amused with its ingenuity and humor. The manner in which Swift enumerates as disadvantages the very points which should be in the litigant's favor, is intensely bitter. Yet, with all the extravagance and injustice of the invective, some of the matters assailed by Swift were, as the state of the law was in his day, fairly open to grave censure. The reforms that have taken place have done much to remove these various defects and grievances. Above all, the reproach of the tardiness of justice is no longer warranted—at least to any great extent—and instead of a suit taking thirty years to bring it to a close (as sometimes happened in Swift's time), there are few that are not terminated long before the expiration of three.

"In the trial of persons accused for crimes against the state, the method is much more short and commendable: the judge first sends to sound the disposition of those in power, after which he can easily hang or save a criminal, strictly preserving all due forms of law."

Here my master, interposing, said it was a pity that creatures endowed with such prodigious abilities of mind as these lawyers, by the description I gave of them, must certainly be, were not rather encouraged to be instructors of others in wisdom and knowledge. In answer to which I assured his honor that in all points out of their own trade they were usually the most ignorant and stupid generation among us; the most despicable in common conversation, avowed enemies to all knowledge and learning, and equally disposed to pervert the general reason of mankind in every other subject of discourse as in that of their own profession.

CHAPTER VI

A Continuation of the State of England Under Queen Anne —The Character of a First Minister of State in European Courts.

MY master was yet wholly at a loss to understand what motives could incite this race of lawyers to perplex, disquiet, and weary themselves, and engage in a confederacy of injustice, merely for the sake of injuring their fellow-animals; neither could he comprehend what I meant in saying they did it for hire. Whereupon I was at much pains to describe to him the use of money, the materials it was made of, and the value of the metals; that when a *Yahoo* had got a great store of this precious substance he was able to purchase whatever he had a mind to—the finest clothing, the noblest houses, great tracts of land, the most costly meats and drinks. Therefore, since money alone was able to perform all these feats, our *Yahoos* thought they could never have enough of it to spend or to save, as they found themselves inclined, from their natural bent, either to profusion or avarice. That the rich man enjoyed the fruit of the poor man's labor, and the latter were a thousand to one in proportion to the former. That the bulk of our people were forced to live very miserably by laboring every day for small wages to make a few live plentifully.

I enlarged myself much on these and many other particulars to the same purpose; but his honor did not understand, for he went upon a supposition that all animals had a title to their share in the productions of the earth, and especially those who presided over the rest. Therefore he desired I would let him know what these costly meats were, and how any of us happened to want them. Whereupon I enumerated as many sorts as came into my head, with the various methods of dressing them, which could not be done without sending vessels by sea to every part of the world, as well for liquors to drink as for sauces and innumerable other conveniences. I assured him that this whole globe of earth must be at least three times gone round before one of our better female *Yahoos* could get her breakfast or a cup to put it in. He said that must needs be a miserable country which cannot furnish food for its own inhabitants; but what he chiefly wondered at was, how such vast tracts of ground as I described should be wholly without fresh water, and the people put to the necessity of sending over the sea for drink. I replied that England, the dear place of my nativity, was computed to produce three times the quantity of food more than its inhabitants are able to consume, as well as liquors extracted from grain, or pressed out of the fruits of certain trees, which made excellent drink; and the same proportion in every other convenience of life. But, in order to feed the luxury and intemperance of the males and the vanity of the females, we sent away the greatest part of our necessary things to other countries, whence in return we brought the materials of diseases, folly, and vice, to spend among ourselves.

That wine was not imported among us from foreign countries to supply the want of water or other drinks, but because it was a sort of liquid which made us merry, by putting us out of our senses, diverted all melancholy thoughts, begat wild, extravagant imaginations in the brain, raised our hopes and banished our fears, suspended every office of reason for a time, and deprived us of our limbs, till we fell into a profound sleep, although it must be confessed that we always awoke sick or dispirited, and that the use of this liquor filled us with diseases which made our lives uncomfortable and short.

But, beside all this, the bulk of our people supported themselves by furnishing the necessities or conveniences of life to the rich and to each other. "For instance, when I am at home, and dressed as I ought to be, I carry on my body the workmanship of a hundred tradesmen; the building and furniture of my house employ as many more, and five times the number to adorn my wife."

I was going on to tell him of another sort of people, who get their livelihood by attending the sick, having, upon some occasions, informed his honor that many of my crew had died of diseases. But here it was with the utmost difficulty that I brought him to apprehend what I meant. He could easily conceive that a *Houyhnhnm* grew weak and heavy a few days before his death, or by some accident might hurt a limb; but that nature, who works all things to perfection, should suffer any pains to breed in our bodies, he thought impossible, and desired to know the reason of so unaccountable an evil.

I told him we fed on a thousand things which operated contrary to each other; that we ate when we were not hungry, and drank without the provocation of thirst; that we sat whole nights drinking strong liquors, without eating a bit, which disposed us to sloth, inflamed our bodies, and precipitated or prevented digestion; that it would be endless to give him a catalogue of all diseases incident to human bodies, for they would not be fewer than five or six hundred, spread over every limb and joint—in short, every part, external and intestine, having diseases appropriated to itself. To remedy which, there was a sort of people bred up among us in the profession, or pretence, of curing the sick.

But, besides real diseases, we are subject to many that are only imaginary, for which the physicians have invented imaginary cures. These have their several names, and so have the drugs that are proper for them; and with these our females *Yahoos* are always infested.

"One great excellency in this tribe is their skill at prognostics, wherein they seldom fail; their predictions in real diseases, when they rise to any degree of malignity, generally portending death, which is always in their power, when recovery is not; and, therefore, upon any unexpected signs of amendment, after they pronounced their sentence, rather than be accused as false prophets, they know how to approve their sagacity to the world by a seasonable dose." *

I had formerly upon occasions discoursed with my master upon the nature of government in general, and particularly of our own excellent constitution, deservedly the wonder and envy of the whole world. But having here accidentally mentioned a minister of state, he commanded me, some time after, to inform him what species of *Yahoo* I particularly meant by that appellation.

I told him that a first or chief minister of state, who was the person I intended to describe, was "a creature wholly exempt from joy and grief, love and hatred, pity and anger; at least he makes use of no other passions but a violent desire of wealth, power, and titles; that he applies his word to all uses, except to the indication of his mind; that he never tells a truth, but with an intent that you should take it for a lie; nor a lie, but with a design that you should take it for a truth; that those he speaks worst of behind their backs are in the surest way of preferment; and when he begins to praise you to others or to yourself, you are from that day forlorn. The worst mark you can receive is a promise, especially when it is confirmed with an oath, after which every wise man retires and gives over all hopes.

"There are three methods by which a man may rise to be chief minister. The first is by knowing how, with prudence, to dispose of a wife, a daughter, or a sister; the second, by betraying or undermining his predecessors; and the third is by a furious zeal, in public assemblies, against the corruptions of the court. But a wise prince would rather choose to employ those who practice the last of these methods; because such zealots prove always the most obsequious and subservient to the will and passions of their master. That these ministers, having all employments at their disposal, preserve themselves in power by bribing the majority of a senate or great council; and, at last, by an expedient called an act of indemnity (whereof I described

---

* Swift is almost as hard upon the physicians as he is upon the lawyers, and seems to have had as little love for the one profession as for the other .

the nature to him), they secure themselves from after-reckonings, and retire from the public laden with the spoils of the nation.*

"The palace of a chief minister is a seminary to breed up others in his own trade; the pages, lackeys, and porter, by imitating their master, become ministers of state in their several districts, and learn to excel in the three principal ingredients, of insolence, lying, and bribery. Accordingly, they have a subaltern court paid to them by persons of the best rank; and sometimes, by the force of dexterity and impudence, arrive, through several gradations, to be successors to their lord.

"He is usually governed by a decayed wench or favorite footman, who are the channels through which all graces are conveyed, and may properly be called, in the last resort, the governors of the kingdom.' "

One day, in discourse, my master, having heard me mention the nobility of my country, was pleased to make me a compliment which I could not pretend to deserve: that he was sure I must have been born of some noble family, because I far exceeded in shape, color, and cleanliness, all the *Yahoos* of his nation, although I seemed to fail in strength and agility, which must be imputed to my different way of living from those other brutes; and, besides, I was not only endowed with the faculty of speech, but likewise with some rudiments of reason, to a degree that, with all his acquaintance, I passed for a prodigy.

I made his honor the most humble acknowledgments for the good opinion he was pleased to conceive of me; but assured him, at the same time, that my birth was of the lower sort, having been born of plain honest parents, who

---

* In this description of a minister Swift indulges in all the acrimony of a man who has himself suffered political disappointment, and wreaks his vengeance on those who have slighted him. .t is not improbable that in attributing the quality of lying to a minister, our author intended to characterize Thomas, Earl of Wharton, whom he seems to have intensely hated, and certainly abused unsparingly.

were just able to give me a tolerable education; that nobility, among us, was altogether a different thing from the idea he had of it; that "our young noblemen are bred from their childhood in idleness and luxury, and when their fortunes are almost ruined, they marry some woman of mean birth, disagreeable person, and unsound constitution (merely for the sake of money), whom they hate and despise. The imperfections of the mind run parallel with those of the body, being a composition of spleen, dulness, ignorance, caprice, sensuality, and pride.

"Without the consent of this illustrious body no law can be enacted, repealed, or altered; and these nobles have likewise the decision of all our possessions without appeal."

CHAPTER VII

The Author Relates Several Particulars of the Yahoos— The
Great Virtues of the Houyhnhnms—The Education and
Exercise of Their Youth—Their General Assembly.

As I ought to have understood human nature much better
than I supposed it possible for my master to do, so it was
easy to apply the character he gave of the *Yahoos,* from
time to time, to myself and my countrymen; and I believed
I could yet make further discoveries from my own observation. I therefore often begged his honor to let me go
among the herds of *Yahoos* in the neighborhood, to which
he always very graciously consented, being perfectly convinced that the hatred I bore these brutes would never
suffer me to be corrupted by them; and his honor ordered
one of his servants, a strong sorrel nag, very honest and
good natured, to be my guard, without whose protection I
durst not undertake such adventures. For I have already
told the reader how much I was pestered by these odious
animals upon my first arrival; and I afterward failed very
narrowly three or four times of falling into their clutches,
when I happened to stray at any distance without my
hanger. And I have reason to believe they had some imagination that I was of their own species, which I often
assisted myself by stripping up my sleeves, and showing my
naked arms in their sight, when my protector was with me;
at which times they would approach as near as they durst,
and imitate my actions after the manner of monkeys, but
ever with great signs of hatred, as a tame jackdaw with
cap and stockings is always persecuted by the wild ones
when he happens to get among them.

They are prodigiously nimble from their infancy. However, I once caught a young male of three years old, and

endeavored, by all marks of tenderness, to make it quiet; but the little imp fell a squalling, and scratching, and biting with such violence, that I was forced to let it go; and it was high time, for a whole troop of old ones came about us at the noise, but finding the cub was safe (for away it ran), and my sorrel nag being by, they durst not venture near us.

By what I could discover, the *Yahoos* appear to be the most unteachable of all animals; their capacities never reaching higher than to draw or carry burdens. Yet I am of opinion this defect arises chiefly from a perverse, restive disposition; for they are cunning, malicious, treacherous, and revengeful; they are strong and hardy, but of a cowardly spirit, and by consequence insolent, abject, and cruel. It is observed that the red-haired of both sexes are more mischievous than the rest, whom yet they much excel in strength and activity.

The *Houyhnhnms* keep the *Yahoos* for present use in huts not far from the house; but the rest are sent abroad to certain fields, where they dig up roots, eat several kinds of herbs, and search about for carrions, or sometimes catch weasels and *luhimuhs* (a sort of wild rat), which they greedily devour. Nature has taught them to dig deep holes with their nails on the side of a rising ground, wherein they lie by themselves, only the kennels of the females are larger, sufficient to hold two or three cubs.

They swim from their infancy like frogs, and are able to continue long under water, where they often take fish, which the females carry home to their young.

Having lived three years in this country, the reader, I suppose, will expect that I should, like other travelers, give him some account of the manners and customs of its inhabitants, which it was indeed my principal study to learn.

As these noble *Houyhnhnms* are endowed by nature with a general disposition to all virtues, and have no conceptions or ideas of what is evil in a rational creature, so their grand maxim is to cultivate reason and to be wholly governed by it. Neither is reason among them in a point problematical, as with us, where men can argue with plausibility on both sides of the question, but strikes you with immediate conviction, as it must needs do where it is not mingled, obscured, or discolored by passion and interest. I remember it was with extreme difficulty that I could bring my master to understand the meaning of the word "opinion," or how a point could be disputable; because reason taught us to affirm or deny only where we are certain; and beyond our knowledge we cannot do either. So that controversies, wranglings, disputes, and positiveness, in false or dubious propositions, are evils unknown among the *Houyhnhnms.* In the like manner, when I used to explain to him our several systems of natural philosophy, he would laugh, that a creature pretending to reason should value itself upon the knowledge of other people's conjectures, and in things where that knowledge, if it were certain, could be of no use. Wherein he agreed entirely with the sentiments of Socrates, as Plato delivers them, which I mention as the highest honor I can do that prince of philosophers. I have often since reflected what destruction such doctrine would make in the libraries of Europe, and how many paths of fame would be then shut up in the learned world.

Friendship and benevolence are the two principal virtues among the *Houyhnhnms;* and these not confined to particular objects, but universal to the whole race. For a stranger from the remotest part is equally treated with the nearest neighbor; and wherever he goes looks upon himself as at home. They preserve decency and civility in the highest degrees, but are altogether ignorant of ceremony. They have no fondness for their colts or foals, but the care they take in educating them proceeds entirely from the dictates of reason. And I observed my master to show the same affection to his neighbor's issue that he had for his own. They will have it that Nature teaches them to love the whole species, and it is reason only that makes a distinction of persons where there is a superior degree of virtue.

Courtship, love, presents, jointures, settlements, have no place in their thoughts, or terms whereby to express them in their language. The young couple meet, and are joined merely because it is the determination of their parents and friends; it is what they see done every day, and they look upon it as one of the necessary actions of a reasonable being. But the violation of marriage, or any other unchastity, was never heard of; and the married pair pass their lives with the same friendship and mutual benevolence that they bear to all others of the same species who come in their way, without jealousy, fondness, quarrelling, or discontent.

In educating the youth of both sexes, their method is admirable, and highly deserves our imitation. These are not suffered to taste a grain of oats, except upon certain days, till eighteen years old; nor milk, but very rarely; and in summer they graze two hours in the morning, and as many in the evening, which their parents likewise observe; but the servants are not allowed above half that time, and a great part of their grass is brought home, which they eat at the most convenient hours, when they can best be spared from work.

Temperance, industry, exercise, and cleanliness are the lessons equally enjoined to the young ones of both sexes; and my master thought it monstrous in us to give the females a different kind of education from the males, except in some articles of domestic management; whereby, as he truly observed, one half of our natives were good for nothing but bringing children into the world: and to trust the care of our children to such useless animals, he said, was yet a greater instance of brutality.

But the *Houyhnhnms* train up their youth to strength, speed, and hardiness, by exercising them in running races up and down steep hills, and over hard, stony grounds; and when they are all in a sweat, they are ordered to leap over head and ears into a pond or river. Four times a year the youth of a certain district meet to show their proficiency in running and leaping, and other feats of strength and agility, where the victor is rewarded with a song in his or her praise. On this festival, the servants drive a herd of *Yahoos* into the field, laden with hay, and oats, and milk, for a repast for the *Houyhnhnms*, after which these brutes are immediately driven back again, for fear of being noisome to the assembly.

Every fourth year, at the vernal equinox, there is a representative council of the whole nation, which meets in a plain about twenty miles from our house, and continues about five or six days. Here they inquire into the state and condition of the several districts; whether they abound or be deficient in hay, or oats, or cows, or *Yahoos*; and wherever there is any want (which is but seldom), it is immediately supplied by unanimous consent and contribution.

CHAPTER VIII

A Grand Debate at the General Assembly of the Hou-
yhnhnms, and How It Was Determined—The Learning of
the Houyhnhnms—Their Buildings—Their Manner of
Burials—The Defectiveness of Their Language.

ONE of these grand assemblies was held in my time, about
three months before my departure, whither my master
went as the representative of our district. In this council
was resumed their old debate, and, indeed, the only debate
that ever happened in their country; whereof my master,
after his return, gave me a very particular account.

The question to be debated was, whether the *Yahoos*
should be exterminated from the face of the earth. One
of the members for the affirmative offered several arguments of great strength and weight, alleging "that as the
Yahoos were the most filthy, noisome, and deformed animals which Nature ever produced, so they were the most
restive and indocile, mischievous and malicious; they would
ill-treat and destroy the *Houyhnhnms'* cows, kill and devour
their cats, trample down their oats and grass if they were
not continually watched, and commit a thousand other ex-
travagances." He took notice of a general tradition that
Yahoos had not been always in their country, but that,
many ages ago, two of these brutes appeared together
upon a mountain; whether produced by the heat of the
sun upon corrupted mud and slime, or from the ooze and
froth of the sea, was never known; that these *Yahoos* en-
gendered, and their brood in a short time grew so numerous
as to overrun and infest the whole nation; * that the

* When the reader has become reconciled to the absurdity of
the Apologue, this debate of the Houyhnhnms in grand council
is not a little amusing. Whether in the particular subject of
discussion, or the mode of discussing it, Swift had any special

Houyhnhnms, to get rid of this evil, made a general hunting, and at last inclosed the whole herd; and, destroying
the elder, every *Houyhnhnm* kept two young ones in a
kennel, and brought them to such a degree of tameness as
an animal so savage by nature can be capable of acquiring,
using them for draught and carrriage; that there seemed to
be much truth in this tradition, and that those creatures
could not be *ylnhniamshy* (or *aborigines* of the land), be-

---

question or persons in view, it would be very difficult—perhaps
impossible—now to discover, as there does not appear to be any
clew in the narrative itself to afford grounds for probable conjecture. The tradition put forward as to the origin of the
Yahoos, and the manner in which they came into the country,
is, no doubt, intended to ridicule the various hypotheses put
forward as to the creation of man, as well as the speculations
of ethnologists upon the migrations of peoples. The idea that
man was allied to the monkey was, it is plain, known to and
used by Swift as the foundation of his Yahoo, though the theory
of man's progressive development from the lower animal was
not seriously put forward till half a century later by Lord
Monboddo, who, following the classification of Linnæus, maintained that man at first walked on all fours; that he then
learned to walk upright—as may be seen in the orang-outang,
which he declared to be of the human race—and in due time
made use of his hands, and acquired the art of swimming. This
theory is ridiculed by Horne with grave humor, in a paper contributed to the "Olla Podrida," who argues that man went
originally upon all fours from the universal habit of children,
and the strong propensity he shows to return to it again. Nor
does the want of a tail—a want alike common to the Yahoo and
the man—escape his pleasantry. "The period is altogether
unknown when our nature was first despoiled of an appendage
equally useful and ornamental—I mean a *tail;* for, with an
eminently learned philosopher of North Britain, I am most
firmly persuaded that it was originally a part of our constitution; and that, in the eye of superior beings, man, when he
lost that, lost much of his dignity. If a conjecture might be
indulged upon the subject (and, alas! what but conjectures can
we indulge?) I should be inclined to suppose that the defalca-
tion now under consideration was coeval with the change of
posture discussed above. No sooner had man unadvisedly
mounted on *two,* but his tail dropped off; or rather, perhaps, in
the confusion occasioned by the change, it hitched in a wrong
place, and became suspended from his head."

cause of the violent hatred the *Houyhnhnms*, as well as all other animals, bore them, which although their evil disposition sufficiently deserved, could never have arrived at so high a degree if they had been *aborigines*, or else they would have been long since rooted out; * that the inhabitants, taking a fancy to use the service of the *Yahoos*, had very imprudently neglected to cultivate the breed of asses, which are a comely animal, easily kept, more tame and orderly, without any offensive smell; strong enough for labor, although they yield to the other in agility of body; and if their braying be no agreeable sound, it is far preferable to the horrible howlings of the *Yahoos*.

Several others declared their sentiments to the same purpose, when my master proposed an expedient to the assembly, whereof he had indeed borrowed the hint from me. He approved of the tradition mentioned by the honorable member who spoke before, and affirmed that the two *Yahoos*, said to be seen first among them, had been driven thither over the sea; that coming to land, and being forsaken by their companions, they retired to the mountains, and degenerated by degrees, became in process of much time more savage than those of their own species in the country whence these two originals came. The reason of this assertion was that he had now in his possession a certain wonderful *Yahoo* (meaning myself), which most of them had heard of and many of them had seen. He then related to them how he first found me; that my body was all covered with an artificial composure of the skins and hairs of other animals; that I spoke in a language of my own, and had thoroughly learned theirs; that I had related to him the accidents which brought me thither; that when he saw me

* In arguing that Yahoos could not be aborigines because of the violent hatred the Houyhnhnms bore to them, and of the fact of their not having been rooted out of the country, Swift probably intends a censure upon the cruel manner in which the European discoverers treated the natives of America, first invading their territories, then hunting, inclosing, and subjugating them, and finally exterminating them.

without my covering I was an exact *Yahoo* in every part, only a whiter color, less hairy, and with shorter claws. He added how I had endeavored to persuade him that in my own and other countries the *Yahoos* acted as the governing rational animal, and held the *Houyhnhnms* in servitude; that he observed in me all the qualities of a *Yahoo*, only a little more civilized by some tincture of reason, which, however, was in a degree as far inferior to the *Houyhnhnm* race as the *Yahoos* of their country were to me; that among other things, I mentioned a mode we had of dealing with *Houyhnhnms* when they were young, in order to render them tame; that the operation was easy and safe; that it was no shame to learn wisdom from brutes, as industry is taught by the ant and building by the swallow (for so I translate the word *lynhannh*, although it be a much larger fowl); that this invention might be practiced upon the younger *Yahoos* here, which, besides rendering them tractable and fitter for use, would in an age put an end to the whole species, without destroying life; that in the mean time the *Houyhnhnms* should be exhorted to cultivate the breed of asses, which, as they are in all respects more valuable brutes, so they have this advantage, to be fit for service at five years old, which the others are not till twelve.

This was all my master thought fit to tell me at that time of what passed in the grand council. But he was pleased to conceal one particular, which related personally to myself, whereof I soon felt the unhappy effect, as the reader will know in its proper place, and whence I date all the succeeding misfortunes of my life.

The *Houyhnhnms* have no letters, and consequently their knowledge is all traditional. But there happening few events of any moment among a people so well united, naturally disposed to every virtue, wholly governed by reason, and cut off from all commerce with other nations, the historical part is easily preserved without burdening their memories. I have already observed that they are subject to no diseases, and therefore can have no need of physicians. However, they have excellent medicines, composed of herbs,

to cure accidental bruises and cuts in the pastern or frog
of the foot by sharp stones, as well as other maims and
hurts in the several parts of the body.

They calculate the year by the revolutions of the sun and
moon, but use no subdivisions into weeks. They are well
enough acquainted with the motions of those two lumin-
aries, and understand the nature of eclipses; and this is the
utmost progress of their astronomy.

In poetry they must be allowed to excel all other mortals,
wherein the justness of their similes, and the minuteness as
well as exactness of their descriptions, are indeed inimitable.*
Their verses abound very much in both of these, and
usually contain either some exalted notions of friendship
and benevolence, or the praises of those who were victors
in races and other bodily exercises. Their buildings, although very rude and simple, are not inconvenient, but well
contrived to defend them from all injuries of cold and heat.
They have a kind of tree which at forty years old loosens in
the root and falls with the first storm; it grows very
straight, and being pointed like stakes, with a sharp stone
(for the *Houyhnhnms* know not the use of iron), they stick
them erect in the ground, about ten inches asunder, and
then weave in oat straw, or sometimes wattles between
them. The roof is made after the same manner, and so
are the doors.

The *Houyhnhnms* use the hollow part between the pastern
and the hoof of the fore-foot as we do our hands, and this
with greater dexterity than I could at first imagine. I have
seen a white mare of our family thread a needle (which I
lent her on purpose) with that joint. They milk their
cows, reap their oats, and do all the work which requires

* This is a sneer at the poetasters of his day, most of whom
his friend and contemporary, Pope, has condemned to never-
ending punishment and exposure in the pillory of his immortal
verse. Just at this very time Swift assailed them, in his advice
to the Grub Street verse writers, with bitter pleasantry. One
of the best of Swift's poetical productions is his "Rhapsody on
Poetry," in which he lashes all the tribe, from Colly Cibber, the
laureate. down to Welsted.

hands in the same manner. They have a kind of hard flints, which, by grinding against other stones, they form into instruments that serve instead of wedges, axes, and hammers. With tools made of these flints, they likewise cut their hay and reap their oats, which there grow naturally in several fields; the *Yahoos* draw home the sheaves in carriages, and the servants tread them in certain covered huts to get out the grain, which is kept in stores. They make a rude kind of earthen and wooden vessels, and bake the former in the sun.

If they can avoid casualties, they die only of old age, and are buried in the obscurest places that can be found, their friends and relations expressing neither joy nor grief at their departure; nor does the dying person discover the least regret that he is leaving the world, any more than if he were upon returning home from a visit to one of his neighbors. I remember my master having once made an appointment with a friend and his family to come to his house upon some affair of importance. On the day fixed, the mistress and her two children came very late; she made two excuses, first for her husband, who, as she said, happened that very morning to *lhnuwnh*. The word is strongly expressive in their language, but not easily rendered into English; it signifies, "to retire to his first mother." Her excuse for not coming sooner was, that her husband dying late in the morning, she was a good while consulting her servants about a convenient place where his body should be laid; and I observed she behaved herself at our house as cheerfully as the rest: she died about three months after.

They live generally to seventy or seventy-five years, very seldom to fourscore. Some weeks before their death they feel a gradual decay, but without pain. During this time they are much visited by their friends, because they cannot go abroad with their usual ease and satisfaction. However, about ten days before their death, which they seldom fail in computing, they return the visits that have been made them by those who are nearest in the neighborhood, being

carried in a convenient sledge drawn by *Yahoos*, which
vehicle they use, not only upon this occasion, but when
they grow old, upon long journeys, or when they are lamed
by any accident: and therefore when the dying *Houyhnhnms*
return those visits, they take a solemn leave of their
friends, as if they were going to some remote part of the
country where they designed to pass the rest of their lives.

I know not whether it may be worth observing that the
Houyhnhnms have no word in their language to express
anything that is evil, except what they borrow from the
deformities or ill qualities of the *Yahoos*. Thus they denote
the folly of a servant, an omission of a child, a stone that
cuts their feet, a continuance of foul or unseasonable
weather, and the like, by adding to each the epithet of
Yahoo. For instance, *hhum Yahoo, whnaholm Yahoo,
ynlhmndwiklma Yahoo,* and an ill-contrived house, *ynholm-
hnmrohlnw Yahoo.*

I could, with great pleasure, enlarge further upon the
manners and virtues of this excellent people; but intending
in a short time to publish a volume by itself, expressly
upon that subject, I refer the reader thither; and, in the
mean time, proceed to relate my own sad catastrophe.

CHAPTER IX

The Author's Economy and Happy Life Among the Houy-hnhnms—His Great Improvement in Virtue by Convers-ing with Them—Their Conversations—The Author Has Notice Given Him by His Master that He Must Depart from the Country—He Falls into a Swoon for Grief, but Submits—He Contrives and Finishes a Canoe, by the Help of a Fellow-servant, and Puts to Sea at a Venture.

I HAD settled my little economy to my own heart's content. My master had ordered a room to be made for me, after their manner, about six yards from the house, the sides and floors of which I plastered with clay, and covered with rush mats of my own contriving. I had beaten hemp, which there grows wild, and made of it a sort of ticking; this I filled with the feathers of several birds I had taken with springs made of *Yahoos'* hairs, and were excellent food. I had worked two chairs with my knife, the sorrel nag helping me in the grosser and more laborious part. When my clothes were worn to rags, I made myself others with the skins of rabbits, and of a certain beautiful animal, about the same size, called *nnuhnoh*, the skin of which is covered with a fine down. Of these I also made very tolerable stockings. I soled my shoes with wood, which I cut from a tree and fitted to the upper leather; and when this was worn out, I supplied it with the skins of *Yahoos* dried in the sun. I often got honey out of hollow trees, which I mingled with water or ate with my bread. No man could more verify the truth of these two maxims, that "Nature is very easily satisfied," and that "Necessity is the mother of invention." I enjoyed perfect health of body and tranquillity of mind; I did not feel the treachery or inconstancy of a friend, nor the injuries of a secret or open enemy   I had

no occasion of bribing or flattering, to procure the favor
of any great man or of his minion. I wanted no fence
against fraud or oppression; here was neither physician to
destroy my body, nor lawyer to ruin my fortune; no in-
former to watch my words and actions, or forge accusations
against me for hire; here were no gibers, censurers, back-
biters, pickpockets, highwaymen, housebreakers, attorneys,
buffoons, gamesters, politicians, wits, splenetics, tedious
talkers, controvertists, murderers, robbers, virtuosoes; no
leaders or followers of party and faction; no encouragers to
vice by seducement or examples; no dungeons, taxes, gib-
bets, whipping-posts, or pillories; no cheating shopkeepers
or mechanics; no pride, vanity, or affectation; no fops,
bullies, or drunkards; no ranting or expensive wives; no
stupid, proud pedants; no importunate, overbearing, quarrelsome, noisy, roaring, empty, conceited, swearing companions; no scoundrels raised from the dust upon the merit
of their vices, or nobility thrown into it on account of their
virtues; no lords, fiddlers, judges, or dancing-masters.

I had the favor of being admitted to several *Houyhnhnms*
who came to visit or dine with my master, when his honor
graciously suffered me to wait in the room and listen to
their discourse. Both he and his company would often
condescend to ask me questions and receive my answers.
I had also sometimes the honor of attending my master
in his visits to others. I never presumed to speak, except
in answer to a question; and then I did it with inward
regret, because it was a loss of so much time for improving
myself; but I was infinitely delighted with the station of
an humble auditor in such conversations, where nothing
passed but what was useful, expressed in the fewest and
most significant words; where, as I have already said, the
greatest decency was observed without the least degree of
ceremony; where no person spoke without being pleased
himself and pleasing his companions; where there was no
interruption, tediousness, heat, or difference of sentiments.
They have a notion that when people are met together,
a short silence does much improve conversation. This I

found to be true; for, during those little intermissions of talk, new ideas would arise in their minds, which very much enlivened the discourse. Their subjects are generally on friendship and benevolence, on order and economy; sometimes upon the visible operations of Nature, or ancient traditions; upon the bounds and limits of virtue; upon the unerring rules of reason, or upon some determination to be taken at the next great assembly, and often upon the various excellencies of poetry. I may add, without vanity, that my presence often gave them sufficient matter for discourse, because it afforded my master an occasion of letting his friends into the history of me and my country, upon which they were all pleased to descant, in a manner not very advantageous to human kind; and for that reason I shall not repeat what they said; only I may be allowed to observe that his honor, to my great admiration, appeared to understand the nature of *Yahoos* much better than myself. He went through all our vices and follies, and discovered many which I had never mentioned to him, by only supposing what qualities a *Yahoo* of their country, with a small proportion of reason, might be capable of exerting; and concluded, with too much probability, "how vile as well as miserable such a creature must be!"

I freely confess that all the little knowledge I had of any value was acquired by the lectures I had received from my master and from hearing the discourses of him and his friends; to which I should be prouder to listen than to dictate to the greatest and wisest assembly in Europe. I admired the strength, comeliness, and speed of the inhabitants; and such a constellation of virtues, in such amiable persons, produced in me the highest veneration. At first, indeed, I did not feel that natural awe which the *Yahoos* and all other animals bear toward them; but it grew upon me by degrees, much sooner than I imagined, and was mingled with a respectful love and gratitude, that they would condescend to distinguish me from the rest of my species.

When I thought of my family, my friends, my country,

men, or the human race in general, I considered them, as
they really were, *Yahoos* in shape and disposition, perhaps
a little more civilized, and qualified with the gift of speech;
but making no other use of reason than to improve and
multiply those vices whereof their brethren in this country
had only the share that nature allotted them. When I
happened to see the reflection of my own form in a lake or
fountain, I turned away my face in horror and detestation
of myself, and could better endure the sight of a common
Yahoo than of my own person. By conversing with the
Houyhnhnms, and looking upon them with delight, I fell
to imitate their gait and gesture, which is now grown into
a habit; and my friends often tell me, in a blunt way,
that I trot like a horse; which, however, I take for a great
compliment: neither shall I disown that in speaking I am
apt to fall into the voice and manners of the *Hoyhnhnms*,
and hear myself ridiculed on that account without the
least mortification.

In the midst of all this happiness, and when I looked
upon myself to be fully settled for life, my master sent
for me one morning a little earlier than his usual hour.
I observed by his countenance that he was in some perplexity, and at a loss how to begin what he had to speak.
After a short silence he told me he did not know how I
would take what he was going to say: that in the last
general assembly, when the affair of the *Yahoos* was entered
upon, the representatives had taken offence at his keeping
a *Yahoo* (meaning myself) in his family, more like a *Houyhnhnm* than a brute animal; that he was known frequently to converse with me, as if he could receive some
advantage or pleasure in my company; that such a practice was not agreeable to reason or nature, or a thing
ever heard of before among them; the assembly did therefore exhort him either to employ me like the rest of my
species, or command me to swim back to the place whence
I came: that the first of these expedients was utterly
rejected by all the *Houyhnhnms* who had ever seen me at
his house or their own; for they alleged that because I had

some rudiments of reason, added to the natural gravity of those animals, it was to be feared I might be able to seduce them into the woody and mountainous parts of the country, and bring them in troops by night to destroy the *Houyhnhnms'* cattle, as being naturally of the ravenous kind, and averse from labor.

My master added that he was daily pressed by the *Houyhnhnms* of the neighborhood to have the assembly's exhortation executed, which he could not put off much longer. He doubted it would be impossible for me to swim to another country, and therefore wished I would contrive some sort of vehicle resembling those I had described to him, that might carry me on the sea; in which work I should have the assistance of his own servants, as well as those of his neighbors. He concluded that, for his own part, he could have been content to keep me in his service as long as I lived; because he found I had cured myself of some bad habits and dispositions, by endeavoring, as far as my inferior nature was capable to imitate *Houyhnhnms*.

I should here observe to the reader that a decree of the general assembly in this country is expressed by the word *hnhloayn*, which signifies an exhortation, as near as I can render it; for they have no conception how a rational creature can be compelled, but only advised or exhorted; because no person can disobey reason without giving up his claim to be a rational creature.

I was struck with the utmost grief and despair at my master's discourse; and being unable to support the agonies I was under I fell into a swoon at his feet. When I came to myself he told me that he concluded I had been dead; for these people are subject to no such imbecilities of nature. I answered, in a faint voice, that death would have been too great a happiness: that although I could not blame the assembly's exhortation or the urgency of his friends, yet, in my weak and corrupt judgment, I thought it might consist with reason to have been less rigorous: that I could not swim a league, and probably the nearest land to theirs might be distant above a hundred: that many materials necessary for making a small vessel to carry me off were wholly wanting in this country; which, however, I would attempt, in obedience and grati- tude to his honor, although I concluded the thing to be impossible, and therefore looked on myself as already devoted to destruction; that the certain prospect of an unnatural death was the least of my evils; for, supposing I should escape with life by some strange adventure, how could I think with temper of passing my days among *Yahoos,* and relapsing into my old corruptions, for want of examples to lead and keep me within the paths of virtue? that I knew too well upon what solid reasons all the de- terminations of the wise *Houyhnhnms* were founded, not to be shaken by arguments of mine, a miserable *Yahoo;* and therefore, after presenting him with my humble thanks for the offer of his servants' assistance in making a vessel, and desiring a reasonable time for so difficult a work, I told him I would endeavor to preserve a wretched being; and if ever I returned to England was not without hopes of being useful to my own species, by celebrating the praises of the renowned *Houyhnhnms,* and proposing their virtues to the imitation of mankind.*

My master, in a few words, made me a very gracious reply; allowed me the space of two months to finish my boat; and ordered the sorrel nag, my fellow-servant—for so at this distance I may presume to call him—to follow my

* When Swift makes Gulliver swoon at the prospect of being banished from the society of the Houyhnhnms, and condemned once more to associate with his own now hated species, to whom he was to propose the virtues of the former for imitation, he reaches in intensity the climax of that bitter, misanthropic spirit with which he is so painfully animated throughout the entire of this voyage. The speech of the human Yahoo, pre- senting, as it does, the nature of man in so degrading a light, is yet, is must be confessed, thoroughly consistent with the design of Swift in this fable, as expressed to Pope—to "vex the world rather than divert it."

instructions; because I told my master that his help would be sufficient, and I knew he had a tenderness for me.

In his company, my first business was to go to that part of the coast where my rebellious crew had ordered me to be set on shore. I got upon a height, and looking on every side into the sea, fancied I saw a small island toward the north-east; I took out my pocket-glass, and could then clearly distinguish it about five leagues off, as I computed: but it appeared to the sorrel nag to be only a blue cloud; for as he had no conception of any country beside his own, so he could not be as expert in distinguishing remote objects at sea, as we who so much converse in that element.

After I had discovered this island I considered no further, but resolved it should, if possible, be the first place of my banishment, leaving the consequence to fortune.

I returned home, and consulting with the sorrel nag, we went into a copse at some distance, where I with my knife, and he with a sharp flint, fastened very artificially after their manner to a wooden handle, cut down several oak wattles, about the thickness of a walking-staff, and some larger pieces. But I shall not trouble the reader with a particular description of my own mechanics; let it suffice to say that in six weeks' time, with the help of the sorrel nag, who performed the parts that required most labor, I finished a sort of Indian canoe, but much larger, covering it with the skins of *Yahoos*, well stitched together with hempen threads of my own making. My sail was likewise composed of the skins of the same animal; but I made use of the youngest I could get, the older being too tough and thick; and I likewise provided myself with four paddles. I laid in a stock of boiled flesh, of rabbits and fowls; and took with me two vessels, one filled with milk and the other with water.

I tried my canoe in a large pond near my master's house, and then corrected in it what was amiss, stopping all the chinks with *Yahoos'* tallow, till I found it stanch, and able to bear me and my freight; and when it was as complete as I could possibly make it I had it drawn on a carriage very gently by *Yahoos* to the sea-side, under the conduct of the sorrel nag and another servant.

When all was ready, and the day came for my departure, I took leave of my master and lady and the whole family, my eyes flowing with tears, and my heart quite sunk with grief. But his honor, out of curiosity, and perhaps (if I may speak it without vanity) partly out of kindness, was determined to see me in my canoe, and got several of his neighboring friends to accompany him. I was forced to wait above an hour for the tide, and then, observing the wind very fortunately bearing toward the island to which I intended to steer my course, I took a second leave of my master; but as I was going to prostrate myself to kiss his hoof, he did me the honor to raise it gently to my mouth. I am not ignorant how much I have been censured for mentioning this last particular. Detractors are pleased to think it improbable that so illustrious a person should descend to give so great a mark of distinction to a creature so inferior as I. Neither have I forgotten how apt some travelers are to boast of extraordinary favors they have received. But if these censurers were better acquainted with the noble and courteous disposition of the *Houyhnhnms* they would soon change their opinion.

I paid my respects to the rest of the *Houyhnhnms* in his honor's company; then getting into my canoe I pushed off from shore.

CHAPTER X

The Author's Dangerous Voyage—He Arrives at New Hol-
land, Hoping to Settle There—Is Wounded with an
Arrow by One of the Natives—Is Seized and Carried by
Force into a Portuguese Ship—The Great Civilities of
the Captain—The Author Arrives at England.

I BEGAN this desperate voyage on February 15th, 1714-15
at nine o'clock in the morning. The wind was favorable
however, I made use at first only of my paddles; but considering I should be weary, and that the wind might chop
about, I ventured to set up my little sail; and thus, with
the help of the tide, I went at the rate of a league and a
half an hour, as near as I could guess. My master and
his friends continued on the shore till I was almost out
of sight; and I often heard the sorrel nag (who always
loved me) crying out, *Hnuy illa nyha, majah Yahoo* ("Take
care of thyself, gentle *Yahoo*").

My design was, if possible, to discover some small island
uninhabited, yet sufficient by my labor to furnish me with
the necessaries of life, which I would have thought a
greater happiness than to be first minister in the politest
court of Europe; so horrible was the idea I conceived of
returning to live in the society and under the government
of *Yahoos*. For in such a solitude as I desired, I could
at least enjoy my own thoughts, and reflect with delight
on the virtues of those inimitable *Houyhnhnms*, without
an opportunity of degenerating into the vices and corruptions of my own species.

The reader may remember what I related when my crew
conspired against me, and confined me in my cabin; how
I continued there several weeks without knowing what
course we took; and when I was put ashore in the long-

boat, how the sailors told me with oaths, whether true or false, that they knew not in what part of the world we were. However, I did then believe us to be about ten degrees southward of the Cape of Good Hope, or forty-five degrees southern latitude, as I gathered from some general words I overheard among them, being, as I supposed, to the south-east in their intended voyage to Madagascar. And although this were little better than a conjecture, yet I resolved to steer my course eastward, hoping to reach the south-west coast of New Holland, and perhaps some such island as I desired lying westward of it. The wind was full west, and by six in the evening I computed I had gone eastward at least eighteen leagues, when I spied a very small island about half a league off, which I soon reached. It was nothing but a rock, with one creek naturally arched by the force of tempests. Here I put in my canoe, and climbing a part of the rock I could plainly discover land to the east, extending from south to north. I lay all night in my canoe; and repeating my voyage early in the morning I arrived in seven hours to the south-east point of New Holland. This confirmed me in the opinion I have long entertained, that the maps and charts place this country at least three degrees more at the east than it really is; which thought I communicated many years ago to my worthy friend, Mr. Herman Moll, and gave him my reasons for it, although he has rather chosen to follow other authors.

I saw no inhabitants in the place where I landed, and being unarmed I was afraid of venturing far into the country. I found some shell-fish on the shore, and ate them raw, not daring to kindle a fire for fear of being discovered by the natives. I continued three days feeding on oysters and limpets, to save my own provision; and I fortunately found a brook of excellent water, which gave me great relief.

On the fourth day, venturing out early a little too far, I saw twenty or thirty natives upon a height not above five hundred yards from me. They consisted of men, women, and children, sitting round a fire, as I could discover by the smoke. One of them spied me, and gave notice to the rest; five of them advanced toward me, leaving the women and children at the fire. I made what haste I could to the shore, and getting into my canoe, pushed off; the savages, observing me retreat, ran after me; and before I could get far enough into the sea discharged an arrow, which wounded me deeply on the inside of my left knee: I shall carry the mark to my grave. I apprehended the arrow might be poisoned, and paddling out of the reach of their darts (being a calm day), I made a shift to suck the wound, and dress it as well as I could.

I was at a loss what to do, for I durst not return to the same landing-place, but stood to the north, and was forced to paddle; for the wind, though very gentle, was against me, blowing north-west. As I was looking about for a secure landing-place, I saw a sail to the north-north-east, which appearing every minute more visible, I was in some doubt whether I should wait for them or not; but at last my detestation of the *Yahoo* race prevailed; and turning my canoe, I sailed and paddled toward the south, and got into the same creek whence I set out in the morning, choosing rather to trust myself among these barbarians than live with European *Yahoos*. I drew up my canoe as close as I could to the shore, and hid myself behind a stone by the little brook, which, as I have already said, was excellent water.

The ship came within half a league of this creek, and sent her long-boat with vessels to take in fresh water (for the place, it seems, was very well known); but I did not observe it till the boat was almost on shore, and it was too late to seek another hiding-place. The seamen at their landing observed my canoe, and rummaging it all over, easily conjectured that the owner could not be far off. Four of them, well armed, searched every cranny and lurking-hole, till at last they found me flat on my face behind the stone. They gazed awhile in admiration at my strange, uncouth dress—my coat made of skins, my wooden-

soled shoes, and my furred stockings; whence, however
they concluded I was not a native of the place, who all go
naked. One of the seamen, in Portuguese, bid me rise, and
asked who I was. I understood that language very well,
and getting upon my feet, said I was a poor *Yahoo* vanished from the *Houyhnhnms*, and desired they would please
to let me depart. They wondered to hear me answer them
in their own tongue, and saw by my complexion I must be
a European; but were at a loss to know what I meant by
Yahoo and *Houyhnhnms;* and at the same time fell a-laughing at my strange tone in speaking, which resembled the
neighing of a horse. I trembled all the while betwixt fear
and hatred. I again desired leave to depart, and was
gently moving to my canoe; but they laid hold of me,
desiring to know what country I was of, whence I came,
with many other questions. I told them I was born in
England, whence I came about five years ago, and then
their country and ours was at peace. I therefore hoped
they would not treat me as an enemy, since I meant them
no harm, but was a poor *Yahoo* seeking some desolate
place where to pass the remainder of his unfortunate life.
When they began to talk, I thought I never heard or
saw anything more unnatural; for it appeared to me as
monstrous as if a dog or a cow should speak in England,
or a *Yahoo* in *Houyhnhnmland.* The honest Portuguese
were equally amazed at my strange dress, and the odd
manner of delivering my words, which, however, they
understood very well. They spoke to me with great
humanity, and said they were sure the captain would
carry me free to Lisbon, whence I might return to my
own country; that two of the seamen would go back to
the ship, inform the captain of what they had seen, and
receive his orders. In the mean time, unless I would give
my solemn oath not to flee, they would secure me by force.
I thought it best to comply with their proposal. They
were very curious to know my story, but I gave them very
little satisfaction, and they all conjectured that my misfortunes had impaired my reason. In two hours the boat

which went laden with vessels of water, returned, with the captain's command to fetch me on board. I fell on my knees to preserve my liberty, but all in vain; and the men, having tied me with cords, lifted me into the boat, whence I was taken to the ship, and thence to the captain's cabin.*

I gave the captain, Pedro de Mendez, a very short relation of my voyage, of the conspiracy against me by my own men, of the country where they set me on shore, and of my five years' residence there—all which he looked upon as if it were a dream or a vision; whereat I took great offence, for I had quite forgot the faculty of lying, so peculiar to *Yahoos*, in all countries where they reside, and, consequently, the disposition of suspecting truth in others of their own species. I asked him whether it were the custom in his country to say the thing which was not.

* As during his former residence in Lilliput and Brobdingnag, Gulliver was so habituated to a standard of humanity so physically different from his own that he was for a long time after leaving those regions unable to disabuse his mind of the false impressions of size that he had received, so here his estimate of the intellectual and moral standard of mankind is so debased, and his hatred and contempt of his race, as identified in his mind with the odious, irrational, and vicious Yahoo, are so intense, that he cannot endure the thought of returning to their society; that his earnest desire is to seek some desolate place where he may never meet his kind again; and that, if forced to trust himself among them, he prefers the society of the savage to that of the civilized man. From the other countries, it will be remembered too that he always desired to escape, and ever cherished the hope of returning to his family and his native land. But he leaves the Houyhnhnms upon compulsion, and with profound sorrow; and when forcibly saved by the Portuguese seamen, he supplicates for permission to depart, and can only be restrained from escaping by their threat that if he attempts to do so he will be secured by force; and then he has finally to be tied with cords, and so taken into the ship, and placed a prisoner in the captain's cabin. All this is consistent with the character of Gulliver as drawn throughout—a man at once simple and shrewd, of an honest and very impressible nature. The delusion, too—the *mentis gratissimus error*—to which he clings so tenaciously, is highly amusing and admirably well sustained, and gives great liveliness to the narrative.

I assured him I had almost forgot what he meant by falsehood, and if I had lived a thousand years in *Houyhnhnmland,* I should never have heard a lie from the meanest servant; that I was altogether indifferent whether he believed me or not: but, however, in return for his favors, I would give so much allowance to the corruption of his nature as to answer any objection he might please to make, and then he might easily discover the truth.

The captain, a wise man, after many endeavors to catch me tripping in some part of my story, at last began to have a better opinion of my veracity. But he added, that since I professed so inviolable an attachment to truth, I must give him my word and honor to bear him company in this voyage, without attempting anything against my life, or else he would continue me a prisoner till we arrived at Lisbon. I gave him the promise he required; but at the same time protested that I would suffer the greatest hardships rather than return to live among *Yahoos.*

Our voyage passed without any considerable accident. We arrived at Lisbon November 5th, 1715. At our landing the captain forced me to cover myself with his cloak, to prevent the rabble from crowding about me. I was conveyed to his own house; and at my earnest request he led me up to the highest room backward. I conjured him to conceal from all persons what I had told him of the *Houyhnhnms;* because the least hint of such a story would not only draw numbers of people to see me, but probably put me in danger of being imprisoned, or burned by the Inquisition. The captain persuaded me to accept a suit of clothes newly made; but I would not suffer the tailor to take my measure; however, Don Pedro being almost of my size, they fitted me well enough. He accoutred me with other necessaries, all new, which I aired for twenty-four hours before I would use them.

The captain had no wife, nor above three servants, none of which were suffered to attend at meals; and his whole deportment was so obliging, added to very good human understanding, that I really began to tolerate his company.

He gained so far upon me that I ventured to look out of the back window. By degrees I was brought into another room, whence I peeped into the street, but drew my head back in a fright. In a week's time he seduced me down to the door. I found my terror gradually lessened, but my hatred and contempt seemed to increase.

In ten days Don Pedro, to whom I had given some account of my domestic affairs, put it upon me, as a matter of honor and conscience, that I ought to return to my native country, and live at home with my wife and children. He told me there was an English ship in the port just ready to sail, and he would furnish me with all things necessary. It would be tedious to repeat his arguments and my contradictions. He said it was altogether impossible to find such a solitary island as I desired to live in; but I might command in my own house, and pass my time in a manner as recluse as I pleased.

I complied at last, finding I could not do better. I left Lisbon the 24th day of November, in an English merchantman, but who was the master I never inquired. Don Pedro accompanied me to the ship, and lent me twenty pounds. He took kind leave of me, and embraced me at parting, which I bore as well as I could. During this last voyage I had no commerce with the master or any of his men; but, pretending I was sick, kept close in my cabin. On December 5th, 1715, we cast anchor in the Downs, about nine in the morning, and at three in the afternoon I got safe to my house at Redriff.

My wife and family received me with great surprise and joy, because they concluded me certainly dead; but I must freely confess the sight of them filled me only with hatred, disgust, and contempt; and the more, by reflecting on the near alliance I had to them. For although, since my unfortunate exile from the *Houyhnhnms'* country, I had compelled myself to tolerate the sight of *Yahoos*, and to converse with Don Pedro de Mendez, yet my memory and imagination were perpetually filled with the virtues and ideas of those exalted *Houyhnhnms*.

CHAPTER XI

The Author's Veracity—His Design in Publishing This Work—His Censure of Those Travelers Who Swerve From the Truth—the Author Clears Himself From Any Sinister Ends in Writing—An Objection Answered—The Method of Planting Colonies—His Native Country Commended—The Right of the Crown to Those Countries Described by the Author Is Justified—The Difficulty of Conquering Them—The Author Takes His Last Leave of the Reader—Proposes His Manner of Living for the Future—Gives Good Advice, and Concludes.

Thus, gentle reader, I have given thee a faithful history of my travels for sixteen years and above seven months: wherein I have not been so studious of ornament as of truth. I could, perhaps, like others, have astonished thee with strange, improbable tales; but I rather chose to relate plain matter of fact, in the simplest manner and style; because my principal design was to inform and not to amuse thee.

It is easy for us who travel into remote countries, which are seldom visited by Englishmen or other Europeans, to form descriptions of wonderful animals both at sea and land; whereas a traveler's chief aim should be to make men wiser and better, and improve their minds by the bad as well as good example of what they deliver concerning foreign places.

I could heartily wish a law was enacted that every traveler, before he were permitted to publish his voyages, should be obliged to make oath before the Lord High Chancellor that all he intended to print was absolutely true to the best of his knowledge; for then the world would no longer be deceived, as it usually is, while some writers, to make their works pass the better upon the public, impose the grossest falsities on the unwary reader. I have perused several books of travels with great delight in my younger days; but having since gone over most parts of the globe, and been able to contradict many fabulous accounts from my own observation, it has given me a great disgust against this part of reading, and some indignation to see the credulity of mankind so impudently abused. Therefore, since my acquaintance were pleased to think my poor endeavors might not be unacceptable to my country, I imposed on myself as a maxim never to be swerved from, that I would strictly adhere to truth; neither indeed can I be ever under the least temptation to vary from it, while I retain in my mind the lectures and example of my noble master, and the other illustrious *Houyhnhnms* of whom I had so long the honor to be an humble hearer.

> "Nec si miserum Fortuna Sinonem
> Finxit, vanum etiam, mendacemque improba finget."

I know very well how little reputation is to be got by writings which require neither genius nor learning, nor indeed any other talent except a good memory or an exact journal. I know likewise that writers of travels, like dictionary-makers, are sunk into oblivion by the weight and bulk of those who come last, and therefore lie uppermost. And it is highly probable that such travelers, who shall hereafter visit the countries described in this work of mine, may, by detecting my errors (if there be any), and adding many new discoveries of their own, jostle me out of vogue, and stand in my place, making the world forget that ever I was an author. This indeed would be too great a mortification, if I wrote for fame; but as my sole intention was the public good, I cannot be altogether disappointed. For

who can read of the virtues I have mentioned in the
glorious *Houyhnhnms* without being ashamed of his own
vices, when he considers himself as the reasoning, governing animal of his country? I shall say nothing of those
remote nations where *Yahoos* preside, among which the
least corrupted are the *Brobdingnaggians*, whose wise
maxims in morality and government it would be our happiness to observe. But I forbear descanting further, and
rather leave the judicious reader to his own remarks and
application.

I am not a little pleased that this work of mine can
possibly meet with no censures; for what objections can
be made against a writer who relates only plain facts that
happened in such distant countries where we have not the
least interest, with respect either to trade or negotiations?
I have carefully avoided every fault with which common
writers of travels are often too justly charged. Besides,
I meddle not the least with any party, but write without
passion, prejudice, or ill-will against any man or number
of men whatsoever. I write for the noblest end, to inform
and instruct mankind; over whom I may, without breach
of modesty, pretend to some superiority, from the advantages I received by conversing so long among the most
accomplished *Houyhnhnms*. I write without any view to
profit or praise. I never suffer a word to pass that may
look like reflection, or possibly give the least offense, even
to those who are most ready to take it. So that I hope
I may with justice pronounce myself an author perfectly
blameless, against whom the tribes of Answerers, Consid-
erers, Observers, Reflectors, Detectors, Remarkers, will
never be able to find matter for exercising their peculiar
talents.

I confess is was whispered to me that I was bound in
duty, as a subject of England, to have given in a memorial
to a secretary of state at my first coming over; because
whatever lands are discovered by a subject belong to the
crown. But I doubt whether our conquests, in the coun-

tries I treat of, would be as easy as those of Fernando Cortez over the native Americans. The *Lilliputians,* I think, are hardly worth the charge of a fleet and army to reduce them; and I question whether it might be prudent or safe to attempt the *Brobdingnaggians;* or whether an English army would be at their ease with the flying Island over their heads. The *Houyhnhnms* indeed appear not to be so well prepared for war, a science to which they are perfect strangers, and especially missive weapons. However, supposing myself to be a minister of state, I could never give my advice for invading them. Their prudence, unanimity, unacquaintedness with fear, and their love of their country would amply supply all defects in the military art. Imagine twenty thousand of them breaking into the midst of a European army, confounding the ranks, overturning the carriages, battering the warriors' faces into mummy by terrible yerks from their hinder hoofs; for they would well deserve the character given to Augustus— *Recalcitrant undique tutus.* But, instead of proposals for conquering that magnanimous nation, I rather wish they were in a capacity, or disposition, to send a sufficient number of their inhabitants for civilizing Europe, by teaching us the first principles of honor, justice, truth, temperance, public spirit, fortitude, chastity, friendship, benevolence, and fidelity; the names of all which virtues are still retained among us in most languages, and are to be met with in modern as well as ancient authors; which I am able to assert from my own small reading.

But I had another reason, which made me less forward to enlarge his majesty's dominions by my discoveries. To say the truth, I had conceived a few scruples with relation to the distributive justice of princes upon these occasions. For instance, a crew of pirates are driven by a storm they know not whither; at last a boy discovers land from the topmast; they go on shore to rob and plunder; they see a harmless people; are entertained with kindness; they give the country a new name; they take formal possession of it

for their king; they set up a rotten plank or stone for a
memorial; they murder two or three dozen of the natives,
bring away a couple more, by force, for a sample; return
home and get their pardon. Here commences a new
dominion acquired with a title by divine right. Ships are
sent with the first opportunity; the natives driven out or
destroyed; their princes tortured to discover their gold;
a free license given to all acts of inhumanity and lust, the
earth reeking with the blood of its inhabitants; and this
execrable crew of butchers, employed in so pious an expe-
dition, is a modern colony, sent to convert and civilize an
idolatrous and barbarous people.*

But this description, I confess, does by no means affect
the British nation, who may be an example to the whole
world for their wisdom, care, and justice in planting colonies; their liberal endowments for the advancement of
religion and learning; their choice of devout and able
pastors to propagate Christianity; their caution in stocking
their provinces with people of sober lives and conversations from this the mother kingdom; their strict regard to
the distribution of justice, in supplying the civil administration through all their colonies with officers of the greatest abilities, utter strangers to corruption; and, to crown
all, by sending the most vigilant and virtuous governors,
who have no other views than the happiness of the people
over whom they preside, and the honor of the king their
master.

But as those countries which I have described do not

* These observations are a just and eloquent stricture upon
the indefensible conduct of the Spanish and Portuguese in their
invasion and subjugation of America. The course of their proceeding in that country and their inhuman treatment of the
native races are here briefly but truly and forcibly described.
The reader of history will remember, above all, the cruelties
perpetrated, partly through policy but principally through
fanaticism, upon a noble and unoffending people, under the plea
of converting them to Christianity.

appear to have any desire of being conquered and enslaved, murdered or driven out, by colonies, nor abound either in gold, silver, sugar, or tobacco, I did humbly conceive they were by no means proper objects of our zeal, our valor, or our interest. However, if those whom it more concerns think fit to be of another opinion, I am ready to depose, when I shall be lawfully called, that no European did ever visit those countries before me. I mean if the inhabitants ought to be believed, unless a dispute may arise concerning the two *Yahoos* said to have been seen many years ago upon a mountain in *Houyhnhnmland*.

But as to the formality of taking possession in my sovereign's name, it never came once into my thoughts; and if it had, yet, as my affairs then stood, I should perhaps, in point of prudence and self-preservation, have put it off to a better opportunity.

Having thus answered the only objection that can ever be raised against me as a traveler, I here take a final leave of all my courteous readers, and return to enjoy my own speculations in my little garden at Redriff; to apply those excellent lessons of virtue which I learned among the *Houyhnhnms;* to instruct the *Yahoos* of my own family, as far as I shall find them docile animals; to behold my figure often in a glass, and thus, if possible, habituate myself by time to tolerate the sight of a human creature; to lament the brutality of *Houyhnhnms* in my own country, but always treat their persons with respect, for the sake of my noble master, his family, his friends, and the whole *Houyhnhnm* race, whom these of ours have the honor to resemble in all their lineaments, however their intellectuals came to degenerate.

I began last week to permit my wife to sit at dinner with me, at the farthest end of a long table; and to answer (but with the utmost brevity) the few questions I asked her. And, although it be hard for a man late in life to remove old habits, I am not altogether out of hopes in some time to suffer a neighbor *Yahoo* in my company, without the apprehensions I am yet under of either his teeth or his claws.

My reconcilement to the *Yahoo* kind in general might not be so difficult, if they would be content with those vices and follies only which nature has entitled them to. I am not in the least provoked at the sight of a lawyer, a pickpocket, a colonel, a fool, a lord, a gamester, a politician, a physician, an evidence, a suborner, an attorney, a traitor, or the like; this is all according to the due course of things; but when I behold a lump of deformity and diseases, both in body and mind, smitten with pride, it immediately breaks all the measures of my patience; neither shall I be ever able to comprehend how such an animal and such a vice could tally together.* The wise and virtuous *Houyhnhnms*, who abound in all the excellences that can adorn a rational creature, have no name for this vice in their language, which has no terms to express anything that is evil, except those whereby they describe the detestable qualities of the *Yahoos*; among which they were not able to distinguish this of pride, for want of thoroughly understanding human nature, as it shows itself in other countries where that animal presides. But I, who had more experience, could plainly observe some rudiments of it among the wild *Yahoos*.

But the *Houyhnhnms*, who live under the government of reason, are no more proud of the good qualities they possess than I should be for not wanting a leg or an arm; which no man in his wits would boast of, although he must be miserable without them. I dwell the longer upon this subject from the desire I have to make the society of an English *Yahoo* by any means not insupportable; and there-

* In this indignant denunciation of pride, the wounded spirit of Swift finds full utterance. He had suffered too much and too often from the arrogance and supercilious coldness of those in power not to feel that suffering deeply, and express it strongly.

fore I here entreat those who have any tincture of this absurd vice, that they will not presume to come in my sight.*

* There is nothing finer in the volume which we have just finished than this concluding chapter. For vigor of reasoning, for clearness of style, for excellence of composition, and for its moral tone, it is a masterpiece; while in its sarcastic humor it is not unworthy of its author. In reviewing the scenes of his fabled journeyings, Swift declares his motives in bringing them before the world. "I write," he says, "for the noblest end, to inform and instruct mankind: my principal design was to inform, and not to amuse." How far this is a correct account of his object in these travels, and how far he was occasionally animated by a different spirit, we have already endeavored to show in our annotations upon this work.

In concluding our task, we would say a word or two on "Gulliver's Travels" as a whole. Despite of its faults—occasional inconsistencies in the fables themselves, its too frequent indelicacies (which we have presumed to correct), and its too virulent attacks upon political enemies—it is a marvelous work; one which, in its own class, has never been equaled. The general favor and admiration with which it was received at its first appearance when every allusion, personal and political, was well understood and keenly relished, prove that it was a masterpiece. That its popularity has not diminished nor its interest grown less, now that many of those allusions have either ceased to be understood or ceased to be appreciated, is the best proof of its enduring merit.

THE END.